ROUTLEDGE LIBRARY EDITIONS:
POLITICAL THOUGHT AND
POLITICAL PHILOSOPHY

I0130586

Volume 54

THE DEVELOPMENT OF
POLITICAL THEORY

THE DEVELOPMENT OF POLITICAL THEORY

CHARLES VEREKER

Routledge
Taylor & Francis Group

LONDON AND NEW YORK

First published in 1957 by Hutchinson

This edition first published in 2020
by Routledge
2 Park Square, Milton Park, Abingdon, Oxon OX14 4RN

and by Routledge
52 Vanderbilt Avenue, New York, NY 10017

Routledge is an imprint of the Taylor & Francis Group, an informa business

British Library Cataloguing in Publication Data
A catalogue record for this book is available from the British Library

ISBN: 978-0-367-21961-1 (Set)
ISBN: 978-0-429-35434-2 (Set) (ebk)
ISBN: 978-0-367-36976-7 (Volume 54) (hbk)
ISBN: 978-0-367-36980-4 (Volume 54) (pbk)
ISBN: 978-0-429-35216-4 (Volume 54) (ebk)

Publisher's Note
The publisher has gone to great lengths to ensure the quality of this reprint but points out that some imperfections in the original copies may be apparent.

Disclaimer
The publisher has made every effort to trace copyright holders and would welcome correspondence from those they have been unable to trace.

THE DEVELOPMENT
OF POLITICAL THEORY

CHARLES VEREKER

M.A., D.PHIL.

Lecturer in Social Science, University of Liverpool

HUTCHINSON UNIVERSITY LIBRARY

London

HUTCHINSON & CO (*Publishers*) LTD
178–202 Great Portland Street, London, W.1

London Melbourne Sydney
Auckland Bombay Toronto
Johannesburg New York

★

First published 1957
Second edition 1964

*This book has been printed in Great Britain
by litho-offset by William Clowes and Sons Ltd,
London and Beccles*

CONTENTS

Il faut étudier la société par les hommes,
et les hommes par la société : ceux qui
voudront traiter séparément la matière
politique et la morale n'entendront jamais
rien à aucune des deux.

JEAN-JACQUES ROUSSEAU

PREFACE

This short essay on an intricate historical theme, to which it is customary and proper to devote large volumes, has been designed to whet but not to satisfy the appetite. Its perusal will, I hope, provoke a wider and more intense study of social and political thought; for it is not intended to be regarded or used as a substitute for further reading and reflection but as an invitation to prosecute these activities. The very strict allowance of space has imposed a severe selective discipline, which has limited both the questions and the authors chosen for consideration. But in so far as the choice might have been made better or differently, I must take full responsibility for the arrangement of the material. Inevitably, in covering so long a historical period, I have been deeply indebted to those many scholars whose knowledge of particular periods far exceeds my own. The works, both critical and expository, which I have found most valuable, are included in the suggestions for further reading.

Several volumes already published in this series have been specially concerned with political thought or have crossed its frontiers. Students of the subject should not fail to supplement the brief outline in this essay with the more precise studies undertaken in Mr. Mabbott's *The State and the Citizen*, Professor d'Entrèves's *Natural Law*, and Mr. Mackenzie's *Socialism*. I have taken the liberty of saying less than I might have done on the subjects covered in these volumes, for this very reason.

I am particularly indebted to Professor G. D. H. Cole both for encouraging me to begin this book and for his critical understanding of its difficulties. I could ask for no gentler an editor. Professor T. S. Simey, with whom I have been privileged to work in Liverpool, has generously supported my prosecution of a task, liable to be overborne at any moment by the weight of other academic duties. Mr. M. B. Foster was good enough to read the

first chapter and his penetrating comments have been of very
great value to me.

But it is to my wife that I owe the strength to have finished
what I set out to do, and not only because she alone is able to
shorten my sentences. If I were to consider an introductory text
book a worthy offering for any woman, it is to her, I think,
that I should be moved to dedicate this essay in political thought.

Liverpool   C. H. V.

CHAPTER I

JUSTICE

THE terms political and theory are both Greek words, in form so close to the original that it requires considerable imaginative effort to understand the changes which their significance has undergone in the course of a development through more than two thousand years. Not to make this effort condemns the student either to the belief that nothing which the great Greek thinkers taught is any longer relevant or useful for our current political debate or to the habit of interpreting everything they said in the language and values of modern speculation. Both these tendencies are to be regretted. Reflection upon political associations was initiated by the Greeks. 'The first valuable contribution the Greeks made to political theory was that they invented it.'[1] Since that time, the setting has altered often, the emphasis has been moved back and forth, the terms used have changed their meanings, until sometimes they bear almost the opposite of their original significance. But the importance of distinguishing and defining the relationship between human beings which we, like the Greeks, call political and the need to study this relationship systematically have been constantly recognized in European society.

The science of society, unlike the sciences of natural phenomena, has very few neutral and stable terms which can be exactly defined. The Greek city, or polis, even though it is often called a city-state, differs in many respects from those political associations which we have been accustomed to call states during the last four hundred years. But this lack of stability and precision is not altogether a loss; for it serves to emphasize that the historical setting, the views and prejudices of the thinkers concerned and, increasingly, the influence of earlier thought and tradition together mould the meaning and decide the fashion of political terminology.

[1] A. E. Zimmern: 'Political Thought' in *The Legacy of Greece* (Oxford, Clarendon Press, 1921), p. 331

If we loosely call the Greek polis a state, there is a danger that many of the theoretical assumptions held about modern states will be transferred to the Greek background and that in consequence what the Greeks said about themselves will either seem beside the point or else be misinterpreted in terms of modern problems and post-classical theories of man and society.

Before the construction of the polyglot imperial societies ruled over by Macedon and Rome, the Greek world, united in a general way by language and a sense of common ancestry, was divided into numerous settlements round the shores of the Mediterranean. These cities, though sometimes confederating in loose groups for short periods, were for the most part self-governing communities, with small populations of from ten to a hundred thousand, economically poor by later standards and too quarrelsome among themselves to provide stability or security in the face of threats from more powerful or better-organized neighbours. The survival, and above all the achievements in thought, art and civilized living, of this variegated Greek world is one of the miracles of history, a kind of happy accident which does not seem to have recurred since and which might therefore be thought to have little connection with the complex political system which succeeded it. Indeed, the human and economic limitations of the average Greek city were such that it is difficult at first sight to see why reflection upon its problems could remotely concern or interest the social thinkers of later ages.

Men had lived together before the Greeks and were doing so in larger, richer, stronger and more stable societies in Persia and Egypt contemporaneously; but, though we study the history of these great societies, we rarely enquire what they thought about politics, despite the apparent similarity of their scale and success with more modern political achievements. Political speculation had not been separated from the mythical, theological and merely customary traditions on which the administration of these large-scale societies was founded. Their political thinking was proportionately small as their scale, economic, administrative and geographical, was large.

By contrast, the political reflections of Plato and Aristotle, though written at the very end of the classical Greek period and in some measure provoked by the evident failure and confusion of

Greek city-life, have endured as masterpieces ever since, constantly renewing their influence down the centuries and of value to later thinkers precisely because they cannot be reduced to mere commentaries on the contemporary Greek political scene. The specific problems and difficulties faced by the citizens of classical Greek cities, the quarrels of Athens and Sparta, the internecine conflicts of oligarchs and democrats are indeed remote from present-day concerns. But it was because Plato lived through experiences of this kind, because of the shock he received when the Athens of which he was a prominent citizen judicially put to death his friend and master, Socrates, 'a man,' as he said, 'whom I should not hesitate to call the most righteous man then living,' that he was moved to reflect on the purposes involved in human social activities and to try to distinguish the good from the less good. In doing this, Plato penetrated the local and ephemeral events of his own times to discover principles and methods which have significance wherever men come together and are faced with the inevitable problems of their co-existence and contrary purposes.

Plato's particular answers to the questions he raised are less important for later students of politics than his insistence that men are intended by nature to live happily together in harmony and peace, that they fail to do so from lack of knowledge how to attain this end and that it is possible by systematic reflection to discover the proper path to follow, if not necessarily to make sure that everybody follows it. It is this critical and reflective attitude to social affairs which has distinguished subsequent political thought. Later thinkers, such as Augustine, Hobbes, Rousseau and Marx, have remained in this sense in the Platonic tradition. They differ about the cause of disharmony; they offer diverse suggestions for reorganizing social relations in a more satisfactory pattern and they have various specific proposals for the proper institutional arrangements to achieve the desired end; but though provoked by other imperfections than his, they all follow Plato's example in critically reflecting upon man's plight and the most efficacious plan for his rescue.

In a post-Christian, scientific era, we have two major difficulties in understanding Plato's way of seeking answers to these general questions which, nevertheless, are common to both periods. It has been customary during the Christian centuries to believe that many, and at some periods most, of the truths about the way and purpose of human life, individual and social, have either been revealed by God or can be deduced from such a revelation. That Christians argue about the mode and extent of this revelation does not seriously detract from their agreement about its significance. Secondly, during the last three or four centuries, it has been increasingly evident that truths concerning the natural universe, including man as a biological and psychological specimen, are to be discovered by observation and experiment, from experience rather than revelation. This scientific point of view also claims sometimes to provide truths about social relations and about the sphere of human life called politics.

It might be argued that the true knowledge which, Plato holds, would enable us to live harmoniously together in society is a kind of revelation of a divine order. It is perfect as the social and moral life we know in experience is not. But this Platonic vision is not of a God; it does not suggest that the relationship between the knower and the divine truth is personal; and, above all, it is confined to a very small minority of intellectually and morally gifted persons, called in Greek philosophers.

The closest parallel among present-day intellectual disciplines to this mode of knowledge is mathematics. We know, if we are sane, that twice two is four and we remain proof against the temptation to hold that the answer might perhaps be seventeen. It was this kind of certainty which Plato claimed for rational insight into moral and social truths. By contrast, mathematicians do not now expect their study to provide final conclusions concerning events either in this world or the next; and even devout believers in divine revelation do not require a mathematical certainty in the moral truth to which they give their assent.

There is a further difficulty in coming to understand what Plato tells us about the character and purpose of political association, which is that he constantly employs in his description of the kinds of men and social groups which he believes to be the most satisfactory an analogy drawn from technical skill, a favourite argument of his teacher Socrates and one generally more intelligible to their contemporaries in the Greek world than to ourselves.

Unfortunately, most of the terms which we use in modern languages in the west to describe moral and political values have come down to us through more than one translation and have lost in their long journey much of their original Greek or Latin sense. These difficulties of translation have accentuated the unfamiliarity of Plato's analogies. It is difficult to detect in virtue the idea, originally almost neutral, of being good at something, which pertains to the corresponding Greek term *arete* or the Latin *virtus*. We shall find the same difficulty with justice and nature, examples where even the Latin showed signs of deviation from the Greek. Thus, the good man, for Plato, was analogous to the good sailor and the good carpenter, one possessing a special knowledge of a special technique, but the knowledge was of the good life, or, more simply, how to be good at being a man.

This teleological or purposive view of human life is common to both Plato and Aristotle and their tradition has come down to later thinkers. But the idea of what a good man would be like, were he successfully and constantly good, has been modified and sometimes changed out of all recognition. For Christians, this question proved relatively easy to answer, because to be a good man was to be like Christ; a personal model rather than an idea served to exhibit perfection. But when later thinkers try to define the good man as the happy man, the man who successfully satisfies his desires, or the free man, the parallel with Plato's view is no longer a close one. Admittedly, it might be argued that Plato thought of Socrates as his model and had in mind his friend and master's exceptional character and attainments when he described the man of virtue, the man who was best at being a man. But, in his view, only certain kinds of persons were ever likely, from natural endowment and intellectual ability, to attain such a moral status. For most people the essential precondition of a good and morally successful life was the character and constitution of the community, or city, in which they lived. Plato was acutely aware that the cities of which he had experience condemned most of his contemporaries to unhappy, imperfect and frustrated lives. He conceived the science of politics as an enquiry into the right ordering of the relations of the citizens, such that they might help one another to be good men. It is this reordering of the pattern of social relations, the reframing of the constitution or republic, the Latin term which corresponds to the Greek *politeia*, or polity, which is the theme of Plato's most important study in this field, the *Republic*, a conversation-piece whose sub-title is *Concerning Justice*. It would, indeed, be an advantage if we could go back to using the term polity to describe the body-politic uncluttered by secondary meanings.

This first and most famous of all enquiries into the character of the political relationship, of the ways in which men constitute themselves into organized groups and how they could do so more effectively, makes two assumptions which we shall find absent from many later writings on this subject. The same moral qualities which characterize the good and happy man are taken to be those which will ensure the harmonious life of the group also. The citizens fulfil themselves through their membership; they belong together and sustain one another in ways which remind us more of what we should expect of a church than of a modern state. Secondly, of the desirable moral qualities, or patterns of behaviour as we might now say, of which the four principal examples, wisdom, courage, temperance and justice, have since been known as the cardinal virtues, two are aspects as it were of the character of particular sub-groups of members, but the remaining two, temperance and justice, pervade the whole life of the group and its members and represent the harmonious co-operation between the differentiated parts of the whole.

This harmonious society, then, is an achievement dependent on there being men within it capable of making right judgments, because it is this sense of deciding wisely rather than pronouncing according to law which is nearest to the Greek term translated as justice. But Plato's social theory is in the original sense of the word aristocratic. He did not believe that many men were wise; and thus, while different members of the group might individually be specially virtuous, most of them could only be just citizens, that is function in a politically harmonious and co-operative way, through the grace or good luck of belonging to a well-governed, or wisely governed society. Justice might be achieved by the few; it was conferred on the many; and each group required the other to enable both to live in harmony. But the same behaviour required to promote social harmony was that which expressed and at the same time developed the moral character of individual citizens. Thus did Plato see the political relationship as the indispensable prerequisite of moral achievement.

Any social thinker who sets out to do more than describe how the institutions of a society function and speculates on the further question of the ends which the society is pursuing and the distinction, if any, between these ends and those which it ought to pursue is compelled to explain why, in his view, failure in this sphere ever occurs, to give some account, whether naturalistic or otherwise, of the genesis of imperfection. If this new political society, the just society sketched for us in the *Republic*, is Plato's resolution of a moral dilemma, how did the difficulty arise? This problem is distinct from the historical crisis through which Plato lived, which may be described as the occasion of his enquiry. To say that the decline of Greek city civilization into war and faction was due to the popular teaching of the day, the superficial tenets of the Sophists, was to argue that their opinions on the character of the good life and the good society were untruthful and misguided. It did not meet the wider and more difficult challenge of why men, able to envisage a better and more co-operative way of life, are found in fact to be thus misled, at the mercy of what Plato called opinion or belief as distinct from knowledge and somehow unresponsive to the truth.

One of the Sophists' views, which Plato is particularly at pains to discount in his enquiry into the true character of the just polity, is that which holds that social customs, laws and constitutions are merely conventional, artificial agreements, as it were, made between individuals who are in fact bent on satisfying their particular aims and not concerned with any shared end with other members of the group. Against this early version of the social contract theory Plato contends that the bonds of society are natural and, by implication, universal, arising out of the character and needs of man, none of whom is sufficient unto himself.

The simplest definition of social justice is one which can be framed at the economic level; for it is in the necessity of a reciprocal system of needs and services, in which each member of the group helps to supply the lacks of his fellows, that Plato recognizes a universal principle binding men together in a balanced partnership. The material satisfaction of needs provides at this rudimentary economic level for the happy and satisfying co-existence of the members. As in other simplified utopian myths from the Garden of Eden to the Marxist millennium neither sin nor sorrow need disturb the harmony. But Plato, as later were Rousseau and Marx and earlier the author of *Genesis*, was concerned to explain the common experience of imperfection in history, and the enquiry in the *Republic* goes on to describe the development of society beyond primitive organization which satisfies only the barest needs.

It is at this point in the argument that Plato introduces a metaphor which has reverberated down the ages whenever later writers on politics have succumbed to his influence. The simple economic community is described by Socrates in the *Republic* as 'the true one, in sound health as it were' : and its complication by the addition of luxuries as an 'inflammation'. The setting up of a political community is thus likened to the recovery of health after disease and government is seen as the regime of physicians, with special knowledge, able to reconstitute the economic society and maintain it in a healthy condition. In the first, simple state of the society its moral condition, its expression of justice or harmony, lay in its exhibiting the principle of the division of labour. This principle will continue to be manifest in the society which has recovered from its fever ; but in order to prevent a relapse it will include the newly specialized group called by Plato 'Guardians', physicians of the social soul and, after differentiation, defenders of the social body.

Despite this revealing, but also dangerous, metaphor of disease and recovered health, the process in Plato's description is little like the fall from grace, common to Jewish and Christian thought, and only superficially similar to the corruption of primitive innocence which is described by Seneca, Rousseau and pre-Marxian communist writers. Rather does Plato seem to suggest that the growth of a more complex and cultured society, above the level of what Glaucon described in the *Republic* as 'a community of pigs', must involve a period of maladjustment and disharmony to be brought to an end only by a new and different application of the division of labour and of the modes of interdependence, whereby the members of the community can survive. The two sources of disturbance are not in this case primarily imperfections of human character, but the relation between the human tendency to multiply wants and the evident limitations of the conditions in which Plato himself lived: the relative niggardliness of natural resources and the threat of competition from other human groups leading to war. Plato does not take into account situations where, conceivably, these two factors would not be present.

But the aspect of the metaphor from medicine which tells us most about Plato's theory of politics is the profound difference between natural health, which can be experienced without knowledge of its causes, and reconstituted health which depends on obeying the orders of a physician who, by definition, is applying his general knowledge to particular cases. Without pressing the metaphor too far, we can see that Plato tended to think of the specifically political relationship as superimposed on a natural economic system operating according to the division of labour and as being necessitated by the tendency of the simple system to grow complex, unbalanced and incapable, while constituted in this way, of providing its own remedies and re-establishing its previous harmony.

There are two important points to notice here which occur in later arguments about political organization. The first is the assumption that the general supervision and guidance of the society cannot be undertaken by those members already specializing in various trades and economic techniques; the second, the conviction that the new political classes are to be differentiated not merely in respect of special skills but by reason of special moral attributes. Subsequent debate about the freedom of subjects and the duties and status of ruling groups has often been concerned either to defend or criticize the point of view held by Plato.

The special moral attributes of the groups or classes whose function it is to recreate and defend the harmonious system of the city are wisdom and courage, and the arts which they are enabled thereby to pursue are the political art of ruling and the military art of defence and the maintenance of order. Sometimes, Plato speaks of these activities as if they were technical accomplishments like bricklaying or joinery, in which sense he would be adding only two new economic groups to his community. But by suggesting that the qualification for these two special jobs is primarily a moral one he is differentiating them from all the previous groups in a way which makes the latter appear as members of a single class in relation to these two new groups. Like temperance but unlike the other two virtuous conditions, justice itself does not specifically characterize any one of the three social groups. Like health it is a condition of the whole body-politic and may be defined as the balanced relation between its parts. As also in the case of health, we must now distinguish between the earlier unconscious pattern of co-operation of those engaged in economic activities, and the acceptance of the ordered or imposed pattern of co-operation provided by the physician rulers. From this it is evident that the chance of living the just life for most of the citizens of a Platonic society depends upon their being subjected to the rule of adequately wise superiors. But to this must be added the corresponding requirement that if the society is to continue to be harmonious, over a period of time, it is dependent on its being successfully defended by the second class of courageous auxiliaries (as this sub-division of the guardian class is called).

It is, then, hardly fair to interpret Plato's theory as advocating the sacrifice of the individual to the state, which is only to mis-interpret his analysis of the problem in terms of later arguments and a different language. Where wisdom and courage are believed to be rare virtues but necessary to survival, those who are held to lack these qualities will in a sense depend upon those who have them. But the parts of the body-social are strictly interdependent; and Plato's vision of justice is of a new division, by classes, of a different sort of labour, the establishment of harmony, security and happiness, not for one class only but for all the members of the new political community.

The most telling criticism of these arguments, though its roots go back to Christian and Stoic doctrine, was put most clearly by one of Plato's devoted later disciples, Jean-Jacques Rousseau, who proclaimed one of the principal articles of modern democratic faith in his contention that all members of a society were able and should be willing to frame its laws and fight its battles. But this concept of political equality must await later consideration.

Behind the Platonic conception of political order being the gift of the few to the many lay a pattern of metaphysical speculation which, while it can render Plato's views intelligible for us, at the same time limits their significance for a world which for the most part now holds quite different views. The ideas of creation, evolution or even materialism, as explanations of the universal order, all in one way or another deny the view that what is experienced in time consists in chaotic matter informed by a pattern which is universal, intelligible and spiritual.

This view must be studied in works specially devoted to Plato's thought. We need only note here that for him it seemed sensible to suggest that knowledge of the moral virtues was limited in fact to few persons and that therefore a healthy, harmonious society required that most of its members could expect to enjoy this harmony and security only if they handed over the general direction of affairs to specially qualified groups.

In the case of the third, or economic, class, which must not be thought of as a proletariat for it included all the owners of property, a characteristic denied to the guardians, the imposition of political order corresponded to the moulding of matter in accordance with an intelligible form. The members of this class were not temperate as a result of autonomous choice, though admittedly by willing submission.

The second class, the auxiliaries, however, held an intermediate status, for they were the pupils rather than the material of the guardians proper. They were to be trained rather than merely ordered, as men of sufficient intelligence may be taught to care for their own health by being disciplined in the rules on which its maintenance depends.

The first class of rulers, too, had to undergo training, and it is to be noticed that the role of education in Plato's political theory, as in that of many later writers, is of primary importance, but in contrast with the other two classes, they would have to be self-trained. They were in the position of physicians healing themselves, or at least maintaining their own health, for they were part of the triple-class community which their additional function had brought into being; and in so far as ruling was an essential attribute of this new society the rulers had to make laws to which they themselves would be subject.

There is one provision made for the guardian class which has long been cause for comment since Aristotle first criticized it in his *Politics*: this is the special arrangements made for the forswearing

of private property and family life. In so far as this suggestion is
no more than a corollary of Plato's belief in the dependence of
a harmonious society on the political guidance of a gifted aristocracy, his preference for rearing successive generations of the
ruling class, as one would rear thoroughbred animals, over
leaving the procreation of children to the caprice of personal
choice adds little to his theory of politics. But he had two other
purposes in mind. The first was to foster a sense of family unity
in the ruling class ; and, secondly, to remove from the guardians
all temptation to pursue personal ambitions by depriving them
of the economic and familial pressures which tend to limit the
concern of most citizens to their own private needs. The attempt
to find a principle of social unity constantly recurs in subsequent
discussions of political themes ; and, historically, many ruling
groups have tried to achieve an end similar to Plato's by less
revolutionary means. In the ecclesiastical sphere, there is a close
parallel in the life of the monastic orders. What is significant is
that, if such a plan were to be adopted, the group, like monks,
would have to impose this discipline on themselves.

Plato himself does not fully recognize this peculiar position
of the guardians, since he tends to think of the ideal constitution
as depending on the wisdom of Socrates and the other contributors
to the dialogue. But even in the *Republic* he explicitly states its
realization will depend on the city containing a few uncorrupted
philosophers whom lucky circumstances compel to take charge
of it. In his later work, the *Laws*, Plato specifically recognizes that
the wise philosopher-kings will need to be subject to their own
laws. But the implications of the idea of a self-imposed law were
hidden from Plato and belong to later history.

In the *Laws*, Plato is concerned to outline the pattern of a
second-best rather than an ideal political society ; and it is to be
noticed that in this society temperance becomes the most admir-
able virtue. Nevertheless, we learn less about the primary characteristics of the political relationship from Plato's later works than
from his earlier and admittedly visionary treatise.

Politics is concerned with the general direction, control and
harmonious ordering of the multifarious exchanges of goods and
services between the members of a given group. It is, moreover,
itself an example of one of these services, even the most important

of them. Such a group becomes a political entity, a city, when it, or representative members in it, recognizes such a common end, that is the harmony and security of the whole group, and sets itself deliberately to realize it. The maintenance of harmony and security, even if not in themselves specialist activities as Plato held, must be entrusted to special groups within the whole. These groups would have their own specific function, their own particular work to do, just as the different but analogous economic functions are undertaken by the economic class. Everyone in the city is then in a political as well as an economic relationship with everyone else, either in respect of making the rules and regulations or laws, or of obeying them; and all contribute to the total life of the city according to their special skills. Where the laws are wise, the soldiers courageous and everyone obedient, the society will be happy, harmonious and in the special Greek meaning of the word, just. Finally, only in such a society can most men, for the very rare cases of philosophers might be excluded, find this same justice in their own souls.

Thus does Plato distinguish for us the political from the economic order, and the moral life from the acceptance of mere custom; and, further, in the self-dedication of the guardians and philosopher-kings, hints something of the later importance of the modern doctrine of political freedom.

.   .   .   .   .

It is tempting in passing from Plato to Aristotle to emphasize those aspects of the latter's teaching which most differentiate it from Platonic doctrines. To compare and contrast the thought of these two most famous names in classical philosophy has long been a favourite and not unrewarding sport. To the initiated the distinction between them is marked; but, in the long history of political speculation, it is their similarity which is the more striking: just as Oxford and Cambridge by contrast with each other seem to their devotees places infinitely apart, whereas to those who know them only from afar there is little to choose between their shades of blue.

Aristotle was born into the succeeding generation to Plato's and was related to him as pupil to master, and afterwards remained a member of Plato's Academy for seventeen years.

Unlike his master, he was not a politician turned philosopher, not a member of the privileged Athenian ruling class and, if anything, rather less aware than Plato of the disastrous trend of political events in the fourth century B.C. As Alexander the Great's tutor, Aristotle was closer than most of his contemporaries to the centre of world power at the time, and yet the picture he gives us of the workings of political society, whether ideal or actual, is still that of the Greek city whose independence was finally doomed by Alexander's victorious imperial career.

But also doomed for the greater part of two thousand years was the development of free, scientific enquiry which had flourished in the social and political atmosphere of the Greek cities and which Aristotle's inquisitive mind and wide interests notably represented. Up to the fifteenth century, and, for many people, much longer, Plato and Aristotle remained synonymous with learning for cultured Europe.

We are indebted, therefore, to Aristotle for giving us, at what in retrospect seems to have been the last possible moment, a masterly survey, summary and encyclopaedic review of the realms of knowledge with which the classical Greek mind was acquainted. Himself perhaps primarily a biologist, Aristotle took the whole of natural life for his province and what he has to tell us about human life in cities is only one aspect of his catholic concern with the discovery of truth. In some respects, notably in what he has to say about the ideal life for the individual capable of attaining the highest excellence, Aristotle is no less speculative than Plato. Nevertheless, there is greater emphasis in his academic enquiries on the careful observation of what was happening, on empirical investigation into events ; and although in the political field most of Aristotle's researches are lost to us, the account we have of the political life of the Greek city corresponds closely to the norm of political and moral ends accepted by the Greek world on the eve of its succumbing to Macedonian imperialism.

Aristotle's treatise, the *Politics*, is a very different work from Plato's *Republic*. Scholars have debated even whether in its received form it is Aristotle's own composition, attributing the relative disorder of the material to an accidental compilation of students' notes. At all events the *Politics* has none of the advantages of a connected discourse framed as a work of art which we

enjoy in the *Republic*. But the loss is less serious than a first
reading might suggest.

For one thing, two distinct themes may be clearly enough
distinguished : that concerned with political ends, purposes and
ideals and that which analyses the constitutions of Greek cities
as Aristotle himself knew them. The order in which these subjects
are treated is not very satisfactory, but the two aspects of politics,
what we should now call theory and institutions, remain distinct.

The first, theoretical, argument, which is our primary concern
in this essay, though at times critical of Plato, is at one with the
Platonic conception of politics on two very important issues.
Aristotle agrees that politics is natural, an activity necessarily
bound up with man's specific character and destiny ; and he agrees
too that the political life is a means, an essential means to a
moral end. It is possible that in the present century we are return-
ing to the first, if not also to the second, of these views, but we
must remember that for long periods in the interval one or other
or both of them have been denied.

To Aristotle's second theme our greatest debt is linguistic ;
but it must be added that like other debts it is sometimes embar-
rassing. The analysis of contemporary Greek institutions was
plainly a valuable enquiry at the time, though its interest for us is
now largely historical. But the terms which Aristotle used,
monarchy, aristocracy, oligarchy, democracy, tyranny, have
reverberated down the ages and are still, however drastically
redefined, terms either of honour or abuse in our current political
arguments. Polity, one of Aristotle's most useful, because least
emotive, terms has regrettably shown least survival value. This
is not an altogether happy issue, bedevilling not only our analysis
of modern political institutions, but also our understanding of
Aristotle's own point of view.

It is now commonplace to remark that Aristotle's discussion
of politics as an activity corresponds more closely with Plato's
treatment of the subject in the *Laws* than with his outline of the
ideal community. But for Aristotle this is less a second-best
concern than a sober appraisal of what is best in the circumstances,
of what can in fact be achieved. While Aristotle agreed that
politics was natural, he did not wholly agree with Plato about
man's nature. In one very important respect, he disagreed

fundamentally; and this psychological division of opinion has had a profound subsequent effect on political speculation.

For Plato, the pattern of the good life could be known theoretically, at least by a gifted minority of persons; and if known, then taught, caught or imposed. This was the essence of political life. But for Aristotle, scientific knowledge, knowledge of necessary and universal truths, did not include moral and political truths; that is to say these latter truths were not apprehended by an intellectual faculty called reason, but rather by a practical judgment, refined in everyday experience. What was possible was no abstract pattern of living to which actual conditions must be made to conform, but rather itself to be discovered progressively in experience. The practical life is, then, to be considered separately from the theoretical life and the truths of the former are learned not by the contemplation of eternal verities (though this, Aristotle would admit, is the highest human activity) but by careful attention to experienced events and by a judgment of each particular situation, guided and supported by a disciplined moral disposition.

This empirical approach to pragmatic truths is in close harmony with Aristotle's biological interests. He saw different forms of life in various stages of development, and without propounding an evolutionary doctrine in modern terms, nevertheless interpreted the behaviour of living creatures as the organized pursuit of ends given to them in conformity with their particular characters or natural dispositions. The natural destiny of an organism was to strive to be self-sufficient, by satisfying its several needs; and it was in this sense that organized human communities were natural. The proper nature of any living organism was its final developed state, that state in which it was most perfectly itself. It was in this sense that man, specifically rational, could find his true self only in community, could achieve his highest development only in the polis, and could thus properly be defined as a political animal. Moreover the priority which Aristotle claims for the polis over its individual members is to be similarly explained; it is a moral and natural priority rather than, in the modern usage of the term, constitutional; for the polis is a necessary precondition of the morally fulfilled lives of its members.

This state of moral fulfilment is described by Aristotle in a word usually translated in English as happiness.[1] But this happiness is the reward rather of good judgment than good fortune, and it is less a state than an activity, less an achieved end than an acquired and constantly maintained harmony or balance; and without their political relationship, their living together subject to the laws of the city, the citizens would never achieve this desirable state, never be completely men or thoroughly happy in Aristotle's sense.

Up to this point, Aristotle's description of a political society as the natural and necessary framework for the successful moral development of its members is not markedly different from Plato's. But because he is more interested in what can best be done in the circumstances than what might be done ideally and convinced that knowledge of moral and political ends derives from practical judgment rather than scientific theory, Aristotle does not phrase his political thought primarily in terms of restoration, as does Plato, but as recommendations for the maintenance of an already functioning order.

This is not to say that there is no consideration of why and how human communities go wrong and fail to work. Aristotle's famous section (Book V) on the 'Causes of Revolution and Constitutional Change' is still one of the best of the essays on this perennial political problem which may be recommended to students.

It might in general be argued that for Aristotle, as for Plato, the prime factor which disintegrates a human society is ignorance. As for Plato too, some people are more likely to be ignorant than others. Slaves, unfitted to rule themselves, are thus properly enslaved and necessarily dependent. But it is ignorance of a different kind from that described by Plato. The section of the community, the citizens proper, which is competent to redress social disequilibrium, though a minority in the city, is not the same type of minority as the Platonic guardians. They are not people specially qualified to legislate by reason of a superior knowledge of the good life, derived from natural endowment and

---

[1] Sir Ernest Barker, in his edition of the *Politics* (Oxford, Clarendon Press, 1946), has a valuable section on Aristotle's vocabulary. See in particular pp. lxxv–lxxvi for his discussion of the Greek concept *eudaimonia*.

rigorous training, but men of sound sense and common prudence, self-controlled and well-schooled in moderation and balanced judgment, and therefore capable of administering good laws. They could not do this, however, were they not practised in living the political life; and they are a minority because only those in the community free from daily economic toil will have the opportunity to exercise a capacity for political activity, to accept office and to pursue those liberal ends which Aristotle calls leisurely.

Thus, for Aristotle, citizenship is the privileged status of the ruling group, able to practise the good life and therefore learn more about it, and free to do so only because it is a leisured class, with time and energy to devote its talents to specifically political tasks.

But this ruling group of citizens defines for Aristotle the limits of citizenship; and his idea of the polis as an association for the pursuit of the good life limits its members, unlike the scheme in the *Republic*, to those capable of undertaking administrative, leisured, non-economic, political or military activity. Aristotle does not suppose that such a city will not require economic support, but these illiberal and menial activities, though necessary to the life of the city, are no more than preconditions of its good life. Those who pursue them are mere subjects, not competent or free to take their turn, as are the citizens, in the administration of law.

Less inclusive in this respect than Plato, whose lower classes participated in the organic whole as parts of it, Aristotle at the same time makes fewer demands on his citizens in respect of their political duties. They must be ready to take turns, capable of being both rulers and ruled, for it is in this equal relationship that their political status specifically consists. Moreover, they are not deprived of the ownership of property, the guarantee not only of their economic independence but also of the happiness and satisfaction which is attendant on the pursuit of the higher, political activities. Aristotle's citizen group is, thus, pursuing similar ends to Plato's guardians but by different means in different conditions.

A citizen, then, is to be defined as one 'who enjoys the right of sharing in deliberative or judicial office'; and a properly constituted city 'in its simplest terms, is a body of such persons adequate in number for achieving a self-sufficient existence'.[1] Self-sufficiency is the essential characteristic of an association which may be said to be fully developed. It completes the natural growth of the group as the satisfaction of narrower, more primitive needs began its natural development in, for instance, the family. That Aristotle could argue that the comparatively small political entities of the Greek world were good examples of completely developed human groups may sound unfashionable to us to-day, but does not deprive his discussion of political principles of all relevance for later ages.

Self-sufficiency, for Aristotle, carried with it the sense of independence, wholeness, functional fitness and the organic relationship of the parts of the self-sufficient, self-directing whole. It differed according to the needs believed to be natural to the organism being studied. Indeed, the ability of an organized group to satisfy the needs of its members depends to some extent on which needs the members choose to put first. Man had more than the simple biological needs satisfied by the family, more than the simple social and economic needs satisfied by the village or other small community. He became only the best of animals when perfected, when his special moral characteristics, the life of virtue made possible by the unique gift of language, had full play; and it was only in the life of the city that adequate scope could be found. Without justice, man would be worse than the beasts; without the order, harmony and opportunities for living under law bestowed by the city, justice was impossible.

'Justice,' Aristotle affirms, in a famous definition, 'belongs to the polis; for justice, which is the determination of what is just, is an ordering of the political association.'[2] This is not to say anything seriously different from Plato's own ideal. Man cannot live well alone. His association with his neighbours, determined naturally by biological and economic interdependence, is no less naturally determined by moral interdependence. It is only at the political level that the group becomes independent and self-directing; and to do this it must differentiate within itself special organs, in particular a political class proper, to serve the several

[1] *Politics*, p. 95
[2] *Politics*, p. 7

needs of the group life. Herein is to be found the good life at once natural, perfected and truly human.

Aristotle analyses with some care the different possible structures of his citizen class; for the expression of just balance in the community requires not only the determining of the right qualifications for sharing in the privileges of citizenship, but also an attempt to see that the rewards and honours granted to different citizens accord with a rational and morally satisfactory principle. This latter principle, which is called distributive justice, is Aristotle's answer to the claims of egalitarianism. Equality should express a balance between social function and the corresponding status and reward rather than the unbalanced and, in the Greek view, unjust attempt to disregard this differentiation of social function in favour of an equality which is universal, but disproportionate. Aristotle would agree that the community should ask from each according to his ability, but he would amend the later eighteenth-century slogan to read to each also according to his ability.

The perennial problem of what in modern centuries has been called sovereignty, which in the context of the Greek city was the question of which group of citizens should make the final administrative decisions, is also considered at some length by Aristotle. This question resolved itself for Plato in the setting up of the guardian class; whereas Aristotle, looking at the problem in its empirical setting, considered the claims of the rival groups customarily found in human societies: the well-born, the wealthy, the single outstanding man, the tyrant, and the citizens as a whole. But his conclusion is that the justly ordered city should be as little dependent as possible on the decisions of persons 'subject as persons are to the passions that beset men's souls; and that it is better to rest it [the sovereignty] in law'.[1] 'Rightly constituted laws should be the final sovereign; and personal rule, whether it be exercised by a single person or a body of persons, should be sovereign only in those matters on which law is unable, owing to the difficulty of framing general rules for all contingencies, to make an exact pronouncement'.[2]

Behind this preference for the superiority of the law to the decisions of social groups, however carefully chosen, lay the

[1] *Politics*, p. 122
[2] *Politics*, p. 127

relatively unchanging character of Athenian law, the rules of which were not enacted and altered as by a modern legislature, but a permanent background of regulations against which current decrees, should any be passed, might be measured.

Aristotle revered this system in so far as it represented the stable, prudent and balanced rule of reason, but at the same time he saw that there was no obvious guarantee that a body of law was merely by prescription good and just. Laws, he saw, might themselves be biassed in favour of one group in society against the others, the situation which according to Marx normally obtains. 'The one clear fact,' he concludes, as was Montesquieu to do later, 'is that laws must be constituted in accordance with constitutions; and if this is the case, it follows that laws which are in accordance with right constitutions must necessarily be just, and laws which are in accordance with wrong or perverted constitutions must be unjust.'[1]

But by constitution Aristotle did not mean only or primarily, as we do now, the division of authority and the arrangement of offices; for this definition leaves out of account the supremely important question of the purpose or end served by the political structure so classified. A king can be just or tyrannical; oligarchies selfish or genuinely aristocratic; and democracies mere examples of mob-rule or representative of the general prudence and wisdom which is often to be found in a cross-section of the population. If the proper end of the community is to be organized for the pursuit of the good life, only governments which consider this common interest have the right, or morally satisfactory, constitution. Only authority exercised in pursuit of this common interest is just. Conversely, whenever any sectional concern is paramount, and in particular the special selfish interests of a ruling person or group, the constitution, according to Aristotle, is perverted and the laws will be unjust and not properly a final court of appeal.

The question of which form of constitution is best in the administrative sense is, thus, secondary for Aristotle. Whether the rich or the poor dominated the constitution, the few or the many, they could do so either for the good of all or for their sectional interest. On the whole, Aristotle himself had highest hopes of the

[1] *Politics*, ibid.

collective judgment of the many, the bulk of the citizens, when it took the form of decisions in favour of the whole polis, and he calls this kind of constitution a polity. But we must remember that the collective assembly had little of the final democratic control claimed by modern legislatures. Its chief functions were to elect the executive officers and to review their work. The term democracy is reserved by Aristotle for the perverted expression of popular government and had not then acquired the much fuller meaning it bears to-day.

In personal as in public life, Aristotle was against extremes. The pursuit of perfection must be along the middle path. It was the prudent not the eccentric man who was to be trusted, the man of regular and well-disciplined habits. So too did Aristotle prefer the middle group of citizens, neither too rich nor too poor. Moreover, it was the quality of the personal life of the citizens which both sustained and was sustained by the political constitution.

As for Plato, the part played by education was a foremost consideration in building the just city. Citizens must be educated in those habits of life which befitted the kind of city they lived in, which would enable the constitution of that city to be maintained. The system adopted should be common to all the citizens and regulated by the political authorities. But what we should call state education was not merely an economic and administrative convenience, but necessitated by the final moral purpose which informed the political structure of the Greek city. It was for this reason that the educational training suggested by Aristotle for an ideal city was concerned to develop natural endowment by schooling the character in good habits and exercising the rational faculty, so that individuals themselves could maintain their own self-control.

In Aristotle, as in Plato, we must beware of interpreting the emphasis he places on the unity of the city as the subordination of its members to an impersonal central control. It is better to think of the co-operation of the citizens as a partnership in the good life; and for both Aristotle and Plato, the political life is ultimately a means to moral perfection, being both its precondition and one of the best ways of exercising the moral character.

But for Aristotle, beyond the practical life lay the higher reaches of pure intellectual activity, the theoretical life proper; for it was in contemplation of universal, scientific truth that a man, had he the leisure, ability and wisdom, could expect to be most completely happy and in which he would fulfil himself most satisfactorily as a man. This was the life of the greatest self-sufficiency, least dependent on outside support; 'for while it is true that the wise man equally with the just man and the rest requires the necessaries of life, yet . . . whereas the just man needs other persons towards whom or with whose aid he may act justly, and so likewise do the temperate man and the brave man and the others, the wise man on the contrary can also contemplate by himself, and the more so the wiser he is; no doubt he will study better with the aid of fellow-workers, but still he is the most self-sufficient of men'.[1]

In the three centuries which elapsed between the death of Aristotle and the consolidation of the Roman imperial system, few of the political principles worked out in the life of the Greek cities could be applied to the changing pattern of the nascent, polyglot imperial communities of the Hellenistic age. But the Greek ideal of the unified and morally satisfying community persisted in the very different circumstances of the great society; although the myriad individuals, often uprooted and adrift, who peopled the urban centres of the Mediterranean world must have felt themselves infinitely far from its realization. It is not surprising, therefore, that there was little scope for political speculation in this confused period, and that the emphasis of the leading schools of thought was on the practical moral problems of the individual, fending for himself in what was often an alien, unfriendly and dangerous world.

It was in this setting that the classical concept of the polis was extended to the wider and more abstract vision of the cosmopolis; and during these centuries that the political virtues of the Greek citizen were less in evidence than the stern, Stoic ideal of suffering the decrees of fate and necessity, while never allowing circumstances to deflect the wise man from his pursuit of duty.

    .   .   .   .   .

[1] *Nicomachean Ethics* (Loeb), X, vii

The relationship between theory and practice in human affairs is inconstant; and possibly never again since Aristotle's day have political practice and precept been as little divided as was the case during the preceding generation. The spread of Greek rule to the middle-eastern empires and the supersession in the Mediterranean world of the loosely connected, self-governing cities by centres of royal, and later imperial, authority caused a gulf between traditional Greek thought about city life and the new institutions of the great society which was never successfully bridged from either side. Developments in the realm of theory remained ideal, disconnected from events and imprecise, while the new institutions of central authority, extended citizenship, universal law and the despotism of the later Roman empire failed to correspond to the only political theory available to interpret them, and for many centuries there was nothing new to replace it.

The growth of new concepts in jurisprudence, designed by Roman lawyers to match the extended imperial responsibilities of the original local civil law of a single city, did not of itself add to the stock of political theory proper. Nor can we argue that the emergence of the important new ideas of universal equality and of the law of nature, striking and significant as they undoubtedly were, constituted the sharp break with the classical Greek past for which it has often been accepted as evidence. These concepts remained ideals, far removed from the daily experience of the large-scale administration which replaced life in the Greek cities. It was the search for justice which remained constant; though it had to be conducted in new and unfamiliar surroundings and the ideal forms in which the Greek and Roman thinkers of the imperial period expressed their conclusions about social life were necessarily imprinted with the institutional patterns of the great society.

The closely-knit political life of the Greek city was affected principally in two ways. The city itself ceased to be a self-governing entity with wide initiative in the administration of its own laws and in the conduct of relations with other cities. This result became increasingly evident as Roman imperialism supplanted Macedonian and the central power ceased to be in Greek hands. But at the same time Greek thought and culture, language and custom, spread east and west and, at least until the counterattack of the middle-eastern religions, gave to Hellenism a pre-eminence on a universal scale which Athens in her prime had never rivalled.

The inhabitants of this new, extended and uprooted world developed an outlook on life at once less parochial and more individualized. They were members, if not yet citizens, of a society wider than and different from the cities of their fathers' allegiance. But the increased mobility in the Mediterranean world, the confusion of races, languages and cultures, and the diminished chances of local advancement threw the individual back on his personal life and resources. There was as yet no theory to distinguish the individual from the social realm, to differentiate the provinces of private and public life, such as developed in later centuries, but the experiences which demanded such an interpretation became the common lot of the generations which succeeded the deaths of Alexander and Aristotle.

The Roman imperial system which finally brought together the warring, post-Alexandrian states was no organic social development of the kind which could find a place in Aristotle's theory, but an efficient administration superimposed on a congeries of diverse cities, bereft of their freedom but saved from one another. It depended for its success on a competent civil service, a well-trained standing army and the wide, though diffused and unrepresented, popular support of the many peoples for whom the benefits of Roman rule outweighed subjection to its control, taxation and overlordship.

But the new experiences of social life in an imperial age had no immediate repercussions in the realm of theory; and the Hellenistic and early imperial centuries represent a classical example of the difficulties of interpreting new social phenomena in terms of traditional concepts and theories. The first effects of these momentous changes were modifications and differences of application rather than any attempt at the revolutionary restatement of the Greek theory of politics. There was available no historical pattern of progressive or dynamic social thought, such as we find in Condorcet or Hegel or Marx and their followers. In theory it was a static, unchanging social order; in practice subject to the most catastrophic and revolutionary changes.

2

The characteristic distinction between the Greek and the barbarian, for instance, was transmuted, under pressure of the experience of a cosmopolitan world, into the general distinction between the wise and the foolish; and it was the wise, as formerly it had been Greeks, who were specially favoured by heaven. There was still a pattern of the virtuous life which could be known intellectually by the gifted and taught to others; but these special truths were open to any individuals with the right endowment and not reserved for a special, political class. Moral individuals took the place of political classes and their unity was universal, mysterious and unseen. The concept of citizenship remained valid and valuable; but even the wide extension of this coveted privilege by the early third century A.D. failed to incorporate the great masses of the Roman proletariat; and the philosophers could offer to the unprivileged only the doubtful consolation of keeping their souls free, however enslaved and undernourished their bodies. In the privileged classes the ideal of the moral life as the service of the political body either administratively or judicially remained valid and important, at any rate up to the founding of the empire, as we can see from the life and writings of Cicero; but for those to whom such opportunities were not open there grew up the practice of regarding private, social relationships and service as morally no less satisfactory.

Parallel with the continuance of the old values and habits there developed new loyalties and customs outside and wider than those of the polis. In the new social patterns of cosmopolitan society, in the growth of the popular religions, and in the great polyglot cities such as Alexandria, Antioch and, finally, Rome herself we can see the birth of a new pattern of social and political relationships and sometimes catch hints of the radical new theories which later served to interpret this great social experiment in terms which proved intelligible to its sponsors.

But at least until the end of the third century A.D., that is to say for six centuries after the death of Aristotle, the primary concern of the successive governments of the Mediterranean world was that of secular administration, informed by such moral purpose and legal equity as the combined wisdom of Greece and Rome together could supply. In Sir Ernest Barker's words: 'A Roman development meets a Greek conception. That is the genesis of the conception of the Roman Empire.'[1] Differently phrased, as Maine had said earlier, 'the Greek theory of a law of Nature was applied to the practical Roman administration of the law common to all Nations'.[2] This was as close as the realms of theory and practice ever came; and even here the divorce of the theory from the facts was more in evidence than their assumed harmony and congruence.

The social thinkers of the Hellenistic age, excluded for the most part from direct political activity, concentrated on those problems of personal conduct which most commonly beset their unsettled contemporaries. The search for the good life continued in the new conditions and the concepts of wisdom and self-sufficiency continued to serve the theme of individual moral character where before they had described the pattern of political life in the city. Indeed, the cosmopolis or world city with its life of virtue was the old polis, purified, idealized and writ large.

The quest was common to all the great schools of thought, Stoics, Epicureans, Cynics and later the modified version of Latin Stoicism, of which Seneca and the Emperor Marcus Aurelius are the most famous examples. But if the dominant theme was still in terms of the Platonic insistence that the moral life was one of co-operation with a man's fellows in communal activity and of Aristotle's ideal of self-sufficient independence, the centre of this co-operation was no longer the self-sufficient polis and independence itself became an attribute of the individual rather than of the community. The effect and appearance of much of this teaching was, thus, negative and often unworldly. Among the Cynics, of whom Diogenes is most often remembered, it became anarchical and anti-social. For the Epicureans, at their best very different from the self-indulgent aesthetes of popular legend, the emphasis was clearly on a withdrawal from public responsibility, on the studied avoidance of anxiety and care, which left them with little noticeable influence on social thought and behaviour. Even in the case of the Stoics, by far the most persistent and influential of all the schools, the principal message was that a man

[1] Barker: 'The Conception of Empire' in *The Legacy of Rome* (Oxford, Clarendon Press, 1923), p. 60
[2] Sir Henry Maine: *Ancient Law* (10th ed., London 1884), p. 55

should suffer fate and fortune with equanimity and without complaint, do his duty with resolution rather than enthusiasm and, should the situation become intolerable, withdraw finally in the act of suicide. Marcus Aurelius austerely exemplified the first ideal; Seneca, whose fate included the service of Nero, sadly followed the latter path. The ideal polis was no longer a possibility within the confines of the new order. Athens could not serve as a satisfactory symbol. There was only the mystical community of the wise, the universal city of gods and man, or else some utopian dream of vanished innocence or paradise to come. In these theoretical realms the manifest injustice and inequality of social life could be remedied more effectively than even Rome with all her power and prestige was able to achieve.

The positive contribution of the later Greek philosphers to the interpretation of social and individual problems came to be expressed in the development of the concept of nature. At once the most fruitful and the most elusive and confusing of all social ideas, nature and the natural has enjoyed a continuous conceptual career from Greek times to our own. But the continuity has been verbal only, for both the variety of the meanings attached to these terms and the estimation of their value and significance have been wider and less stable than in the case of almost any other long-lived political concept.[1]

The distinction between the natural and the conventional in human affairs was traditional in Greek thought. Both Plato and Aristotle set out to show that political life was natural for man, the morally proper exercise of reason in society, the forum of the good life. Furthermore, for Aristotle, inclined to draw upon biological analogies and even to see political bodies as varying examples of an organic type, the term natural served a dual purpose. It described behaviour which fitted the circumstances, which, therefore, in terms of political justice, allowed for some variation, and also the constitution which most closely resembled the norm of good development. To be natural was to be harmonious and normal, empirically adjusted to circumstances and also ideally fully developed. Constitutions are not identical everywhere, but 'in all places there is only one form of Government

---

[1] For the difficulties involved in the long history of natural law theory, see, in particular, Professor A. P. d'Entrèves's essay, *Natural Law*, in this series.

that is natural, namely, the best form'.[1] This conception of the natural as that which achieved its end not merely as best it could but in the fuller sense of the unconditionally best way for any particular species is not Aristotle's usual use of the term. We must be careful to see that it is an extension and not a contradiction of his customary usage, because he would not have argued that defective examples of civic or any other bodies were unnatural or that the harmoniously constituted but less than perfect polis was thereby rendered merely conventional.

But it was this further use of the term natural, to mean an ideal pattern of relations and development which should serve as a criterion of judgment for assessing experienced events, which came to be fashionable among Aristotle's Stoic successors. The confusion between the idea of nature as a causal system of physical and biological changes and its use as a universal moral norm has remained with us to this day.

Thus it was that Zeno, founder of the Stoic school and significantly an alien from Cyprus with probably a Phoenician ancestry, began to argue that the only social order which could be called natural was universal and that limited political bodies, precisely in respect of their narrowness, were conventional. This was not to divorce social and political relationships from the moral life, but to say that only in a very much wider community could the moral life successfully be lived. This not only implied a condemnation of the scale of the Greek city-life, but even hinted that its central doctrine that political and moral ends were at one might have to be questioned in the changed circumstances. With the suggested widening of the scale of the polis came the first awareness that perhaps no earthly community could satisfy man's moral aspirations.

If there is any theme which unites the divergent uses of the idea of nature during these centuries, it is perhaps the emphasis on necessity. We are accustomed to-day to distinguish clearly between physical and moral necessity. Furthermore, it is obvious that men are subjected to the causal sequences of the physical order and to the social pressure of custom whether they understand them or not, whereas the awareness of a moral obligation must

[1] *Nicomachean Ethics* (Loeb), V, vii, 5. See also M. B. Foster's comment in *Masters of Political Thought* (London 1942), vol. I, pp. 193–94.

involve some kind of rational comprehension. But in a system of values such as Stoicism, where the emphasis was strongly on submission to the pattern of events and in which moral virtue was accredited primarily to the way in which the wise man passively accepted his fate, the distinction between a physical accident, a bereavement, and, say, an act of injustice suffered by an individual was not of primary importance. For the Stoic, nature was the total system of necessary events: it was the character of a man's reaction to this system which established his moral status. In the Roman version of the creed, as we find it in Seneca, there is the reiterated reference to the unchanging, perpetual factors in life, the echo of the Greek insistence that that which changes least is most real, most excellent, nearest to the divine. For Cicero, too, nature usually means the true order of living, carrying with it the double sense of that which must be because it is ordained of God and that which ought to be, by comparison with human behaviour as we know it.

Whereas, however, the political and legal structure of the empire fulfilled many of the demands of the philosophers, this service was not done in compliance with their theories and both the oppression and the inequalities of the imperial system could only be stigmatized as unnatural. If there were a cosmopolis of the wise with its franchise open to all, it was evidently not in the Roman world and until the triumph very much later of Christian doctrine with its kingdom not of this world and its ecclesiastical organization within it, citizenship remained the special privilege it had always been in Greek theory.

By the end of the third century B.C. the Stoa had become the most influential and eminent of the Athenian schools of philosophy and for the succeeding four or five hundred years its teaching retained a hold over many of the best minds in the Greek and Roman worlds. Where Epicureans saw the political relationship as a matter of convenience, maintaining the Sophist tradition of earlier centuries and in some respects foreshadowing modern utilitarian theories, the Stoics insisted on the natural, rational and positive bond of all men subject to a universal law of justice, ideally to be expressed in a world community, but also to be realized to some extent in the fulfilment of whatever social duties fell to a man's lot. Where the Cynics had preached the free anarchism and non-political brotherhood of the wise, another recurring theme in social thought, Stoics could welcome and serve the law and order of the empire, using their own concept of a universal natural law less as an alternative and higher allegiance than as a standard in the light of which the positive achievements of Roman law could be assessed.

There are many references to the all-embracing, universal and harmonious city idealized by Stoic teaching. It was more a moral, even religious, concept than strictly political. Yet we can discern the lineaments of the old Athens in this Hellenistic vision, with the purified and universal law common to all its members, its citizenship open to the wise, its bond of brotherly concord, from which Zeno taught that only a man's own folly need exclude him. Two centuries later, Posidonius saw both gods and men as co-citizens of this single, universal order; and the vision of the true law, promulgated by divine decree and necessarily known to all men by virtue of their common rationality, was expressed by Cicero in one of the most famous passages of his *De Re Publica*. 'True law is right reason in agreement with nature; it is of universal application, unchanging and everlasting; it summons to duty by its commands, and averts from wrongdoing by its prohibitions. And it does not lay its commands or prohibitions upon good men in vain, though neither have any effect on the wicked. It is a sin[1] to try to alter this law, nor is it allowable to attempt to repeal any part of it, and it is impossible to abolish it entirely. We cannot be freed from its obligations by senate or people, and we need not look outside ourselves for an expounder or interpreter of it. And there will not be different laws at Rome and at Athens, or different laws now and in the future, but one eternal and unchangeable law will be valid for all nations and all times, and there will be one master and ruler, that is, God, over us all, for he is the author of this law, its promulgator, and enforcing judge. Whoever is disobedient is fleeing from himself and denying his human nature, and by reason of this very fact suffers the worst penalties, even if he escapes what is commonly considered punishment. . . .'[2] The terms which Cicero uses here,

---

[1] Cicero does not mean sin in the Jewish or Christian sense. The Latin reads 'nec . . . fas est' which means literally 'neither is it right by divine law', but this is a law apprehended in the Greek sense by reason, not revealed.

[2] *De Re Publica* (Loeb), III, xxii, 33

constans, sempiterna, immutabilis, will be found used of the law of nature to this day; and the suggestion that its severest sanction lies in a man's own conscience has similarly survived the changes of two thousand years.

There was a similar agreement on the question of the universal equality which was directly entailed by the rational system of laws to which all men were held equally to be subject. This doctrine of equality, the emergence of which is sometimes held to be the distinguishing mark of post-Aristotelian social thought,[1] is, once again, less a radically new development than an extension and adaptation in changed circumstances of Aristotle's own argument that one of the desirable characteristics of a functioning citizen body is that its members should all enjoy equal status. With the extension of the cosmopolitan concept of citizenship went a similar extension of the corresponding equality. Neither ideal was in fact realized in the Roman world.[2] The theory remained an ideal construction. But once wisdom and virtue were theoretically within all men's reach, and so long as these qualities remained the criteria of membership, then the equality and citizenship of the cosmopolis were open to all. 'There is no human being of any race,' as Cicero put it, 'who, if he finds a guide, cannot attain to virtue.'[3]

In practice there were not enough guides or else an unexplained indisposition on the part of most men to follow them. It was plainly difficult and unsatisfactory to transpose the Platonic doctrine of a city guided and guarded by philosophers into the circumstances of a cosmopolitan empire. Cicero, who refers vaguely to the bad habits and false opinions which deflect the weaker brethren, was forced back on a general statement that the most important conclusion of the philosophers' discussions was the 'full realization that we are born for justice, and that right is based, not upon men's opinions, but upon nature'.[4] It is a con-

---

[1] Notably in R. W. and A. J. Carlyle: *A History of Mediaeval Political Theory in the West,* vol. I, ch. 1
[2] See W. W. Tarn: *Hellenistic Civilisation* (London 1927), pp. 272–73. The Stoic world state was in practice unrealizable, he says, 'for the world was composed of ordinary men, ruled by people who were not philosophers and had no knowledge of the Universal Law'.
[3] *De Legibus* (Loeb), I, x, 30
[4] *De Legibus,* ibid., 28

viction not unlike Rousseau's famous declaration that men are
born for freedom, but Cicero had no adequate theory of the
character of the chains to which Rousseau's exposition was
primarily devoted.

Equality, thus, became an equality of moral expectation based
upon common humanity. Cicero relates his general argument
directly to 'a clear conception of man's fellowship and union with
his fellow-men. For no single thing is so like another, so exactly
its counterpart, as all of us are to one another.'[1] We ought, therefore, to live in a just society. This would be the natural, proper
and morally best condition of human social co-operation.

But Cicero, still using the concepts of Greek political thought,
reiterates that the very being of a political body depends upon its
just constitution; and that the absence of justice renders the
republic a disconnected multitude. The language, however, has
become Latin and legal. 'The commonwealth is the affair of the
people, but the people is not any assemblage of men, gathered
together in any fashion, but a gathering of the multitude united
together under a common law (*consensu iuris*) and in the enjoyment
of a common well-being.'[2] The organization of such political
bodies, whether by way of preserving existing examples or by
founding new ones, still claimed Cicero's loyalty as an activity of
the highest value : 'For there is really no other occupation in which
human virtue approaches more closely the august function of the
gods. . . .'[3]

It was, however, the purpose of the political body, its pursuit
of communal well-being by means of submission to a common
law, rather than the precise mode of government and administration which, for Cicero as for Aristotle, conferred its true status,
morally and politically, on the commonwealth. An unjust government destroyed the very being of the commonwealth; and conversely Seneca in the following century agreed with Cicero that it
was not the form of the government but its moral end which was
of primary importance.

When Rome with its own civil law resting largely on custom
came to be responsible for administering the Mediterranean

[1] *De Legibus*, ibid., 28, 29
[2] *De Re Publica*, I, xxv, 39 (Carlyle's translation)
[3] *De Re Publica*, I, vii, 12

world, the strong central authority of the principate, which this immense task provoked, continued to be derived in theory from the consent of the people, just as in practice it rested on wide popular support. We must not interpret this democratic language in modern terms. It was never suggested that the people made the law; and, indeed, for Cicero himself, the justice which the law of a valid political body expressed was decreed by heaven. In theory, law was perceived by reason and therefore obeyed; in practice it was decreed and enforced by the political authority.

Side by side with the extension of Roman civil law there developed the wider law of nations or *ius gentium* under the aegis of which all those alien and foreign subjects of Rome who enjoyed no citizen status could nevertheless obtain justice. The precise interrelations of these two branches of Roman law and their interpretation in the light of the universal application of natural law principles is extremely confusing. But there seems little reason to suppose, despite passages in some Roman jurists to the contrary, that the Roman lawyers responsible for the development and administration of these codes were wont to consider the question from the point of view of philosophical political theory. 'It is indeed very difficult to construct a coherent doctrine from the different views which are expressed on the subject in the passages quoted in the *Digest*.'[1]

Despite Cicero's tendency to exalt natural law to a position of legal rather than solely moral pre-eminence, it seems agreed that in practice its decrees never enjoyed the status of a higher law but were held rather to be ideal principles of criticism. If the congruence of *ius naturale* and *ius gentium* was the point of contact between theory and practice under the imperial administration, it would seem that it was only in theory and not in practice that they ever approached each other really closely.

The achievements of Rome were doubtless idealized by later centuries deprived of the benefits of her rule, but they were not unappreciated by many of her subjects at the time. Nevertheless, however competent her civil servants, however impartial her system of universal laws, Rome could not disguise the fact that her central authority rested increasingly as time went on upon

---

[1] D'Entrèves, op. cit., p. 24. The full discussion of these difficulties in Chapter I of Professor d'Entrèves's essay should be consulted.

despotic military power. There were many critics of public affairs; and just as Cicero regretted the decline of the old republic, Seneca despaired of the service of the empire, personified in Nero, and declared that only the service of mankind in the invisible bond of the cosmopolis remained open to the wise for whom the republic had proved unworthy.

The equality and freedom which might be lacking in the lives of the subjects of the empire could, in the Stoic sense, be found perhaps in their souls. To some extent the wise man by limiting his desires to the measure of his circumstances could establish in his own life the balance and harmony which was not to be found in public service. But it was less easy to find a realm in which the ideal community, displaced from historical events, could in any satisfactory sense be experienced.

Seneca himself imagined a golden age mythically relegated to the beginning of time and his criticism of Posidonius, who had described civilization as the work of reason, has been likened to the Christian vision of paradise and the fall. An almost exactly similar theme was used by Rousseau to illustrate the theory that life according to nature was innocent and the arts and crafts progenitors of luxury and avarice. Seneca's views, although different in very important respects from Christian doctrine, notably in the maintenance of the Greek view that the pursuit of evil is a kind of rational error, do give one significant hint of the change which was to come over social thinking in the succeeding centuries. 'Justice was unknown to them, unknown prudence, unknown also self-control and bravery.'[1] In this ideal myth of the natural society the established Platonic virtues were not in evidence because they were not required; the ends which they subserved were common practice. Here indeed we have a classical parallel to the idea that these social virtues flourish only in a world gone astray and are in some sense provoked by its sinful condition.

The gaps, however, between body and soul and between the political reality and the natural vision were too great to be bridged even by a modified theory of Greek morals and politics. These divided realms remained unreconciled. There had, however, been other signs in the Graeco-Roman world of a new orientation of thought and values, notably among the secret religious cults

[1] *Epistulae Morales* (Loeb), XC, 46

which became increasingly popular from Hellenistic times onwards. It was from Orphism that the philosophers' tendency to
segregate the spirit and the flesh principally sprang. These
religious groups not only brought together the drifting individuals
of the great society, but provided them with a new centre of
loyalty and companionship and, in their initiation ceremonies, set
aside the converts in a new divine-human unity. They provided
responses to an alien and difficult environment which the individual could not make for himself and which his city no longer
provided for him. Not only is it true, then, that the Hellenistic
religions paved the way for Christianity, which began its career
as only one popular religion among rivals, but also that they fore-
shadowed the growth of a new social institution, the church,
within and set over against the political body.

The consequences for political thought and practice of this
division of spheres were profound and continuous. But the
influence of Christianity has not meant the abrogation of the ideal
of justice either in its Greek or Roman sense, but rather a re-
definition of the purpose, limitation and character of the political
relationship in terms of ideals which were no longer to be centred
in a single human social institution, the city, whether Athens or
Rome, but to be shared between two realms and two institutions,
the church and the secular order.

CHAPTER II

PEACE AND ORDER

'I AM under an obligation both to Greeks and barbarians, both to the wise and to the foolish.'[1] That the Gospel of Christ, which Paul felt constrained to preach to all men, marks a new development in social thought does not require to be argued. But this deliberate use of the terms customarily employed to categorize the different social groups of the Hellenistic world is evidence that we must look with suspicion on attempts to assimilate Christian doctrine too closely to contemporary pagan views. It is the novelty of this development which requires to be emphasized. St. Paul's message cut wholly across the accepted divisions of the Gentile world. It was not to be confined either to those who could have claimed Aristotelian citizenship or to those who aspired to become Stoic sages. Whatever similarities can be discovered between Christianity and other contemporary movements of thought, and many must be admitted, the Gospel both in principle and in practice was preached to all men. It enshrined an equality and built up a brotherhood which had hitherto enjoyed little more than the theoretical status of an aspiration.

No social or intellectual barrier limited entry to the new fraternity; and it was perhaps for this reason that the communities which it fostered had, at the outset, few or no characteristics which could at that date properly be called political. Yet it is plain that they fulfilled many of the social and moral demands left unsatisfied by the decline of independent city-life. Moreover, the religious rites of these nascent churches provided a far profounder experience of incorporation than was given by the largely formal cults of the civic divinities in the pagan world. Nor did the release from anxiety and loneliness offered to the faithful convert require to be gained at the cost of the depravity and self-indulgence which too often characterized the practices of the mystery

[1] *Rom.* i, 14

religions.[1] But we must not attribute the advanced moral level of personal and social behaviour, characteristic of Christian aims, solely or even primarily to the personality of Paul. That he was a gifted organizer of a widespread system of Christian cells, called churches, is agreed and certainly the institutional framework of the church owes much to his energy and genius. But the doctrine which he preached and certainly the teaching which brought him converts was the teaching and message of Christ.[2] There is no call to sustain the view that the Gospels themselves contain no social thought or that there is a special category of doctrine, known as Pauline Christianity, to which we require to confine our attention.

The unusual features of the new religion were presented, however, in a setting familiar enough to the Gentiles. It is commonplace to emphasize that the demand for salvation in one form or another was widespread at the time. In company with the other and earlier established religious groups, Christianity offered freedom from the supernatural control of demonic forces, release from the shackles of fate, and a spirit of indifference to the vagaries of fortune. But in place of a negative submission to the pattern of events, a self-centred salvation which issued in apathy and a philosophic detachment which sometimes ended in despair, the new religion brought a conviction of joyous purpose, a sense of close social unity with the brotherhood, and, above all, initiation into a divine-human commonwealth with rewards in this world and hereafter many times more substantial than those predicated of the cosmopolis. Belief in the reality of Christ's resurrection, which was, and still is, the central article of the new faith, served not only to unite the disparate realms of God and man, but to bring together the divorced spheres of mind and body, and to interpret the mystery of death more convincingly than any of its rivals. We must then ask ourselves what other new beliefs provided the Christian church with its initial driving force and the power to build itself into an institution of parallel significance and authority with the Roman empire until, in later centuries, it was

---

[1] That some early Christian groups interpreted the freedom of the Gospel as a general licence to misbehave and modelled themselves on the mysteries is obvious from St. Paul's very strong condemnation of sexual extravagance throughout his writings and particularly in his letters to the Christians in Corinth.

[2] II *Cor.* iv, 5

able to challenge the secular power for the position of final arbiter in the ordering of man and society.

The foremost of the conceptions which Christianity owed to its Jewish background was the linked ideas of sin and redemption. Compared with the Greek distinction between ignorance and wisdom, which tended to separate the two groups of those who could not and those who could attain to the truth, the emphasis was shifted to the sphere of achievement; for sin was primarily a failure to do or be something, a falling short of an ideal, a missing of the mark. The character of revelation, whether according to the Old or the New Testament, was such that it was open to all men who were privileged or able to hear it. The chosen people were all in the Greek sense philosophers, except that they lacked the Socratic gift of identifying the life of virtue with the knowledge of it.

The distinction between those who hear only and those who hear and obey is frequent and significant in the New Testament. 'Not every one that saith unto me, Lord, Lord, shall enter into the kingdom of heaven; but he that doeth the will of my Father which is in heaven.'[1] Those that hear and do are likened to the wise man who built his house on a rock. Paul, treating the same theme in a famous passage in *Romans* ii, repeats that it is not the hearers but the doers of a law which are just before God, and the Greek term used in this passage for hearers could almost be rendered students in the sense of people who attend lectures.

There arose, then, a new pattern of unity or brotherhood, the new Israel, which was to become the world-wide church. The members had in common not only their knowledge of the divine truth but their common experience of failure or sin and their common hope of being ransomed from this predicament and restored to divine favour. Paul often suggests that faith alone will justify this restoration; James prefers works; but for both there is a unity of sinners and redeemed and the significant division becomes one between God and the sinner rather than that between the mind and the body of the individual or the educated and the uninstructed in the community. The familiar distinction in the New Testament between life after the spirit and after the flesh

[1] *Matthew* vii, 21

must not be confused with the higher and lower aspects of human nature referred to in pagan philosophy, but seen rather as the contrary claims of the divine kingdom and the sinful self conflicting in the individual's life.

But the opportunities for repentance, forgiveness and reconciliation were no less characteristic of the life of the new community than its conviction of failure and disobedience. Other religious movements offered release and various forms of purgation, but none so effectively united its devotees in a closely corporate group, centred on a loyalty to a divine founder whose presence among them was no less real and far more influential than that of the many social and political pressures to which they were subject in the secular world.

It is often said that the divinely revealed law is not incompatible with the provisions of natural law as they were set forth by classical social thinkers. The later assimilation of the two codes supports this contention. But whereas there is little evidence that the moral pronouncements of natural law theory were ever more than ideal standards or criteria, the effect of the divine law on the faithful was immediate and binding. Gentiles, Paul tells us, deprived of direct knowledge of God's will, may nevertheless act in accordance with it, 'do by nature the things of the law'; but he adds that in this case they 'are a law unto themselves', responding only to their own consciences.[1]

From the very beginning of the new movement we may detect signs of the profound effects which a conscious response to the divinely revealed law was to entail. This was especially true of the part which the church was later to play, by comparison with other religious groups, in its relation with the civil authorities. In Paul's condemnation of the insubordinate Christian cell at Corinth, he draws attention to the continuance of a practice no longer necessary among Christians, the reference of quarrels among the brethren to a civil court. To have a lawsuit with a fellow-Christian is already to have lost the case. Paul castigates it as a shameful procedure; for while he recognizes that differences of opinion and interest may occur, he holds that their resolution is always possible and ought to take place within the brotherhood.[2] There was no

[1] *Rom.* ii, 14, 15
[2] I *Cor.* vi, 1–11

suggestion that divine law excused the convert from compliance with the civil law, an issue clarified by Christ himself in perhaps the most often quoted verse[1] in this context, when the claims of God and Caesar were precisely differentiated; nor that the rigours of the Jewish law could be evaded in favour of licentiousness, an interpretation on the part of some early converts which Paul was particularly at pains to discount. The new argument presented here, which was destined to affect the social relations of the whole of a great society and to dominate Europe for a millennium, is that just as God is the final judge in his own causes, no less than Caesar in his, so must the community of the faithful, the new Israel, be the first and final court of appeal in all questions of dissension among its members.

The moral distinction between Christian ideals and natural law is not perhaps very great; the pattern of Christian living has many points in common with the approved virtues of sage and philosopher in the classical world; but the founding of a corporate body recognizing a supreme final seat of authority and from the beginning preferring its own tribunals was an institutional innovation of very great consequence.

The prevention of dissension or, failing that, the promotion of reconciliation became a principal aim of the new community. There was from the first an emphasis on the relations between the members and supremely on their relations individually and corporately with God. It is this latter element which differentiates the new doctrine from the harmony and justice of the Greek city, with which otherwise it shares many characteristics. Paul specifically warns the Corinthians against the pursuit of self-sufficiency, of which Aristotle on the contrary would certainly have warmly approved, as would probably many of Paul's Gentile converts. 'Not that we are sufficient of ourselves . . . but our sufficiency is from God.'[2] This dependence on divine aid and support was as characteristic of the church as of the individual. In its pursuit of a peaceful pattern of relations between God and man and man and his fellows, the church relied on God just as did the individual in his concern for salvation from his sinful predicament.

God was not a source of confusion but of peace, as Paul told

[1] *Matthew* xxii, 21
[2] II *Cor.* iii, 5

the Corinthians :[1] and earthly rulers must be concerned to provide the conditions in which the peace of God might be made manifest in the church. Paul asks Timothy to pray for 'kings and all that are in high places ; that we may lead a tranquil and quiet life in all godliness and gravity'.[2] This has remained a consistent Christian attitude to this day. As an ideal, it was not so much a substitute for the just city as an addition to it. Order must be kept in civil affairs no longer as a morally desirable end in itself, but subsidiary and preconditional to a further spiritual end, the peace and tranquillity of the faithful.

It took many centuries for the full implications of this view to be worked out and some of the consequences were very strange indeed. But it is significant that from the very first the purpose of the new sect was expressed in a political metaphor : the building up of the kingdom of heaven. It was a Hellenistic rather than a Greek metaphor proper, though, later, Augustine went back to the idea of a city, and it probably derived something of its character from the post-exilic intensifying of Jewish national aims ; but Christ's assertion before Pilate that 'My kingdom is not of this world', however variously interpreted down the ages, clearly stated the claims of a new jurisdiction and as clearly distinguished it from Pilate's own authority.

The influence of the concept of the heavenly kingdom on social theory and relations would make a single and fascinating enquiry in itself and cannot be pursued here. We must content ourselves with drawing attention to one or two aspects of this political setting for a religious group which have had subsequent and far-reaching effects. There have been times during later centuries when the emphasis has been placed on the heavenly rather than on the kingdom and attempts have been made to give the whole idea an entirely other-worldly setting. Were this the right or the only possible interpretation, many of the less tractable problems of church and state might have been avoided. But though the source of authority may be in heaven, and even this is an equivocal statement for an incarnational religion, the scope of the jurisdiction is undeniably in this life and world. There is a double sense in which the kingdom is not yet come but is already

[1] I *Cor.* xiv, 33
[2] I *Tim.* ii, 2

constituted. This has always been perplexing; and it was in answer
to an enquiry about when the kingdom should come that Christ
replied: 'The kingdom of heaven is within you,' and condemned
the Pharisaic desire for signs and portents by pointing out that
superstitious observation was of no avail.[1] A similar transference
of location is implied in *John* xiv, where the divine peace itself is
spoken of as not of this world; and many of Paul's Jewish converts must have winced when they were told that 'he is a Jew,
which is one inwardly; and circumcision is that of the heart, in
the spirit, not in the letter'.[2]

As a condition of the individual soul, inward states of grace,
wisdom, release or other forms of sanctity and salvation were
commonly experienced in the Hellenistic and Roman worlds. But
such unity and interrelationship as these persons enjoyed was
notional and ideal. Membership in the cosmopolis had no social
consequences. The revolutionary impact of Christianity lay
precisely in the unity and community of the church being at once
a society of the redeemed in Christ and a well-organized system of
cells operating within the secular order, in the world but not of it,
subject to civil authority but recognizing at the same time a higher
allegiance.

There are two passages in the Pauline Epistles in which the
Greek brings out very clearly the new bond of unity which over-
rode all the recognized divisions of creed and race and status. In
both of them significant political terms are used. The Gentiles are
told in *Ephesians* that they must not think of themselves as
strangers or foreigners but as sharing a common citizenship with
other Christians.[3] A parallel term is used in *Philippians* where Paul
says 'Our civic body originates in heaven', a phrase which catches
both the dual domicile of the Christian church and its new sense
of incorporation as a constituted and functioning body of
believers, neither of which senses has survived the beauty of
biblical translation.[4] Dr. Wand has happily paraphrased this
declaration as 'We . . . are colonists from Heaven',[5] which, though

---

[1] *Luke* xvii, 21   [2] *Rom.* ii, 29
[3] ii, 19
[4] iii, 20
[5] J. W. C. Wand: *The New Testament Letters* (Oxford University Press
1946), p. 133. Cf. *The New English Bible*: 'We, by contrast, are citizens of
heaven . . .'

it is to read between Paul's lines, emphasizes just that quality of peaceful penetration and eventual suzerainty which was to characterize the operations of the church in the world. That the new doctrine did not seek to abrogate the civil authority of kingdom but rather to enhance the claims of earthly rulers is much more clearly understood. The famous New Testament passages which support these claims have been quoted times without number. 'Be subject to every ordinance of man for the Lord's sake';[1] 'Put them in mind to be in subjection to rulers, to authorities, to be obedient';[2] and, most famous of all, the opening verses of *Romans* xiii, which begin: 'Let every soul be in subjection to the higher powers'; where it would probably be more satisfactory to translate powers as authorities. The citation could then continue 'for there is no authority except God's; and existing authorities are appointed by God, so that he who opposes such authority is setting himself up against God's administration.'[3]

It has sometimes been argued that the admitted preoccupation of the early church with the imminence of the Second Coming sufficiently accounts for this acceptance of subjection to temporal authority. It was motivated more by the indifference of those who expected the whole secular structure to be superseded at any moment than by a coherent policy for guiding the behaviour of the faithful during a normal earthly sojourn. Against this view, however, we must balance the established tradition in both Jewish and Hellenistic circles of the earthly ruler's being the Lord's anointed or at any rate a candidate for deification. The post-Alexandrian Greek kingdoms were not slow to borrow the cloak of divine authority to which their middle-eastern subjects were accustomed. This was particularly noticeable in Ptolemaic Egypt; and it was probably in Alexandria, where Hellenistic and Jewish ideas came most closely into contact that the wisdom literature of the first century before Christ was composed.

At all events it is in the apocryphal book of *Wisdom* that kings are admonished as servants, or inferior officers, of God's kingdom to give heed to the divine law and conduct themselves in accordance with God's counsel. 'For dominion is given you from the

---

[1] I *Peter* ii, 13   [2] *Titus* iii, 1
[3] Cf. *The New English Bible*, Library Edition, pp. 273–74, published in 1961, after the publication of this book, in which the translators also prefer the term 'authorities'.

Lord and power from the Highest.'[1] To see the relationship of
temporal and divine authority in proper perspective, it is as
important to bear this reference in mind as the better-known
citation from *Romans*. The responsibility of the ruler to God is
ultimately of greater moment, as in later centuries it became of
greater concern, than the subject's duty of obedience to the
divinely appointed authorities.

It was not until the fourth and fifth centuries of the Christian
era that the implications of the precise subordination and relationship of the dual authority in church and empire began to have
serious consequences in social theory and practice. To begin with,
the Roman administration tolerated the Christian sect as one
oriental cult among others. Later, Christians were persecuted
because they refused inexplicably to recognize the sole authority
of the emperor, who slowly graduated in time to the status of
a deified, oriental despot. As the church increased in numbers and
in institutional complexity, its position both as an exotic cult and
as a persecuted minority could no longer be accepted as valid.
The heavenly colonists had become in practice the paramount
power; and it was again by the use of a political metaphor that
the most famous of their classical apologists, Augustine of Hippo,
sought to distinguish the *civitas dei* from the *civitas romana* and
to regulate their relations one with the other.

.   .   .   .   .

The extent of the influence of Augustine's writings throughout
the middle ages and after the Reformation has been considerable.
Nevertheless, we must distinguish carefully between the Bishop of
Hippo's confrontation of the problems of his own day and the
Christian saint's continuous impact on the community of the
faithful. Augustine himself was a product of classical culture,
profoundly modified by Christian influence but still recognizably
at home in the Platonic tradition. Living at the turn of the fourth
century, he enjoyed the advantages in his later years of being
an adherent of an official and no longer proscribed religion; but
it was scarcely a century since the severe persecutions under
Diocletian; and to offset the contemporary good fortune of the
Christian community, heathen barbarians without and powerful

[1] *Wisdom of Solomon* vi, 1–5

heretical sects within constantly menaced the security of the catholic church. The occasion of Augustine's writing his treatise, *De Civitate Dei*, was the need to answer those critics who wished to attribute to the new faith the blame for Rome's inability to defend herself against the Visigoths, and in particular for the barbarian sacking of the city in 410. Nearer home, in his own episcopal see in North Africa, Augustine was in conflict with Donatist heretics who claimed that membership in the church excused its adherents from all civil obligations.

For thirteen years, Augustine contended with these contemporary issues during his composition of a work in which few of the questions asked by moral and political thinkers are not raised and considered. It is too narrow a judgment to confine *The City of God* to a treatise on the relations of church and state; and it is false to read into it a discussion of late mediaeval problems wholly foreign to the times in which Augustine lived. Yet it is true that 'no one can understand the Middle Ages without taking it into account'.[1]

Augustine accepted not only the dual institutional structure which the recognition of the church had introduced into the organization of the empire, but a further duality of purpose, implicit in earlier Christian teaching, which characterized the entire universal order whereby men and angels could be differentiated according to their ultimate allegiance to God and his law of love or to the rebellious self-interest of Satan. Augustine's classification of human groups is thus fourfold; but it is difficult sometimes not to equate the heavenly city with the church militant, its most evident representative body on earth, and the earthly city with the civil power, with which in certain circumstances it can be closely allied.

Augustine himself undoubtedly recognized a parallel between the unifying effect of the imperial administration on the individuals who were subject to it and the corresponding unity of the faithful in Christ. In a sense it was in a similar way that church and empire set about their distinct tasks. Yet the difference in purpose was more striking than the similarity in organization; and we begin to see how profoundly Christianity was modifying classical

[1] J. N. Figgis: *The Political Aspects of S. Augustine's 'City of God'* (London 1920), p. 1

conceptions when Augustine tells us that civil power is little better than brigandage, if it lack justice. The term used echoes Cicero and Plato; but the intention of the passage is to argue that God also should have his due, and that no civil society fulfils a proper purpose if it does not safeguard the freedom of the faithful to worship in peace. Augustine, indeed, goes further and in criticism of Cicero asserts that only a group united by true religion is properly a people. Civil justice, whether in Plato's or Cicero's sense, is therefore subordinate; and Augustine is claiming that it is the duty and sole justification of the civil power to safeguard a religious institution and way of life which it can neither emulate nor provide from its own resources. In terms of Greek thought, this was a revolutionary change. To say that the emperor, who might not even be a Christian, was nevertheless the defender of the faith, and to argue that the cosmopolis had reality only as the city of God, which the Stoic emperor, Marcus Aurelius, had himself half understood, was to envisage the characteristic relations of men with one another and with God differently from those obtaining in a Socratic republic or a Stoic universal society. It implied, indeed, a new psychology, a fuller ideal embracing life on earth and beyond death, and a society with twin institutions.

That Augustine uses the term city to designate each of his wider communities, heavenly and earthly, is a link between his thought and the ideal Platonic polis. But he extends the original concept to include God and the angels; and we have to find new terms for the corresponding but not identical reflections of the two cities in time. If we borrow the term *respublica* for the civil power, we can distinguish it from both the classical polis and the Augustinian city by seeing that it is no longer self-sufficient in Aristotle's sense, and no longer a primary centre of loyalty. Nor is the church on earth the Christian's first object of allegiance. Augustine recognizes no social division between the natural and the supernatural. There is a single universe of God and his creatures; but consequent upon the fatal clash of heavenly wills which deprived the divine society of Satan and his followers, God created new candidates to fill their places and the temporal system within which to train them. Temporal institutions are secondary, and definable in auxiliary terms as they impede or further the divine purpose. The primary division among men is then allegiance to God or the devil, though Augustine's use of the term earthly city for the latter's party does little to clarify these complex categories. The two loyalties are not to be identified with ecclesiastical and civil allegiance in this world. Indeed, from another point of view both church and empire are instruments of God's will, channels for his mercy and judgment respectively. But the officers of these two institutions do not necessarily pay allegiance where their proper loyalty is due. Either temporal body is likely to be misused if seen out of relation to its eternal purpose.

It is not indeed possible to explain this new grouping of human societies and aspirations in terms of classical social and psychological thought. From the Judaic origins of Christian doctrine, Augustine had inherited both the idea of the creation of the temporal order as a dramatic working out of the relations of God and man and the concept of sin to describe the deliberate withdrawal of human co-operation in this joint enterprise. Estimates of the incidence, extent and effects of sin have varied during the Christian centuries. Augustine took an extreme view, justified no doubt by the troubled times in which he lived. Most men, in his view, had their wills deflected from the divine purpose and were led astray by selfish, temporal interests. To use the special, theological term they were reprobate. As in the case of the ignorant, there was a remedy for this condition, but one provided not by an aristocratic élite but by God. Only the grace of God could rescue sinners and, in the life and death of Christ, this redemptive force had been made available to all men. It was the office, but not the exclusive right, of the church to reincorporate the repentant sinner in the divine society. For men could be divinely chosen, elect as it is called, despite themselves and regardless of their formal membership of the church. Herein lay the important distinction between the twin manifestations of the divine society.

There is a similar distinction between the two expressions of what we may now properly call the secular order. In its wider manifestation, as the company of those in rebellion against God, it might number adherents from any human group, not excluding the church, and it extended as the *civitas terrena* throughout time and beyond space. The group is constituted, Augustine tells us, according to the object of the devotion of its members. The earthly citizens choose the lesser, narrower, self-concerned interests. In the precisely temporal sense, however, the civil power and administration is not to be identified with the satanic city, but, like the sinner saved only by grace, is liable to devote itself to worldly needs alone unless sanctified by the presence of the church in its midst, for the defence and preservation of which it must recognize responsibility.

There is room in this classification for much confusion; but the student of politics can nevertheless see clearly that at best the civil authorities were expected to play an auxiliary role compared with the moral and spiritual dominance of the rulers of the Greek city and at worst Augustine did not think it too much to dub them brigands and to relegate secular power to the realm of Satan.

It is not only, then, that Augustine recognizes a different pattern of impediment to the good life from that envisaged by Plato or Aristotle, but that he expects no final improvement in the situation in this world. Something can be done about human disharmony, but it is almost true to say that in Augustine's view only God can do it or at least that no one can be saved from the predicament of sin without divine help, whether mediated through the church or otherwise. Moreover, the redemptive effects of divine grace are experienced in this world primarily as an expectation of glory to come, a trust in the working out of the providential plan for the rebuilding of the kingdom in eternity. Men must live, in Augustine's words, *in spe* not *in re*, not looking for present enjoyment during their sojourn in this world, but confident that despite suffering now, and even because of it, they will experience the fullness of God's love hereafter as befits those whom Christ died to save. *The City of God* has in one sense a misleading title. It is only incidentally a study of politics in the Greek sense. Its Christian setting and the debt which it owes to Old Testament traditions of thought give it the character of a theodicy, a justification of the ways of God to man.

As products of the temporal process, man's most characteristic social institutions, such as government and property (Augustine would add slavery as normal in the classical world), are themselves the effects of his sinful will, the results of self-concern, and essentially imperfect. Yet, it is impossible to escape the all-pervading divinely, imposed order in the universe. Whether in harmony with it or in rebellion against it, man is inevitably subject. When sinful, he experiences the divine order as a judgment limiting and disciplining his desires. When co-operative and obedient, he experiences this same order as peace and harmony, fulfilling his desires. Because of this dependence, human institutions, however sinful in origin, become instruments of God's will. Thus the order imposed by civil authorities, though less perfect than ideal Christian equality, prevents the effects of inequality from being totally disruptive. Property, an evident imperfection by the standards of a primitive Christian communism or even of the Platonic guardian class, at least limits and controls the greed inherent in the desire to have and to hold. Augustine is less convincing in his argument that slavery is also remedial as well as a manifestation of man's evil will. Even interpreted as punishment, slavery still affects only one group in the community and there seems to be no discoverable correlation between the sins of particular members of this subject class and their membership thereof.

The inconveniences and imperfections of these institutions must be suffered as a kind of vicarious punishment by those who are subject to them. Civil justice is not the same as divine justice, but it is within the same dispensation, modified and adjusted as it were to the conditions of this world. We may compare Aristotle's description of the best possible polity in the prevailing circumstances. But the Christian insistence on the propriety of obedience to civil rulers tends to limit the scope of rational criticism of imperfect civil authorities. The extreme form of this. doctrine caused many heart-searchings in later centuries. But the profits of obedience to the civil order greatly outweighed, in Augustine's view, its incidental disadvantages. He was too clearly aware of the services rendered to society by the Roman administration to be likely to underestimate the excellence of secular peace and order, even though it were provided by pagans. This earthly peace could be used by the citizens of the divine kingdom for heavenly ends, and was indeed the precondition of their safe pilgrimage through the world. Thus the eternal body politic 'observes and respects this temporal peace here on earth, and the

coherence of men's wills in honest morality, as far as it may with
a safe conscience; yea, and so far desires it, making use of it for
the attainment of the peace eternal'.[1]

The burden of the secular government is the judgment of God
upon sin. Evil is neither chance nor the social by-product of
ignorance, but due to a defect of the human will. It is to be
remedied by a divine discipline exercised through the very institutions to which the defect has given rise. The Judaic tradition
has here taken precedence of the Platonic; and the Christian
insistence on a harmony of belief and action issuing in love has
replaced the functional harmony of the Greek city which was the
product of the enlightened reason contemplating ideal intellectual
forms.

To hold that the will rather than the intellect is both the
master faculty of the human psyche or personality in its pursuit
of perfection and the source of its experienced disharmony is
characteristic of Jewish and Christian thought. Some Christian
apologists, such as Augustine, hold this view more extremely than
others who have allowed their thought to be modified by the
constant influence of classical philosophy. The will seeks the satisfaction of desire, the state which Augustine describes as peace
and which is finally achieved only in the perfected divine-human
love relationship. But there are an infinite number of lesser loves,
seducing the soul from its true end and substituting transient,
imperfect and only partially satisfying experiences of peace. The
conflict of these diverse purposes makes up the sum of the
individual's painful pilgrimage on earth. But there is a concomitant aspect of satisfaction, the obverse of the coin, for which
Augustine uses the term order rather than peace, though often
the words are almost interchangeable. We may define order as the
peace imposed on the erring will by the divine discipline and
judgment. History, as the scene of providential operation, is the
dramatic outcome of the divine judgment expressed in successive
events. Augustine gives as an example the peace imposed by
conquest.

Human society is, then, a distorted image of its true nature,
a fallen world, subject to imperfect institutions yet having in the
church the promise of paradise to come. It is easy to detect the

[1] *De Civitate Dei*, XIX, xvii (Healey's translation)

Platonic influence on this Christian description of social institutions. Nevertheless, the differences are profound. No provision is
made for the natural attainment of the ideal social harmony. The
distinction between secular and ecclesiastical institutions corresponds neither to the functional division of the three class system
nor to the psychological distinction between the enlightened and
the dependent. Perfection and harmony, though both setting a
standard and having the status of an expectation, have no permanent place in the temporal order. Both the church and the
civil administration are ancillary to the attainment of the heavenly
peace, but it is not to be located within their jurisdiction, either
severally or together. Membership in the church is not confined
to the elect. Correspondingly, Augustine makes clear that civil
society, though good in itself, is imperfect in the eyes of God,
for it can realize only a relative justice and peace, in the sense of
conformity to a lesser order than the unattainable peace and
order of heaven. But it is by the highest, or divine, justice that
the validity and authority of the earthly justice is to be tested.
The very unity and being of a secular society depends on this
other-worldly reference. 'So then, where justice is not, there can
be no society united in one consent of law, therefore no people.
. . . If no people, then no estate of the people, but rather of a
confused multitude. . . .'[1]

Justice in this world, then, is relatively imperfect in this
Christian translation of the Greek original. But Augustine uses
the idea of peace to convey an active state of concord and harmonious relationship, not in terms of Platonic social functions
but as a quality or condition of the new Christian idea of love.
It is a social concept, for Augustine's voluntarist psychology con-
nects the individual at all points through decision and action with
his environment and his fellows. The peace of the reasonable soul
is 'a true harmony between the knowledge and the performance'.
It is in this passage, too, that we hear further Pauline echoes.
'The peace of mortal men with immortal God, is an orderly
obedience unto His eternal law, performed in faith. Peace of man
and man, is a mutual concord : peace of a family, an orderly rule
and subjection amongst the parts thereof : peace of a city, an
orderly command, and obedience amongst the citizens : peace of

[1] *De Civitate Dei*, XIX, xxi

God's City a most orderly coherence in God, and fruition of God : peace of all things, is a well disposed order.'[1]

Of all Christian apologists, Augustine, as we learn from his confessions, was perhaps the most acutely aware of the barriers which frustrated the attainment of peace. Within himself and in the troubled, crumbling world of the early fifth century, he perceived discord, evil, ignorance and sin. From his classical upbringing he inherited the idea of moral conflict as a tension between irrational appetites and the rational soul. From St. Paul he had learned the significance of disharmony between knowledge and performance. But he welcomes the conflict for the peace which, by God's grace, lies beyond it. Society is at best very fragile; individuals for the most part doomed. Nevertheless, church and empire represent, however imperfectly, an embryonic system of right relations between man and God and man and man, dependent in either case on the faith, or trust, that God himself desires the perfection of these relations in love and is working to preserve them and, when they are broken, to restore them. It is the restoring of harmony between man and God and man and his fellows, an idea very close to the Platonic, which Augustine calls justice. The reconstituted concord he calls order and the experience of this harmony by those to whom it is vouchsafed is peace.

The civil authorities, under God, have a recognizable and important part to play in this work of reconciliation. If they can do little to promote it, being themselves often the chief offenders, they can seek to limit the worst effects of sin. In a sense, this negative role of the civil administration was made possible by the theory of the two institutions and the assumption that positive direction and guidance, as demanded by Plato, was the office of the church.

The characteristic Greek virtues of wisdom, courage, temperance and justice are no longer seen as natural dispositions and they are not to be acquired unaided by sinful men. They have become subordinate to those three states of the soul known as the theological virtues: faith, hope and love; for without these gifts of God, the temporal virtues would fail to issue in harmonious social action. Only with the support of trust in

---

[1] *De Civitate Dei*, XIX, xiii

providence and hope in the eternal city, and fulfilled through the peculiar Christian *caritas*, were the Greek virtues either to be acquired, maintained or expected to bear fruit.

The citizens of the heavenly kingdom passed as pilgrims through the alien, secular city. Augustine's description reads prophetically in the light of the troubled period which was to come. Nevertheless, we must beware not to read into his text references to the problems of the later middle ages which he could not possibly have foreseen. Nothing in Augustine can justify us in holding that he was in favour of a dominant ecclesiastical power. Christians, as other men, owed obedience to civil laws, but it was a limited obedience confined to secular affairs.

It was easier, however, to outline this distinction between the two realms and to justify a possible conflict of duties than to resolve the conflict when it occurred or to distinguish the boundaries of civil and ecclesiastical jurisdiction in precise historical conditions. In one way and another, these difficult problems have remained with us to this day, reappearing in a sharpened intensity at the Reformation and no less urgent in the setting of the modern welfare state.

Augustine's distinction between the two cities sharpened the dilemma concerning extra-political allegiance. Was it due to the church as a corporate institution or to the conscience of each individual? Why, for instance, should the elect submit to the church militant? This division of opinion was inherent in Augustine's whole theory; and after the Reformation both catholic and protestant could justly claim his support. Historically, the drawing of a distinction between the religious and secular realms has been more evident in catholic social theory; among protestants, the tendency has been to distinguish between an inner, spiritual, personal jurisdiction and the whole of the external, temporal order.

Some blame, too, must be attached to Augustine for his overlapping conceptions of the church and the heavenly city. It became customary to speak of the church on earth in quasi-political language; and it is difficult not to see here a source of the later mediaeval tendency to think of the church as a self-sufficient corporation, on the analogy of an Aristotelian polity, having in itself alone all things necessary to the perfection of society. Something at least of the secular reaction against the authority of the church in temporal affairs must be attributed to these pretensions; but we cannot find more than the seeds of these developments in Augustine's own thought. Between this educated citizen and administrator of a still functioning Roman empire and the complex quarrels of pope and emperor in the high middle ages lay half a millennium of barbarism, disorder and catastrophe. But the message of Paul and Augustine helped to guide the men of those times back to a condition of society in which their successors could once again study the wisdom of Plato and Aristotle.

. . . . .

During the thousand years which separate the Augustinian twilight of the classical empire and the dawn of the modern era which we call the Renaissance, Christian concepts of life and society were either dominant or strongly influential. The middle ages, customarily so called because they lie between these very different periods of history, never lost touch with the impressive example of Roman law and administration and remained faithful to a Christian interpretation of events which were rarely either peaceful or orderly. Distinguished from the earlier age by their barbarian vitality and from our own by their primitive economic organization and methods, the men who lived from the fifth century to the fifteenth were at one in either believing or being converted to believe, as had Augustine, that the efforts of the civil power could never suffice to satisfy all man's desires. This further realm, which lay outside or beyond politics in the classical sense, was represented for them by the Christian church. The tradition of imperial government and the experience of incorporation in the Body of Christ constitute the twin themes of mediaeval political history.

There is, however, throughout this period, a strange dichotomy between the ideas which might properly be included in a survey of social thought and the events and practices which occurred in the lives of the barbarian people who overran and inherited the imperial system and subsequently developed into the settled communities of the modern world. 'They do not realize the facts of the present, because they move in the theories of the past.'[1] To some extent men do this in every age; but the middle ages are pre-eminent for the width of the gap nearly always to be observed between the social institutions through which public affairs were conducted and the ideas customarily used to interpret and explain the theory of their functioning.

It is impossible to convey the complexity of this situation in a short essay; but in order to underline the inherent contradiction between the claims of the past and the embryonic patterns of the future, we shall consider first the impact of the universal concepts of church and empire and proceed afterwards to sketch the growing influence of the indigenous customs and practices of mediaeval communities, out of which the political pattern of the modern world was developed.

In some ways, Christian social thought was no less teleological than Aristotle's; and the two great institutions which represented the spiritual and temporal powers could in a sense be explained in terms of the functions of a Platonic republic. Ultimate ends were being served, but were sufficiently distinct in character to warrant separate organizations to achieve them. It was not, however, suggested that, therefore, a human community consisted in two societies or that there was ever more than one source of authority, because that authority was ultimately God. The Christian framework of the social theories of this period is always apparent, but the language and many of the arguments remain persistently classical.

More than seven hundred years divide the completion of the *De Civitate Dei* from the appearance of the next considerable attempt at a systematic treatise on social thought to follow it. It was not until 1159 that we meet the *Policraticus* of John of Salisbury. Yet much of the language and many of the arguments used by this twelfth-century thinker seem to have come down almost unchanged from their Greek originals. Admittedly, the commonwealth now has separate spiritual and temporal powers, but they should be closely co-ordinated for the attainment of communal well-being. The work and duties of lesser groups must be harmonized into a single whole of diverse functions,

---

[1] E. Barker: 'Introductory: Mediaeval Political Thought' in *The Social and Political Ideas of some great Mediaeval Thinkers* (London 1923), p. 9

strikingly like a Platonic community; and the comparison of a human society to the unity of soul and body in a person, what may loosely be called the use of the organic metaphor, is employed by John of Salisbury and often met in other mediaeval writers.

But there are characteristics of this apparently organic theory which, on a closer view, bespeak the Christian influence of the intervening period. The common good of the whole is made up of the virtue of the individual members; and this virtue depends less on the achievements of the citizens than on the effects of the grace of God. If the virtue is frustrated, it is sin not ignorance which stands in the way; and for that too there is only a divine remedy.

A better-known example of the survival value of classical thought is to be found in the writings of St. Thomas Aquinas in the following century. This time it was an Aristotelian interpretation of political purpose which was being accommodated to the values and assumptions of Christian thought. St. Thomas's undertaking was important and in some ways revolutionary and we shall have to return to a further consideration of his arguments. But at this point it is interesting to remark that he seems to accept Aristotle's contention that the body politic is a natural phenomenon and represents the highest and best form of organization for the achievement of the common good. Submission to political rule is not wholly to be explained in Augustinian terms as the wages of sin; for 'there is another form of subjection in virtue of which the master rules those who are subject to him for their own good and benefit'.[1] But, plainly, St. Thomas could not leave out the office of the church in his account of the life of virtue; and he distinguishes between those overt acts which can best be controlled by the civil jurisdiction and the inner life of meditation and worship which comprises the ecclesiastical sphere. But Thomas Aquinas sees these realms in harmony where Augustine more often saw them at variance. The thirteenth-century saint extended rather than transformed Aristotle's analysis. He agreed that the end of human society was the virtuous life; but the highest virtue for Thomas consisted in the individual's enjoyment

---

[1] *Aquinas: Selected Political Writings*, edited A. P. d'Entrèves (Oxford, Basil Blackwell, 1948), p. 103

3

of God, and he did not think that the final end of the association could be different from that of the individual. 'Thus the final aim of social life will be, not merely to live in virtue, but rather through virtuous life to attain to the enjoyment of God.'[1] Only divine grace can ensure the fulfilment of such an end. Therefore the Aristotelian city achieves its final end only in concert with the Christian church.

The persistence or recrudescence of these classical theories even in their Christian disguise kept alive the Greek conviction that the study of politics was part of a moral discipline, and served to modify the extreme Augustinian view that it was a subject to be subsumed under the heading of criminology, and the state a divine device for the control of delinquency. St. Thomas himself strikes a renewed positive note. He accepts from Aristotle that politics is a practical science; 'for reason not only knows but also creates the city'.[2]

More striking, however, than the continuity of classical theories of political relationship was the undiminished belief in the constitution of the empire as a functioning political institution. It was rarely this in practice; but the shadow of past greatness exercised a kind of fascination on the new groups who peopled the Roman lands; and as they slowly fashioned new patterns of political order and eventually new political boundaries, they were moved to try to describe these events in terms of continuing imperial concepts. 'The mediaeval empire was to them continuous with the ancient empire, and in their theory should have possessed and exercised the same power, and yet obviously enough it did not do so.'[3] This reference is to the theory of the civilian lawyers of the thirteenth century; but it states the problem which faced many mediaeval observers.

Undoubtedly, the prestige, administrative competence and economic stability of the Roman see did much to preserve the pre-eminence of Rome and of the imperial tradition during the centuries when the power and authority of the western empire was crumbling away. But it is significant that later attempts to

---

[1] *Political Writings*, p. 75
[2] *Political Writings*, p. 197
[3] R. W. and A. J. Carlyle: *A History of Mediaeval Political Theory in the West* (2nd ed., Edinburgh and London 1938), vol. v, pp. 465–66

extend settled rule over the western provinces were seen by their instigators as recreations, or in Otto III's term a renovation, of an empire which had in a sense never entirely passed away. The most notable attempt, that made by Charlemagne in the eighth century, short-lived though it was, seems to have been consciously modelled on the imperial past and to have been seen in theory as a unified society at peace under the rule of a single monarch. The Christian empire was the expression of the Christian ideal society in a Roman imperial setting. One of the articles of a statement of policy, issued in 789, reads: 'Let peace, concord and unanimity reign among all Christian people, and the bishops, abbots, counts and our other servants, great and small; for without peace we cannot please God.'[1] Charles himself knew that exhortation did not imply practice; but his purpose was clear.

Attempts to recapture the past proved easier in the realm of theory than in the often chaotic conditions of early mediaeval Europe. They were supported by the steady resurrection of classical learning and tradition which became possible with the relatively more settled life of the eleventh and twelfth centuries. Centres of learning began to be founded. Important texts, such as that of Aristotle, were once more available; and, most significantly of all, the great codes of Roman law were studied again and made possible the filling out of the concept of imperial authority with some of the details of its legislative administration. Already in John of Salisbury we find a theoretical discussion of royal power not in the feudal language proper to mediaeval kings but as representative of the general interest of the community. These views echoed the classical imperial tradition and mirrored hardly at all the current practices of the twelfth century.

In a society in which law was largely customary, the idea of a centre of legal initiative as it were, with the emperor a law-maker, bore little relation to the way in which mediaeval kings either behaved or thought. But it presaged future developments no less than reflecting the practices of an almost forgotten past. Primed by Aristotle, St. Thomas supports the uncontemporaneous ideas that those not called upon to direct affairs would be virtuous enough if they obeyed the commands of a ruler, and that the

[1] Quoted by J. M. Wallace-Hadrill: *The Barbarian West 400–1000* (London, Hutchinson University Library, 1952), pp. 103–4.

individual bears the same relation to the community as does the part to the whole. But for St. Thomas all secular rule was finally subject to that natural law which was itself an image of the divine law in the lives of men.

Later thinkers, notably the lawyers grappling with the increasingly difficult problems of temporal rule, were very ready to see the emperor, or at any rate secular rulers, as the source of law, a doctrine which they learned from studying Justinian's *Digest*. But they found it awkward to assess the precise standing of the ruler's authority. Roman legal theory had allowed for a popular origin of authority, treating the emperor as a representative rather than an absolute monarch. The difficulty was to decide whether his power had been handed over irrevocably or whether in some sense it remained delegated by the community. The latter theory was more in consonance with current mediaeval doctrines. There was the further complication in mediaeval society that the functioning rulers of the kingdoms were not emperors while the emperor himself often exercised either a weak or a narrow jurisdiction. The Roman theory of the principate had become disconnected from a reigning *princeps*.

There is little doubt that this situation had to some extent been created by the survival of the universal church as a functioning administration and that it was exacerbated during the middle ages proper by the growth of the power and prestige of the church and its repeated efforts to secure a dominant position in Christian society in relation to the empire. Two factors in particular helped to condition the often flagrant disharmony between the imperial and sacerdotal authorities, which in theory should have conducted their affairs separately but in harmonious concord. One was the inherent dualism of Christian doctrine, the early confrontation of the church and the world, the divided allegiance between God and man, which affected the whole of Christendom. The other was peculiar to the west, for the tension worked itself out differently with the Byzantine emperors. During the barbarian centuries when imperial jurisdiction virtually faded away, papal prestige was enhanced; but later during the uncertain conditions following the break-up of the Carolingian empire, Rome became dependent for military and economic security on the good offices of the civil power.

Once the western empire had become officially Christian, two authorities hitherto opposed both in theory and function began to pursue a common interest. What may be called the normal theory of their divided spheres and jurisdictions and of the relation between them was already set forth before the end of the fifth century, and came to be known as the Gelasian theory, after Pope Gelasius I, or the doctrine of the two swords. Briefly, it posited a single community or commonwealth of persons which was pursuing two distinct ends of unequal excellence, one spiritual, which St. Thomas calls salvation, and the other worldly, temporal, in some writers carnal, which St. Thomas calls civil welfare. This society is governed by two authorities, unequal in dignity but equal in jurisdiction and indeed necessary to each other. Each power, sacerdotal or imperial, derives its authority direct from God, through Christ, on whose behalf it wields the sword of justice in its respective sphere both for itself and on behalf of its fellow power. Thus the church promotes the spiritual salvation of the citizens and expects in return the defence of its temporal interests.

One twelfth-century writer speaks indeed of this Christian commonwealth as the church in the wider sense of the whole community of the faithful, but he recognizes the distinction of two ways of life and jurisdictions. St. Thomas, who in general supports the Gelasian theory, sees a difference of functions within the single community, while according to the spiritual power a higher status, as.it were. Admittedly, he writes of kings being subject to the Vicar of Christ, 'as to the Lord Jesus Christ himself. For those who are concerned with the subordinate ends of life must be subject to him who is concerned with the supreme end and be directed by his command.'[1] But he does not support the extreme papal pretensions to a final authority covering also the management of temporal affairs. It is only in John of Salisbury that we find it suggested that the superiority of the clergy, the soul of the commonwealth, to the prince, its head, carries with it a superior power as well as status. The temporal sword, says John, was received first from the church which originally held both from God.

It was this theory of two harmonious social authorities

[1] *Aquinas: Selected Political Writings*, p. 77

co-operating in the dual concerns of serving the needs of men's souls and bodies, their survival in this world and their salvation in the next, which was challenged on more than one occasion by ambitious popes between the eleventh and the fourteenth centuries. Finally, it may be said that the challenge failed and the doctrine of the two swords continued to express the point of view of most Christians. But in the event the Holy Roman Empire and the mediaeval papacy, exhausted perhaps by their quarrels, were transformed out of recognition, never in practice to regain their former unique authority and prestige. In a sense, although the occasions of these disagreements were characteristic of mediaeval society, their causes were perennial and remain with us to this day. A spiritual society which claims to control behaviour, which requires property for its economic support, which stands in need of defence, must at many points risk an overlapping of decisions and administration with any civil power which it does not wholly control or for which it cannot substitute its own jurisdiction.

The particular quarrels of Gregory VII and Henry V, of Innocent IV and Frederick II, of Boniface VIII and Philip of France, which may be studied in histories of the period, cannot concern us in detail here. The possibility of provocation was always present in the special circumstances of the feudal structure of mediaeval society. The higher prelates were almost always feudal magnates as well. When few but clerics were educated, civil administration was frequently placed in ecclesiastical hands. In a society whose wealth was concentrated in the land, its ownership constituted the sole source of economic security. In these facts alone lay ample cause for dissension. But, to increase the tension, the proper limits of ecclesiastical authority in its own sphere were inherently uncertain and ill defined. Where were the bounds of the spiritual life, of the moral realm? Could excommunication of a lay ruler absolve his subjects from their allegiance? Was it a sin to disobey papal authority in temporal concerns, for instance in the paying of taxes?

Although there was little hope in the general conditions of feudal Europe, with an active and often hostile papacy, that the imperial cause could have triumphed and established universal peace, the possibility was seriously mooted in theory. In Dante's *De Monarchia*, written in the early fourteenth century, the

resolution of the tension is seen in the re-establishment of a
dominant temporal and universal authority. Dante's vision was
impracticable but true to the reiterated demand for universal
peace and order put forward by Christians in all ages. The
pursuit of the ends proper to man required tranquillity, 'Whence
it is manifest that universal peace is the best of all those things
which are ordained for our blessedness.'[1]

Dante's contention that temporal authority derived directly
from God and not through the church was in support of the
traditional theory; but when he argues that temporal power in
the hands of the church is out of harmony with its true character,
that final authority should rest with the emperor, and that even
the pope should submit to the authority of councils and the
scriptures, the pattern of future events is already discernible.

The contentious relations of the spiritual and temporal powers
throughout the high middle ages are at once events of the greatest
significance for the later development of European theory and
institutions and yet somehow irrelevant to the settled convictions
and thought of their contemporaries. This great question, write the
Carlyles, 'did not, in itself and directly, contribute anything to
the development of the other political ideas or institutions of the
Middle Ages. . . . But . . . in its relation to the general principles
of human life and its organization, no development in history is
more significant than this of the independence of the spiritual life
and its organization.'[2] We may argue that the conditions of the
times tempted the church to overplay its hand, but it is important
to remember that the position it was defending, however ill-
advised the choice of means, was the independence of the moral
life of individuals from the arbitrary control of the civil power,
an office which in Augustine's terms might be described as the
taming of the brigands with justice.

Although the quarrels of pope and emperor were doubtless
vivid enough for those directly involved in them, their seeming
irrelevance to the more immediate concerns of mediaeval life and
thought must be attributed firstly and perhaps largely to the per-
vasive influence of the one unifying theme in mediaeval theory
and practice, the reverence for law, an institution at once divine

---

[1] *De Monarchia*, I, iv
[2] *Mediaeval Political Theory*, vol. v., pp. 451–52

and human and superior in status, scope and universality to all
other potentates whatsoever.

In the earlier centuries, the slow break-up of the western
empire into barbarian tribal territories had allowed time for the
mingling of tribal custom, already fairly coherent from its
common Germanic origins, with the established legal practices
of the settled Roman community. This Roman foundation,
though modified in time, helped to stabilize and universalize
barbarian practices. It provided, moreover, an aura of eternal
justice derived from the prestige of the former imperial administration and the canon law of the church. By the tenth century, law
had become a universal system of just and equitable principles
and in its positive sense was an attempt to apply these principles
to the conditions of everyday living.

This process of application was, as the term legislation itself
implies, rather the recognition of the proper tradition than the
taking of administrative initiative. Historical changes had altered
the spirit of the old Roman law, while maintaining its prestige
and framework. Law was not made, but discovered and promulgated ; and there was a clear understanding that rulers and ruled
were mutually obliged to maintain the established law which
neither group precisely authorized or decreed, but to which both
were subject. *Lex facit regem*, Bracton's famous phrase, reflected
the normal belief of the times. The king did not make the law,
but neither did anybody else. It was a universal characteristic of
the total community, one of those unifying concepts incor-
porating those subject to it into an intelligible whole. A king
unrecognized by the law or claiming to be above it had no status
in mediaeval society. There was a sense, according to St. Thomas,
in which a ruler was free from the constraint of the law in that
he could not be proceeded against, at least in theory ; but this
view by no means implied that a king was free morally to disregard the law or to substitute for it his own will.

Christian doctrine had contributed to the Roman imperial
tradition of a single central authority in civil affairs the more
exalted notion of a similar authority in the universe. The presence
of the church militant gave this conception an embodiment and
immediate significance which were lacking in the universalism of
the Stoic cosmopolis. 'Human government derives from divine

government and should imitate it,'[1] St. Thomas writes; and his words succinctly summarize the lesson which the church had taught to the new European peoples.

St. Thomas himself was living and writing in that period of the thirteenth century when the renewed influence of Aristotelian thought was in conflict with the traditional Augustinian social concepts of the Christian centuries. He represented the new positive spirit of a more settled and stable society and his advocacy of Aristotle's naturalism did much to modify and counteract, though it never superseded, the sharp division between the life of the spirit and the claims of the world which marked Augustine's treatment of secular concerns. St. Thomas accepted the natural life and secular politics as a necessary stage in the pilgrim's progress to heaven rather than a threat to its successful achievement. The two patterns of life ran together successively and were not liable to be at variance. Grace, he thought, was the complement of nature not its destruction. Faith was not contrary to reason but confirmatory. Active virtue was the proper training for beatific contemplation.

Like the contemporary efforts to upset the balance of the doctrine of the two swords, Thomist Aristotelianism had more significance for later developments than for mediaeval thought itself. It was the first step in that rehabilitation of the classical idea of rational living which flowered in the humanism of the Renaissance. But St. Thomas himself never disconnected his body of rational ethical principles from its divine source. They were codified under the traditional concept of the law of nature. This he defined as 'participation in the eternal law by rational creatures'.[2] But eternal law was itself 'the rational guidance of created things on the part of God'. Thus law in the political sense can be defined as 'nothing else than a rational ordering of things which concern the common good, promulgated by whoever is charged with the care of the community'.[3] This definition came very close to what most of St. Thomas's contemporaries thought about the character of law.

St. Thomas's ethical acceptance of the natural and civil life

---

[1] *Aquinas: Selected Political Writings*, p. 155
[2] *Political Writings*, p. 115
[3] *Political Writings*, p. 113

as having value, albeit subordinate, and as being ancillary rather than antagonistic to the life of grace had one very important consequence. It reversed the traditional Augustinian attitude to property and submission. 'For neither private possession nor servitude were imposed by nature; they are the adoptions of human reason in the interests of human life. And in these cases the natural law is not altered but is added to.'[1] St. Thomas does not go so far as to make property natural; but to argue that it is rational is very different from regarding it as a divine remedy for the sin of avarice. Sin had not detracted from man's ability to know the truth, but only from his competence to act in accordance with it. This traditional Christian doctrine supported the Thomist defence of reason in the ordering of temporal affairs. Beyond reason, faith apprehended the divine law, which directed man to his further and higher purpose, the end of eternal blessedness.

In St. Thomas's vision of the interlaced systems of divine, natural and positive law, unified, majestic and for the most part unchanging, we see something of the awesome character of this sovereign authority of the mediaeval world. God himself maintained the peace and order of the universe and everything in it with an authority and superiority which dwarfed the pretensions of pope and emperor, kings and councils. This august conception came down from heaven to meet the very different world of custom and precedent, prescriptive right and feudal due, which was the daily pattern of mediaeval living. That the two met and fused was both the strength and the glory of the mediaeval achievement. It was a world opposed to change, dominated by the past, resisting very often its own development. St. Thomas does not ignore this very important aspect of an orderly society, for 'in the observance of law, custom is of great importance: so much so, that any action which is opposed to general custom, even if itself of little importance, always seems more serious. So when law is changed its coercive power is diminished, to the extent that custom is set aside.'[2] But the stability of customary procedure was not in fact the same as the divine ordering of the universe, however well the two remained in harmony. It represented the

[1] *Political Writings*, p. 127
[2] *Political Writings*, pp. 143–45

contribution to mediaeval society, neither of Rome nor of Jerusalem, but of the barbarian peoples from the north.

. . . . .

The idea of law as the rational reflection of the divine order in a natural society of men was more closely in harmony with the traditional folk-law conception of the Germanic tribes than the Augustinian belief in secular rule as a remedy for sin. With the revival of the study of Roman law, particularly in the new universities, from the eleventh century onwards, the theoretical assumption that the authority behind the law was that of the whole people formed an even closer link between the two theories.

In practice, the Roman and barbarian systems had met and mingled many centuries earlier. Already by the eighth century, and even before that in Spain, the established customs of tribal law were beginning to be written down. At first these collections represented the traditional pattern of social behaviour by which a particular people lived. But the largely common origin of the invading tribes helped to avoid too great differences between their codes.

As the different groups settled in their embryonic kingdoms in the Roman world, the custom-pattern of a people gradually became attached to a specific territory. This process of relating social practice to place rather than person had the effect of attaching the laws applicable to each area to the principal temporal overlord of the district; and what became known as king's law or common law was thus distinguished from the smaller units of local customary practice. This development carried with it no implication that the king did more than promulgate the law for his lands; but it laid the foundation of the later transformation of mediaeval *regna* into modern nation-states.

The conviction that law was promulgated or made known rather than created or decreed was universal. Law was to be discovered by a process of ascertainment which involved research rather than decision. Behind this conviction lay the deeper belief that practices which had survived from the past were right and just. It was this agreement concerning standard practice which gave unity and a sense of incorporation to the people who shared

the corpus of custom. The experience of the organic whole preceded in a sense any theory of social interpretation.

Legal processes, thus, took the form of careful investigations;
in which all the parties concerned, and representatively the whole
people, sought to establish the prevailing practice. The agreement
was an act of recognition of the right pattern of behaviour and
at the same time a judgment of any admitted deviation. It has
been argued that in this process we can discern something like
the consent of the governed which played so great a part in later
theory. At all events, mediaeval law was never decreed by any
particular group or person. It grew out of and with the life of the
people. If the estates of the realm consented to the laws, they
were recognizing facts rather than concurring with decisions.

Prescription established right in this system of traditional
practice. Inherited from times when custom was not written down
but preserved by the elders, the important criterion was length of
establishment. What could be shown on good evidence to have
formerly been the case had now acquired the right to be enforced.
The origin of these prescriptive rights was of less moment than
their persistence. They were attached not to individuals, but to
particular social groups in respect of their functions, the property
they held and their place in the ordered hierarchy. Property,
status and duties had sometimes in fact been granted by particular
kings; but it was custom and prescriptive right which preserved
them.

This complex of customs, rights and laws established a communal peace, a condition of harmonious co-operation between
the members of the community. It came to be known, as it still
is in this country, as the king's peace. To break it was literally
to place oneself outside the communal unity; and outlawry, being
not so much beyond the law as no longer within its protection,
represented this disruption of the communal peace by breaking
loose from it. The wrongdoer could be received again into the
community, but he must first make restitution and give assurances
of future good behaviour.

The establishment of settled conditions like this over wide areas,
apart from the brief achievement of the Carolingian empire, was
the work of the later mediaeval centuries. If the dreams of a
Christian imperial commonwealth indulged by churchmen and

supported by Dante as late as the fourteenth century were never very close to being realized, it was also a slow and gradual process to bring into being the centres of regional authority or *regna*. 'Political integration,' as Professor Wallace-Hadrill has written, 'was an ideal to the churchmen; it was an accident to the Frankish war-lords.'[1] The distribution of authority in western Europe, ultimately sanctioned by time and custom, did not originate in justice.

In marked contrast to the universal institution of the church and the would-be central authority of the emperor, such order as was achieved in the lands of the western empire was everywhere local and often ephemeral. From as early as the third century onwards, the breakdown of central order had been hastened by the slow decay of the economic life of the towns. The development of large country estates, increasingly self-sufficing as conditions grew less secure, was encouraged by the later emperors themselves setting an example of this pattern of living. With the decline of general trade, the risks and expense of distant transport, and the emphasis on local defence, the country estate with its villa, manor-house and in later centuries castle became the normal economic and often political unit. It was an age of villages rather than towns, of an argicultural economy based on the land as against the imperial trading community centred on the Mediterranean. Inevitably, loyalty was local and the centre of authority often local also. Later, Vikings, Saracens and Hungarians beset the land-locked Christian commonwealth on every side; and whether we attribute the growth of the feudal system of local authority to the military needs of an agricultural community lacking sea-power or to the development of economic and political patterns already to be observed in the late Roman empire, the building up of the embryonic national groups into kingdoms was a considerable achievement, however far it fell short of the ideal theories of imperial unity.

It required nearly the whole span of the middle ages to transfer the concept of a central political authority from the emperor, who rarely disposed of sufficient power, to the kings who lacked the recognized status. Descended from the tribal war-leaders, mediaeval kings began by being officials who performed certain

[1] *The Barbarian West*, p. 114

functions rather than persons of a particular status. It was this emphasis on their ability rather than their constitutional position which perhaps made them the final heirs of imperial, secular authority.

The office of king gradually developed from that of the war-leader to being the hub of the network of feudal loyalties, maintaining the complex of rights and privileges of a hierarchical society, and finally to its unique position as representative of the public interest, guarantee of the common law and the meeting-point of ecclesiastical and lay authority.

At any rate until the fourteenth century, the revival of the Roman conception of a centre of legislative authority remained academic and theoretical, not seriously affecting the exercise of royal authority in its feudal setting. The source of this authority was neither simple nor easily defined. Its earliest origin was doubtless the acclamation or acceptance of a worthy and competent leader by the people; and this popular origin of political authority, though very different from the ascription of imperial authority to popular decision in Roman times, remained an integral element in the attributes of a lawful king up to the time of the absolute monarchies of later centuries. This recognition by the community, almost a kind of election, was reinforced by the hereditary custom of feudal society. Inheritance would not normally hold against incompetence and to begin with did not necessarily follow a law of primogeniture, but the eldest son, or at least one of the children of any feudal overlord, and particularly of the king, had a prescriptive right to be seriously considered as successor to the office. Finally, royal authority derived from God, and in being accepted by the church added providential approval to its other claims to obedience. The king, as *primus inter pares*, had good grounds also for becoming the first and in due course the only estate of the realm. It was out of this office that the concept of the nation-state arose.

But the early national groupings with their changing frontiers and often dominant local magnates depended for such political coherence as they exhibited upon an intricate pattern of inter-relationship, known as the feudal system. Theories of church and empire took little account of it; and one of the gravest difficulties of explaining mediaeval kings in relation to classical theory was that they were primarily feudal overlords and for many centuries did not exercise anything approaching the central authority attributed to the emperor. When in countries like France, England and Spain, central monarchies began to exercise quasi-imperial power, the theory was modified to agree with the facts and kings declared to be emperors within their own domains.

As with the transfer of economic and political initiative from the towns to the landed estates, so with the establishment of a static society in fixed hereditary castes, we find the first steps to have been taken during the declining period of the Roman western empire. Many trades became hereditary by law in the third century and in the fourth tenant farmers were legally attached to the estates where they worked.[1] This was not in itself a feudal system, but it provided the economic and social framework within which the barbarians developed their own pattern of hierarchical relations. It was the way in which the parties to a feudal relationship envisaged their responsibilities which characterized this society as distinct from its predecessors and successors, in which mutual rights and obligations were guaranteed and enforced by a dominant central authority. By contrast, feudal interdependence arose out of a pattern of mutual obligations, in which the central act was an oath of fealty.

Loyalty to an oath has been described as the greatest of the barbarian virtues.[2] In a tumultuous and sometimes chaotic period, the moral tie of mutually accepted obligations was perhaps the principal social force making for ordered living. It gave life and purpose to the stagnant class-structure of late Roman society; it fitted in with the moral standards of the church at least in principle; and it helped to cement those local centres of loyalty which became a military necessity in the face of continuing invasions from beyond the frontiers of Christendom.

A feudal society was, therefore, fragmentary. The chief overlord had few direct relations except with his immediate vassals. It was also confused, for more than one lordship could subsist in a single property and kings in one land could be counts in another. The relationship was not political either in the classical or

[1] For an account of the effects of the economic decline of the empire, see F. W. Walbank : *The Decline of the Roman Empire in the West* (London 1946).
[2] *The Barbarian West*, p. 110

the modern sense; and yet, for all its dependence on personal fealty and overtly recognized obligations, it constituted in practice the most important political and legal relationship of the age. Militarily, legally, economically, the mediaeval hierarchy of estates achieved its immediate social purposes largely through the successful functioning of this intricate institution. With a primitive economy, lack of swift transport, many enemies and a theory of society which never harmonized with events, mediaeval Christendom found in feudal organization an adequate, if often imperfect, substitute for the central government of its unfulfilled hopes.

Economic wealth, such as there was, was concentrated in the land. To correlate the ownership or holding of property with the degree and kind of social service rendered by the holder was a convenient method of paying for the service. The king depended on his baronage for military support and for what corresponded to local government. The lower orders (and the word order had precise significance) in return for a promise to render obedience could expect protection. The whole system was an elaborate exchange of goods and services, but being overtly recognized and customarily practised required no formal social theory to explain what was happening.

Control was exercised in two ways. Within the pattern of mutual obligation between lord and vassal, the inferior owed obedience to his superior, but could claim no obedience in return. He could, however, expect honest fulfilment of whatever obligation his lord had undertaken; and it was in default of this that appeal lay to the court. This was not like an appeal to a minister under modern administrative law, for no lord was ever in theory judge in his own cause. The reference went to the assembled members of the court for adjudication, and they were expected to reach a united decision regarding the rights of the case and to be jointly responsible for enforcing the decision. In theory, this procedure was equally valid in the king's court. A decision against the king was not revolutionary, as it became in later centuries, but the upholding of the supremacy of the feudal court. Only justly exercised power could command obedience and a king who usurped authority not properly his was rightly deposed by his peers.

It may be argued to what extent the loosely knit personal relationships of the feudal order can be said to constitute a political unity. But this is less important to settle than it is to interpret the social and political structure of the mediaeval world as a method of co-operation between different social units by means of representation. The mediaeval high court of parliament in this country was a representation of the whole community assembled in its orders; and that community, as the German historian Gierke discovered in his researches into group-life, was itself made up of many smaller wholes, not dependent for their creation or functioning on central power or royal licence, but self-regulating, small worlds in themselves, as our term university still denotes.

The great estates of the realm were not the only important groups in the community. Guilds of craftsmen and later of merchants, incorporated bodies of teachers and students, towns which, having grown up under the protection of a great lord, claimed charters of independence, all led vigorous communal lives, small corporations within the greater society of church and Christian empire. These groups formed themselves in accordance with the favourite mediaeval social metaphor into organic corporate unities, and they conducted their affairs for the most part through representative institutions. The best-known surviving examples of these are the British parliament and western European universities. But more important perhaps than the continuity of formal organization is the survival of the concept of representation which, though far less influential during the period of royal absolutism, has been revivified in more recent times to serve a wider purpose in a very different kind of society.

Fissiparous tendencies in mediaeval society constantly operated to reduce its theoretical unity to the ineffectual dream of Dante's imperial vision. Finally, the church itself succumbed to these disintegrating influences. They had long been maturing. The major distinction between the Romance- and Teutonic-speaking peoples was already evident on the morrow of Charlemagne's death; and from that date onwards the slow formation of the future nations of the modern era may be traced. Social, economic and political changes all heralded the transformation of mediaeval Europe; and to meet the new

F

situation, new theories of political authority and purpose were propounded.

More than one mediaeval thinker prefigures the changes in thought which were fully developed only after the Reformation. To one of them, the fourteenth-century Marsilius of Padua, who supported the dominance of the temporal power over the spiritual, we shall have occasion to refer in a later chapter. But it was probably in St. Thomas Aquinas that we can find most hints of developments to come. St. Thomas has, somewhat improperly, been called the first Whig; and it may be suggested that his division between Christian grace and Aristotelian nature left it possible to effect a divorce between these two realms in later centuries. But the influence of Thomist thought is seen more clearly in the reintroduction of Aristotle's concept of the self-sufficient polis, having in itself all the necessary power and authority for the successful satisfaction of human needs.

Which of the late mediaeval groups, failing the church and the empire, were likely to fulfil this definition adequately? In some parts of Europe the new commercial towns did so; in others it was the *regna* held together by something more than feudal loyalty, by the sense of national and linguistic unity, and led by kings who had become more than feudal overlords, who were ready themselves to claim to be the state.

CHAPTER III

RIGHTS

IF Louis XIV announced that the state was himself, he was being platitudinous rather than outrageous. What is interesting about this well-known assertion is that it signified that by the mid-seventeenth century the slow transformation of the complex mediaeval system of estates and corporations into closely-knit sovereign powers ruling over subject nationals had been, at least in some parts of Europe, finally accomplished. The nation-state had for the time being become the norm of successful political organization in western Europe. The event preceded for the most part its theoretical justification and analysis. The first three centuries of what we find it convenient, looking back, to call the modern era, that is from the Renaissance to the French revolution, were spent in the prosecution of the work of understanding this transformation of the mediaeval order. Towards the end of that period and up to our own day, political and social theory has been concerned to reinterpret the nation-state itself, not its external form, but by redefining its internal relations. In this and the following chapter we shall investigate the theories predominant before the revolution; and in the last two chapters those which helped also to provoke it, but which have reached fulfilment only in the nineteenth and twentieth centuries.

The apologists who defended the general structure of the new political communities may be distinguished not very precisely according to whether they held that groups and individuals other than the secular ruler retained any rights against him or whether they were left only with interests. This distinction was not really one of principle, for at bottom it was an argument concerning apportionment of responsibility for the efficient pursuit of communal ends. Both groups accepted the necessity of a dominant, centralized, political authority. Both allowed that it was not onmicompetent and that many activities must be left to individuals. The difference was whether these reserved, in a sense extra-political, fields, should be delimited on pragmatic grounds of expediency or utility in terms of expected results, or whether some questions, notably religious association and worship, the ownership and control of property and the moral criteria of justice were sacrosanct and beyond the scope of political interference and control.

The fifteenth and sixteenth centuries were periods of turmoil. All ages may confidently be described as times of transition, but some of them are more self-conscious about the pattern of change than others. Theory is by no means always as revolutionary as events. There are times, and the sixteenth century would seem to have been one of them, when the complexity and rapidity of the social and political changes were less the product of revolutionary innovations in traditional thought than provocative of them. In these circumstances the new patterns of social relationship which superseded and to some extent caused the breakdown of mediaeval society were described by their observers with the help of concepts and arguments almost all derivative from customary mediaeval thought and practice.

The two claimants to political pre-eminence in the Christian commonwealth had failed to rule in harmony and were unable to provide a unitary and sufficiently powerful regime. It may be possible to blame the papacy for the failure to balance the two swords; but it is to be doubted whether the empire could ever have countered the divisive tendencies of mediaeval Europe. Loyalty, power and authority became increasingly concentrated upon the new national groups, recognizing at least a feudal overlordship in their kings. But feudal practice itself allowed for no such concentration of executive and legislative power. In the emperor, where in theory it might have resided, it was not to be found in fact. It was this dichotomy which presented the theoretical problem of the age.

Other factors ensured that there could be no continuance of the effort to resolve the difficulties in terms of the structure of the mediaeval Christian empire. Ecclesiastical organization was itself influenced by national feeling. The anglican and gallican churches were recognizable entities before the disruption of the Reformation, apart from all questions of doctrine. But they had less theoretical justification than the political *regna* with which they were associated.

In addition to political and religious concerns, the economic transformation of mediaeval society from a land-locked agricultural community to a centre of commercial enterprise, able to outflank the barrier of Islam with ocean-going vessels, promoted influences which were opposed both to the control of the mediaeval church and to the local loyalties, static relations and fixed stratification of feudal society. The new class of traders and merchants and the capitalists who financed their ventures were eager to support any centre of authority which could provide public order, legal enforcement of contracts and safe conditions of transport. They were, in a sense, glad to be dependent on an authority which guaranteed them the means of trade and livelihood.

This social process has been described by Gierke in terms of the development of two new social concepts, the state and the individual: the strong unit which claimed a sovereign power, hitherto reserved for pope and emperor, and the weak unit which claimed liberty within the law. All the multifarious intermediate bodies of the mediaeval world gradually lost status and legislative independence in favour of the enhanced status of a central, and usually royal, authority and of the liberty of the subject, as he now became, to find his own social standing free from feudal limitations and static privileges. This confrontation of crown and subject and the discussion of the relations between them has characterized the whole life and thought of the politics of the modern era.

In this chapter we shall be concerned with the first of the two attempts to reassess the political relationship in terms of independent national states recognizing no superior authority. The priority is not strictly temporal, for an interpretation of the justification of political authority as the satisfaction of the interests of the subjects is to be found as early as that which sought to limit authority within a framework of rights. But the concept of rights is closer to the language and practice of mediaeval society; the concern of its supporters with the question of religious freedom helped to make the theory of more immediate interest in the centuries succeeding the Reformation; and Bodin, whose sovereign power was limited by natural law, wrote nearly a hundred years before Hobbes, whose sovereign was limited only by his own ability to maintain order and suppress opposition.

The first estate of the realm was already being spoken of before the end of the mediaeval period as a quasi-emperor. This carried the suggestion that in any given *regnum* the governing body recognized no external superior. There was no question that this became the fact, sooner or later, in countries like England, France and Spain. Its theoretical justification was not so easy. In support of this local imperialism, resort could be had to the late Roman tradition of the single ruler concentrating all secular temporal power at one point. The gradual supersession in the sixteenth century of the Christian term grace in addressing royal rulers by the secular Latin term majesty illustrates this tendency. But this left open the question whether the sovereign power was representative or absolute, whether it had been transferred unconditionally or only with reservations. Moreover, there could be no sudden return to a pagan past in total disregard of Christian teaching.

Any exercise of power was in theory limited morally, for all power was from God. If it were to be used in new and unfamiliar ways, overriding established custom and precedent, the defence of such a use could not for a characteristic sixteenth-century thinker be solely pragmatic. Some valid right must be produced in support thereof; and all rights were ultimately divine. In this sense, the theory of the divine right of kings, widely appealed to by would-be absolutist monarchs, was a mediaeval argument extended to the special case of the majesty of the state. Moreover, it was widely supported by many of those who welcomed the order and security which the monarchs enforced. It met with opposition when this central authority became too narrowly confined to the hereditary right of particular families to exercise it regardless of the consent of their subjects. In England, where the mediaeval estates system had survived in the institution of parliament, the demand to share the central power and authority led to the seventeenth-century civil war, which issued in the unique compromise of a quasi-mediaeval legislature working in harmony with a strong, royal and later aristocratic executive.

In addition to the theoretical problem of the rights and status of the independent kingdoms, finally cut loose from the mock universal empire, the middle ages bequeathed to succeeding centuries the unresolved tangle of the position of the church in relation to temporal power, intensified by the dissolution of the *Respublica Christiana* into several political entities, claiming to be self-governing. It is idle to debate whether the Reformation either could or should have occurred without disrupting the western church. Attempts to control the papacy by general councils in the fifteenth century had failed. By the time reform was seriously undertaken by catholics who wished to maintain the pre-eminence of the papal see in church government, other groups, notably in north Germany which was notoriously un-friendly to Rome, had already broken loose. Politically, the phenomenon which is of particular interest is that in very many cases the power and authority of local temporal rulers was at the back of the seceding sects. But, more than this, the political authorities in lands still remaining loyal to the Roman see behaved towards church property, for instance, in ways indis-tinguishable from those of German princes or Tudor monarchs. This close interconnection between the new church communions and the emerging nation-states raised the old problem of the relation of spiritual and temporal authority in a peculiar context.

There were three principal responses to this situation. The first, and in some senses the typical, answer was the creation of an established national church. Anglicanism in England, Cath-olicism in France, were severally sponsored by the temporal rulers. But they flourished on the same principle. Both countries had constant trouble with nonconforming sects, of different per-suasions according to the character of the establishment. In England, the tension was finally resolved by toleration ; in France, by disestablishment.

The second possible answer was worked out by the one great theorist of the reforming parties, Jean Calvin. Calvin, dreaming perhaps of an organized protestant movement, having something of the universality of the earlier church, wished to see the govern-ment maintaining true doctrine and suppressing heresy, and wholly subject to the church's interpretation of the word. This renewed attempt to balance the two swords was achieved in Geneva itself and influenced Calvinist churches elsewhere ; but a restatement of the Gelasian position in these terms, when no central organ of the church universal remained and no new organization arose to provide it was bound to be limited in its influence. It was a less ambiguous position to adopt than that of the established church, but by not compromising with events, Calvin's theory forfeited its political future.

Finally, those who did not wish to accept the implied subordination of an established national church, notably catholic thinkers in Spain, reverted to the earlier doctrine of the two societies but suggested that the church was itself a *societas perfecta* and could be self-sufficient and independent. Faced with the breakdown of universal Christendom, growing nationalism even in catholic countries, and the hard problems of temporal allegiance for catholics subject to protestant governments, this way out of the theoretical impasse may be seen sympathetically. But the theory ran contrary to the political and economic current of the times which deprived it of any widespread influence. Churches, catholic or reformed, or both as in England, found themselves bereft of their earlier participation in a universal order, dependent in every way on the new centres of local power. It was in this setting that the significant answers had to be attempted.

The established churches depended too closely upon their royal protectors to be in a position to claim specific rights from them which had not been freely granted. They were in a similar but not identical position to other groups or corporations in the community, subordinate to the majesty of the state. It is frequently argued that the emphasis of protestant teaching on the inviolability of the individual's conscience was the true progenitor of the later inalienability of the individual's rights. But it must be remembered that the widespread belief, not only in protestant but in some catholic circles also, that the universal church had now become a spiritual unity lying behind the fragments of the visible external church, helped to make individual subjects the inevitable repositories of the spiritual power. Rome was far better placed than Geneva or Canterbury to recreate something approaching a universal allegiance, but it has never again approached the quasi-political status and temporal power of the high middle ages. What is loosely called the protestant conscience was the realm of the spirit which Luther distinguished from the body and its goods, as properly beyond the concern of the temporal authority. It enshrined a recognition that, with the centralizing of the power of the state, the only area of divinely accorded rights which remained to be set against those of the king was to be found in the individual.

Wherever it was accepted that the purpose of life went beyond the satisfaction of natural, bodily needs, the divine rights of kings could be justified only in the achievement of the salvation and virtue of their subjects; and for this no theorist would have held they could be wholly responsible. Aristotle's pursuit of virtue, St. Thomas Aquinas's doctrine of natural law, and the newly acquired authority of the scriptures all combined to transmute the divine right of the individual soul to seek salvation into a natural and inalienable right to what its most renowned upholders were later to call 'Life, Liberty and the pursuit of Happiness'.

.   .   .   .   .

The difficulty of describing and justifying the new political unit of the state, evidently neither imperium nor polis, within the accepted conceptual framework of mediaeval thought is strikingly evidenced in the famous work, *De la République*, of the sixteenth-century French lawyer, Jean Bodin. Castigated for the confused thought and illogical conclusions in the six books of this lengthy and ill-drafted work which came out in 1576, Bodin mirrored the impasse to which traditional theory had been brought in his very contradictions. Bodin believed, as did his contemporaries, that political power should be subject to moral control and rational limits; yet he observed that its establishment was often due to nothing better than successful force, and mere force could never construct a satisfactory political community. Paradoxically, however, in the conditions of the time, a morally and legally satisfactory community could be established in no other way. Bodin saw that pragmatically only a centre of power could fashion any community whatsoever. How was this to be distinguished from Augustine's band of brigands? For Bodin was not ready, as was Hobbes in the following century, to divorce the problem of political power from the moral sphere altogether and consider only the success of its results in terms of temporal felicity.

Bodin borrowed much from Aristotle to help him resolve his conundrum, but not the contention that the happiness of the citizens was the purpose of government. Whatever the influence of classical thought, the idea that a political community could be omnicompetent in satisfying all its citizens' needs fitted in too ill with the predominantly Christian social assumptions of the period to gain rapid acceptance. But in his discussion of the coming into being of the political body, as distinct from its ends, Bodin adopts Aristotle's naturalistic account of a growth from smaller family units into a wider community. Self-sufficiency was not, for Bodin, an acceptable criterion of the attainment of political embodiment, but self-direction was. The state was that body which exhibited at some point within its structure a power of directing its common activities, with an authority and finality subject to no external control, apart, of course, from that of God himself. Bodin called this seat of human authority a sovereign power.

In this political definition, Bodin is not saying that any body with a government becomes a state, because it is not the method whereby the sovereign direction is exercised which constitutes the state, but the observed presence of such an authority. Its two indispensable criteria are subservience to no other human agency and obedience from all its subjects. Sovereignty and subjection are correlative terms. In practice, the most effective form of government, Bodin thought, would be monarchical; but in this he reflected sober sixteenth-century opinion. The sovereign authority could be exercised by a wider group, as it was, for instance, in Venice. A feeble monarch might be an altogether in-effective sovereign. Nor is Bodin saying that a state must be a national group, although in practice these groups fashioned the most effective states of the succeeding centuries. But this was an accident of history. Bodin's state could comprise various groups, lay or ecclesiastical, differentiated estates of the mediaeval realm, economic guilds and corporations, but they must all be in a condition of subservience to the sovereign power, exercising their privileges and maintaining their customary rights only with the gracious permission of the sovereign.

As a description of how the nascent political communities in western Europe were tending to develop, this definition was a valuable attempt to give these powers some theoretical status. But the difficulty remained of whether Bodin had achieved anything more than a description of events. Any power centre might for a time at least enforce order among weaker groups and defy control from elsewhere; and a situation of this kind, though it might develop in time into a settled political community, was plainly not one in the first instance. Bodin had rejected Augustine's frank acceptance of the wielding of the temporal sword with the single requirement that it be tempered with justice, and he would not go the whole way with Aristotle. Yet, he understood clearly enough, despite the often confused arguments of his text, that there was an important distinction between the exercise of power for tyrannical purposes and what he himself called the well-ordered state.

Good order certainly meant to Bodin something more positive than the absence of disturbance. It implied that the laws should be directed to ends which the subjects had in common: firstly, and obviously, the satisfaction of their temporal needs, and, secondly, the maintenance of conditions which would enable them to lead virtuous lives. Yet the sovereign ruler was the sole source of the law; it emanated from his will; he was answerable to none of his subjects for his decisions; he was absolved even from keeping the law except by his own good grace.

The paradox remained, and Bodin himself never properly resolved it, that if the subjects were obeying mere force they had no moral obligation to do so; but if the laws were justly directed to the end of virtuous living then in a sense the sovereign was as subject to the law as a mediaeval king and no new political principle had been discovered. The truth seems to have been that Bodin never wholly distinguished between his empirical observation of what was in fact occurring in order to maintain any order at all and what he knew ought to occur in order to achieve the conditions of the moral life. He said the sovereign power was above the law, but he knew it ought not to be; for other groups and individuals had rights as well as the sovereign. This difficulty, which in another form perplexed a later French thinker, Montesquieu, was resolved most successfully by the English philosopher, Locke, in the following century.

Bodin's own attempt to express the reservations which he felt compelled to make suggest already in outline some of the arguments which, as we shall see, were to be used later. All minor groups in Bodin's state were in political subjection, with one exception : this was the family from which the wider community naturally sprang. The family remained in a privileged position by reason, it appeared, of its being the very essence of any human community whatsoever ; and as the family itself depended for its continuance on the possession of property, this property was, morally at least, beyond the control of the sovereign power. Over against the public realm of the state Bodin posited a private realm of the natural unit of the family and its economic extension. He reinforced this point of view, moreover, by asserting that the sovereign ruler could not tax his subjects without their consent.[1]

Here, then, we have in outline a pattern of the well-ordered or politically just state : one in which the sovereign power answerable only to God will yet willingly refrain from using legislative authority outside the bounds of natural law, and in particular from invading the privacy or possessions of the family. These reserved areas within the lives of the subjects were not yet overtly described as natural rights : but as against the sovereign they represented rights and their justification was neither political nor ecclesiastical. The later development of a secular theory of natural rights, justified morally in terms of natural law, avoided the confusions of Bodin's analysis and helped to define the concept of constitutional state sovereignty.

Bodin, living in a country rent by religious wars, which was only slowly working towards the unified sovereignty which he wished to see exercised by the French crown, placed his emphasis understandably on the directing authority in the state rather than on its principle of incorporation. It was for an Englishman of a younger generation, no less a supporter of the law-making power of the sovereign state, to draw attention to the pattern of communal, or national life, rooted in history and tradition, which supplied the social framework within which the new political authority could operate.

---

[1] Bodin also applied the principle of the sacrosanct character of property at the national level, for he thought the sovereign should be limited constitutionally by having no right to alienate the domain of the state or to alter immemorial land laws, such as the *Lex Salica*, which forbade females to inherit when male heirs, though more distant, were available.

Richard Hooker, 'that learned and judicious divine', composed his discourse *Of the Laws of Ecclesiastical Polity* towards the end of the sixteenth century. A more coherent thinker than Bodin, Hooker did not share the French lawyer's pragmatic and secular approach. What the sovereign legislator could or could not do did not stop short at any particular unit in the state, not at the family as in Bodin and certainly not at the individual. Hooker's view of a political society might almost be said to be organic. In this, as in many other ways, he carried on the mediaeval tradition of a Christian commonwealth into the very different conditions of English society in the second half of the sixteenth century. Begun as a *livre de circonstance*, Hooker's great work raised most of the abiding problems of political authority, constitution and obligation, and stated, almost for the last time, the mediaeval doctrine of the moral restraints on political power, as applied to the new nation-state. Later restatements of moral limitation are increasingly secular and, though invoking divine sanction, could equally well be interpreted in wholly humanistic terms.

Hooker had been moved to defend the Elizabethan settlement of the established anglican church against criticism and resistance from puritan sects. As with catholics in countries not in communion with Rome, the more extreme protestant groups tended to demand freedom from political control at the expense of admitting that church and state were two separate societies. In place of the pope as extra-territorial authority they put an inspired interpretation of scripture, an inspiration, as Hooker noted, often nicely adjusted to their own most pressing needs. In strong opposition to this disintegrating movement, Hooker upheld the unity of temporal and spiritual membership in a single Christian commonwealth, not indeed the universal mediaeval society, but in whatever organized group an 'independent multitude', as he says, had chosen to live. 'God creating mankind did endue it naturally with full power to guide itself, in what kind of societies soever it should choose to live.'[1] This view repudiated the contention that the two facets of human organization could be distinguished by their being oriented towards distinct ends. A

---

[1] *Of the Laws of Ecclesiastical Polity*, in *Works*, arranged by J. Keble, 7th ed. revised by R. W. Church and F. Paget (Oxford, Clarendon Press, 1888),VIII, ii, 5

Christian people must have its essential purposes in common; 'albeit properties and actions of one kind do cause the name of a commonwealth, qualities and functions of another sort the name of a Church to be given unto a multitude, yet one and the self-same multitude may in such sort be both, and is so with us, that no person appertaining to the one can be denied to be also of the other'.[1] This single national group, for it is primarily of England that Hooker is thinking, need have only one directing authority, which for him was the Queen in Parliament, which would represent the whole people assembled and be competent to consider all its needs. The assumed agreement about Christian essentials went further than could be observed even at the time Hooker was writing. He was outlining an ideal anglican commonwealth which exists still in theory, but has never succeeded in evoking, despite establishment, more than a moderate allegiance even from the English subjects of the British crown.

This relative historical failure does not, however, deprive Hooker's thesis of its great theoretical importance. He based his expectation of general concurrence on the same grounds which we find in St. Thomas, on the possession by man of the God-given faculty of right reason, able to apprehend directly that part of the divine law apposite to human affairs. All men, that is to say, had in their knowledge of natural law a common access to standards of justice and right behaviour quite apart from their agreement, as Hooker calls it, to subject themselves to a political authority. 'The general and perpetual voice of men is as the sentence of God himself. For that which all men have at all times learned, Nature herself must needs have taught; and God being the author of Nature, her voice is but his instrument.'[2]

Hooker went some way with Aristotle in accepting that men were sociable and would find their efforts insufficient to satisfy their needs did they not combine. But man was not naturally a political animal; and the agreement to found the state was conventional. In addition to the law of reason, the universal law of mankind carried written in their hearts, a further law, human and positive law, is necessary for those living in public society. But the authority set up to provide this law is, for Hooker, paramount.

[1] *Ecclesiastical Polity*, VIII, i, 2
[2] *Ecclesiastical Polity*, I, viii, 3

'The public power of all societies is above every soul contained in the same societies. And the principal use of that power is to give laws unto all that are under it; which laws in such case we must obey, unless there be reason shewed which may necessarily enforce that the law of Reason or of God doth enjoin the contrary.'[1]

The laws of God and reason set the bounds to public political power, but so also did the consent of the people to the exercise of political authority. Hooker denied that the noble, wise or virtuous had any natural right to govern the rest. He presumed, as Locke did after him, that social life without political control would encourage contention and violence and 'To take away all such mutual grievances, injuries, and wrongs, there was no way but only by growing unto composition and agreement amongst themselves, by ordaining some kind of government public, and by yielding themselves subject thereunto; that unto whom they granted authority to rule and govern, by them the peace, tranquillity, and happy estate of the rest might be procured.'[2]

With its origin in conventional agreement, Hooker's Christian nation-state becomes a corporate entity, unlimited in time, having all things sufficient for its temporal and spiritual needs, and subjected by consent of its members, not necessarily openly, to a ruling power, with a divinely sanctioned right to make laws for the good of the whole community, as well civil as ecclesiastical. It was an ideal description and it avoided the alternatives of founding political power either in unauthorized force or in a divine authority expressed either papally or biblically outside and superior to the political constitution. The criterion whereby the justice of the laws could be tested was not the scope of their reference but their intrinsic rationality.

It was this tradition which survived in a secularized form through the succeeding two centuries when Hooker's anglican commonwealth drifted ever further from its national ideal. Men might fail to accept an agreed interpretation of scripture; they might deny that the traditional church of England represented the nation; but they could agree about a common humanity and a common rationality founded in nature and nature's God.

. . . . . .

[1] *Ecclesiastical Polity*, I, xvi, 5
[2] *Ecclesiastical Polity*, I, x, 4

The premier exponent of the theory of natural rights within the bounds of a secular natural law was John Locke. A seventeenth-century figure, he looks back to St. Thomas through Hooker, standing between the mediaeval dual society and the unified democratic nation-states which were shaped by the American and French revolutions. To the spread and penetration of his influence in the eighteenth century some of the doctrines and most of the self-justification of these two convulsive historical events may be directly traced. But the occasion of Locke's own concern with the elucidation of the principles of political obedience was the current resurgence of a danger of absolutist government in England under James II.

Locke published his *Letter on Toleration*, first in Latin and then in English, in 1689, but his *Second Treatise of Civil Government* did not appear until 1690, after James's deposition. It is not inapposite to link these writings to the events of the day, but their permanent value and interest transcend the concerns of Whig and Tory apologists and the quarrels of Orangemen and Jacobites.

It is part of the paradox which the Christian tradition has bequeathed to politics that when Locke questions the credentials of the doctrine of the divine right of civil rulers to exercise their authority arbitrarily, he does so in the name of the same divine law by which those very rulers claimed to be justified. For this law still operates, or is still at that date believed to operate, outside the realm of civil authority proper. From this extra-political stance, Locke can criticize the civil order and properly ask how it arises and what ends it serves. More than this, he can discuss what institutional pattern is most just and closest to conformity with that natural law which mediates God's will to rational individual men. In their moral relations with one another, in their natural status as men rather than citizens, the whole world of individuals stands outside the political arena. Echoes of the Christian cell at Corinth, of the mysterious unseen community of the elect, and of the institutional mediaeval church itself may be heard again and again in Locke's defence of individual rights. In the protestant world, every man had become his own pope; and because in the new political pattern of absolutist nation-states, the anointed monarchs of these centralized civil governments had inherited the twin powers of the two swords, Christian social doctrine had in some sense become divided against itself. It is to be doubted whether Locke consciously set out to disentangle this theoretical knot; but we can see, looking back, how successful, in terms of his continuing influence in western states up to the present day, were his analysis and reformulation of the political problems which faced Europe at the end of the seventeenth century.

The significance of Locke's criticism of arbitrary political power is that he prosecutes it from a standpoint theoretically outside the political arena, but not from within the institutional framework of the church, as earlier thinkers might have done. Men considered as bereft of political unity are neither bestial nor warlike nor reprobate, but a collection of moral, rational individuals naturally concerned for the peaceful enjoyment of those rights which nature enjoins for the common good. The attempt to explain or justify political institutions by reference to a theoretically non-political state of nature was almost common form up to the end of the eighteenth century. But the concept of the state of nature, though its roots may be traced to Cicero and Aristotle, owed little to classical thought when used by social thinkers of the seventeenth and eighteenth centuries to define an area of human relations in some sense outside the jurisdiction of civil authority. Moreover, their use of this device to describe men theoretically assumed to be withdrawn from the civil order was by no means consistent or equally illuminating. Hobbes employed the concept to prove it could never enjoy more than a momentary historical reality, whereas for Rousseau it referred rather to an ideal condition, mythically forfeited but able to be regained through reformed political institutions. Only Locke uses this confusing hypothesis to suggest a community of interests which, whether we call it pre-political or non-political, is genuinely natural in the sense of being a necessary substratum in all human relations, and also social in that it unites all the rational individuals in recognition of a single moral code. The concept is undeniably moral, but no longer clearly religious as was the mediaeval theory of the church. It is social, but clearly not political in the classical sense. It is individualistic, but only in respect of the moral equality of the members of the natural society. Locke's non-political rational men had in common their humanity, their reason, the moral law expressing the will of the one God and their community of interests in survival in this world and salvation in the next. But, from the point of view of theory, they had neither church nor state.

The metaphorical language used by political thinkers who posit a pre-civil social condition is usually designated contractual, but it is not always precisely a contract which the various agreements most resemble. Hobbes, who is considering in what way theoretically isolated individuals form a society, uses the term covenant, taken from the Old Testament. Rousseau discusses what steps members of an existing society can take to reform their social and political relations by unanimous agreement to pursue a common moral end. Locke himself is specifically concerned with the method whereby a political regime or government is appointed and controlled, and his own metaphor of a trust more clearly expresses the kind of relationship he envisages. All these thinkers are in fact analysing the political relationship in terms of what they think it either must or ought to be; and the metaphors they use are of less importance than the relationships which they wish to illustrate. Locke is linked to the past in his insistence that the two distinct ends pursued in this world and the next required two separate corporations with differing constitutions. But he prefigures the future in holding that many of the decisions necessary for successful survival and almost all those required by salvation could be safely left to the voluntary action and choices of his rational citizens.

Locke's response to the challenge of absolutist government specifically considers the principal theoretical arguments used to support it. His first treatise attacks the contemporary exposition of the theory of divine right by Sir Robert Filmer and in the second treatise he shows why Hobbes's idea of an anarchical state of nature is an improper premise from which to argue the necessity of a central sovereign above the law. Some men, says Locke, have confounded the state of nature and the state of war; and although he does not go as far as to equate the natural condition with peace and good-will, he believes it to be nearer this state than to enmity and violence. This famous assertion is cast in the form of a simile, not indicatively. Locke's positive definition reads: 'Men living together according to reason, without a common superior on earth with authority to judge between them, is properly the state of nature.'[1] It is the absence of a judge and the corresponding equality of authority of the members of this natural society which Locke wishes to emphasize. But they are not thereby loosed from their moral bonds; 'For truth and keeping of faith belong to men as men, and not as members of society.'[2] They are normally subject to the rule of 'common reason and equity, which is that measure God has set to the actions of men, for their mutual security'.[3]

This description of non-political man, inconceivable to Aristotle, would similarly have surprised Augustine. If the political framework apparently adds so little to natural society, inevitably we ask ourselves on what grounds Locke seeks to justify any government at all. Indeed, the limited authority he permits to the civil power and his insistence that its primary duty is the defence of an intrinsically extra-political domain of individual rights both arise from his conviction concerning rational behaviour. In brief, government is a convenience, even perhaps a necessary convenience, for not all men are constantly obedient to the norms of natural law. Irrational minorities disturb the peace. The supreme natural right to freedom is itself uncertain and constantly exposed to invasion. Property is unsafe and insecure. Men, he says, are 'willing to quit a condition, which, however free, is full of fears and continual dangers'.[4] Further, there is a moral argument. In executing natural justice upon the minority of irrational offenders, men may be biassed in their own favour and carried away by revenge. This consideration, together with the practical concern for executing just punishment upon offenders effectively, which may not always be possible in an unorganized society, persuades Locke that a centrally promulgated law, a known and indifferent judge, and power to pursue and punish anti-social persons are desirable institutions. These political arrangements are justified, then, to achieve certain moral ends, ineffectually defended in the natural society. It is evident that this purpose is in important respects different from the

[1] *The Second Treatise of Civil Government and A Letter concerning Toleration*, edited J. W. Gough (Oxford, Basil Blackwell,1946), p. 11
[2] *Second Treatise*, p. 9
[3] *Second Treatise*, p. 6
[4] *Second Treatise*, p. 62

exercising of God's judgment upon sinners and from the defence
of the church on earth, though it has something in common with
each of these earlier justifications of civil authority.

The natural rights which Locke wished to defend against the
intrusion of ill-disposed persons are summed up in the composite
designation of life, liberty and estate. In one passage, he speaks of
'The great end of men's entering into society' as 'the enjoyment of
their properties in peace and safety'.[1] The terms life and liberty
refer to the self-evident right of men to ensure their own survival,
if possible, and to the presumed right of rational men to arrange
their own affairs without arbitrary interference from others.
Locke assumes a proviso that normally they will make these
arrangements sensibly. But the term estate or property has given
rise to much confusion not only among students of Locke's
theory, but wherever his influence has affected political institutions and practice since his day. In particular, the whole argument
concerning the extent of the civil power's authority to intervene
in regulating economic activities has been bedevilled by the
citation of Locke's theory, even when it was no longer relevant.

Property for Locke was a generic term, used more in its Latin
than its present-day English sense, to cover firstly the person of the
individual, which, if we reject the validity of slavery, is undeniably
his own property. But it included also all those extensions of the
personality due to its operations in the temporal or economic
sphere which could be held to result from the individual's exercise
of his right to live. Locke specifically assumes that these interests
will not normally clash, or need not do so if there is sufficient land
left for others. Land was the standard type of economic property
at the time; other kinds should not be hoarded in excess of their
being liable to be spoiled; and it was by his labour that a man
made good his title to that property on which he had expended it.
Already in his own time the use of money and bank credit was
beginning to render the risk of property being spoiled very much
less. Locke was aware of this new factor but never fully considered
the implications for his theory. The conclusion drawn from this
argument that most economic activities are the concern of the
property owners and that the civil power is set up to defend their
rights has been widely influential and dies very hard.

[1] *Second Treatise*, p. 66

The political implications of the belief that civil authority derives its justification from the adequate defence of natural rights were no less important. Firstly, it could be argued that government, being as it were set up by the members of the natural society, depended upon the consent of these individuals as citizens for its continued authority. If they withdrew it, the government could not properly appeal to God for support. We must beware of interpreting Locke's thought here democratically. Though the idea of consent enters into the concept of modern democratic procedure, the underwriting of the law by the will of the people had little or no part in Locke's theory, except in a remote sense which had no political consequences. He is arguing in favour of the rational recognition of the proper promulgation of natural law through the forms of positive enactments rather than suggesting that we owe no obligation to laws not issuing from our own wills. Consent, Locke admits, is usually tacit, though the founding of new political communities, particularly in the American colonies, was not unknown. Tacit or presumed consent was not invalid for Locke, for the force of his argument lay in the right of the citizen to withdraw allegiance when he perceived a miscarriage of justice or even because he freely wished to alter his allegiance. The assumption that most men, even rulers, obeyed the same moral norm would guarantee that deviations were exceptional.

It was this same assumption that enabled Locke to argue in favour of majority consent in cases of difference of opinion. In one passage he uses the analogy of a physical body, moved 'whither the greater force carries it', to justify following a majority decision. But this argument from expediency is not required by Locke, if his belief that only a minority of citizens ever behaves anti-socially is valid. His true position is expressed in the contention that a *de facto* submission to political authority is no presumption of a rightful exercise of that authority. The standard whereby this right is tested must be external to the political power itself: either the consent of the subject, possibly implied in his enjoyment of property, or the limitation of the political authority within the bounds of natural law. The two tests interlink, for unjust use of political power would quickly forfeit the consent of most of the citizens. It is for these reasons that Locke can speak of the majority 'having . . . the whole power of the community naturally in them'.[1]

The exercise of political power is then, for Locke, limited. Its ends must be confined to 'the peace, safety, and public good of the people'; and its means prescribed at all times according to the law. 'And so whoever has the legislative or supreme power of any commonwealth is bound to govern by established standing laws, promulgated and known to the people, and not by extemporary decrees; by indifferent and upright judges, who are to decide controversies by those laws; and to employ the force of the community at home only in the execution of such laws. . . .'[2] Thus the legislative, judicial, and executive powers reflect the common maintenance of the exercise of rights, theoretically administered by individuals in the pre-civil state. The unification of this procedure in a political society derives its coherence from the law of nature which at the same time renders it just.

It is the position of the legislature, or promulgating body, midway between the law and the people and answerable, as it were, to both, which gives it its supreme position in the state. Yet it is not in any absolute sense sovereign. Locke avoids the pitfalls of the problems of sovereignty by describing the legislature as exercising a trust. This fruitful and helpful concept has been widely and deservedly influential. As trustee of the law for the people, the legislature may rightly claim political supremacy. As beneficiary of this trust, the community itself enjoys a reversionary sovereignty. But it is the law, reflecting natural law and representing God, which receives the ultimate allegiance of the citizens and in the name of which they may properly dismiss their governors. Power must be limited by law and used according to law; and Locke's recommendation for the separation of the executive power from the legislature is both to keep the former subordinate and because he fears for 'human frailty, apt to grasp at power. . . .'[3]

But for a grave cause the citizens retain a final right of appeal to heaven. They may revolt and set up a new political structure. Only the government is dissolved, for the natural society remains

[1] *Second Treatise*, p. 65
[2] *Second Treatise*, p. 64
[3] *Second Treatise*, p. 72

always in being and nothing can destroy 'the native and original
right it has to preserve itself'.[1] Throughout Locke's theory there
is a constant assumption that human beings enjoy a common
rational ability to intuit the same standard of moral behaviour. It
is in terms of this standard that they can estimate not only each
other's performance but the justice and propriety of the laws to
which they consent to submit in civil society.

Locke, indeed, makes a clear distinction between the spheres
of social well-being and personal salvation, though the latter tends
to be displaced to the next world which enhances the immediate
concentration upon temporal affairs. The mode of approaching
these different ends is, however, very similar. The changes in the
relations of individuals to both civil and ecclesiastical authority,
which distinguish this period from mediaeval theory and practice,
are complementary. Only rational persons, as Locke describes
them, could intelligibly operate the kind of civil constitution
which he advocates; and similarly it is individuals of this disposition who can dispense with the corporate and sacramental
support of an organized church. Civil authority is no adjunct of
the ecclesiastical power, but a parallel, independent, secular realm.
Truth is no longer subordinate to the superior test of revelation;
it enjoys secular status and the laws are not concerned 'to provide
for the truth of opinions, but for the safety and security of the
commonwealth, and of every particular man's goods and person.
And so it ought to be for truth certainly would do well enough,
if she were once left to shift for herself.'[2]

In Locke, though we find no support for the subordination of
the temporal order to the spiritual, it remains subordinate to the
rationally perceived natural law; and there is certainly no claim
for the inversion of the traditional roles. Individuals set up states
and churches in the same spirit, but for different ends. If the
commonwealth is a society constituted to preserve and advance
civil interests, a church is also a voluntary society of men 'joining
themselves together of their own accord in order to the public
worshipping of God in such manner as they judge acceptable to
him, and effectual to the salvation of their souls'.[3] The relation

[1] *Second Treatise*, p. 107
[2] *A Letter on Toleration*, op. cit., p. 151
[3] *A Letter on Toleration*, p. 129

between these two realms should be one of mutual toleration. In either, men must be left free to exercise their judgment. If a man may neglect his health or his estate without its being the concern of the civil authority, how much less should he suffer interference in the care of his own soul. Correspondingly, it was not for the church to use civil power to impose uniformity of doctrine. Civil and ecclesiastical absolutism had been closely connected. James II's allegiance to Rome no less than his misgovernment at home was at the root of his subjects' disaffection. Locke's plea for mutual toleration was, then, an integral element in his doctrine of political freedom. But this central contention was itself bound up with a positive view of the status of civil interests. To guarantee liberty under the law in defence of the natural rights of the citizens was to place a different emphasis on the purpose of civil government from the idea that it represented the judgment of God upon sinners and different again from the Greek belief that it was the natural means whereby the ignorant, body and soul, were rescued by the enlightened.

.   .   .   .   .

Locke's influence was widespread in the eighteenth century, partly because his political theory was believed to have provided a justification for the English revolution at a time when the constitutional liberty of Englishmen attracted much admiration, but also because he illustrated for his contemporaries simply and intelligibly their conviction that arbitrary and despotic power ought to be subject to moral restraint. This was particularly the case in France, the most powerful, wealthy and culturally advanced nation-state of the period, in which the centralized monarchical bureaucracy was proving less successful and attracting more criticism than it had done in the previous century. Cultural contacts between the two countries were close throughout the century. In the earlier decades, the virtual exile of Bolingbroke in France, where he formed a close friendship with the young Voltaire, and the latter's visit to England followed by that of Montesquieu, all helped to popularize Locke's theory and English constitutional practice. Reformers in France welcomed support for their criticism of monarchical absolutism; and a social thinker, such as Montesquieu, though his enquiries were framed very differently from Locke's, shared the same purpose of describing the political conditions which would best serve the harmoniously moral co-operation of rational men.

France, however, at that date, had not yet had a successful political revolution; and perhaps for this reason, critics of the regime were more sensitive to the threats to moral and political freedom in the highly organized nation-state. At all events, compared with Locke, French thinkers such as Voltaire and Montesquieu are more historical in their approach to political questions; and Montesquieu himself is notable for the lively interest he takes in the social and economic conditions within which morally responsible governments have in fact to carry out their duties. While Montesquieu is not moved to defend a theory of abstract individual rights, he accepts the same assumptions as Locke with regard to natural law, and in his reiteration that social and political freedom from arbitrary interference is the principal advantage of a well-balanced constitution he is in practice setting a limit to political power at the same point and on the same grounds as did Locke himself. But Montesquieu's analysis of how a consensus of moral opinion is reached and maintained is rather more subtle than Locke's; and he emphasizes more strongly the pattern and structure of political authority which he believes will best permit the development of this moral harmony in particular historical circumstances.

Montesquieu, like Locke, was concerned to criticize political institutions from the standpoint of an assumed universal human nature determined by a universal moral norm. This yardstick governed his interest in the abiding characteristics of social behaviour, as he confidently believed them to be. But Montesquieu did not subscribe only to the view that man in general (it is Voltaire's phrase)[1] shares a common disposition to be rationally moral. He was inclined to agree with the view, which gained ground as the century proceeded, that men were moved more often by their feelings. It was this conviction which promoted his interest in the search for general causes of social behaviour in history; 'for as men at all times have had the same passions, the

[1] 'L'homme en général a toujours été ce qu'il est :' Œuvres (Kehl), xvi, 32. Essai sur les moeurs

occasions which give rise to great changes are various, but the causes are always the same'.[1] Montesquieu's major contribution to this enquiry came out, after many years' work, in 1748. Its title, *De l'Esprit des lois*, is extremely difficult to render into English and not easy to understand in the original French. For this 'esprit' of the laws, which was the subject of such lengthy and varied investigation, refers all the time to two distinct, but inter-connected, characteristics of social law and it was their influence on each other which was the true, but not fully admitted, purpose of his enquiry.

Firstly, Montesquieu wished to discover what may be called the moral purpose of a law, its original intention in terms of some final cause. But he also wished to consider its suitability to the particular circumstances in which it was to operate. Finally these two questions were linked by a third in which he asked, not what was the relationship of law to conditions, but what ought it to be in any particular situation. The conditions, moreover, were to include not only customs and climate, wealth and population, but the character of the political institutions of the community under study. It was the business of reason to adjust the principles govern-ing this complex causal system; and Montesquieu himself applied his mind to just this exercise. Theoretically, his success was not very great; but he did much to expose the weaknesses in the rationalist approach to politics, and his influence, as Locke's, has been no less, and possibly more, widespread by reason of the inaccuracies and confusion of his thought.

The unquestioned assumption which lay behind this appar-ently empirical survey of events was the belief that social historians could disclose a regular pattern in human affairs corresponding to the laws of cause and effect then being discovered by natural scientists. Montesquieu went further and held that the laws of these two realms could be harmonized with each other. With the knowledge of this harmony, a rational political society could be constructed as free from arbitrary despotism as the natural order appeared to be safeguarded from the vagaries of fortune or the irregular intrusions of providence. Such a society would be united in the practice of virtue, not a difficult and costly virtue, but the

[1] *Considérations sur les causes de la grandeur des romains et de leur décadence* (1734), p. 4

result of what seems almost instinctive guidance. Montesquieu had already painted his picture of the natural life with 'its simple customs and ingenuous manners' in an earlier satirical work, the *Lettres persanes* in 1721. In this the Persian visitors to Paris represent the universal rational men, their standards of conduct prescribed by nature rather than the Koran and their political convictions voiced as men and citizens.

History, Montesquieu believed, might reveal the general and regular social habits of the natural man, which other theorists of the state of nature had treated as philosophical assumptions. His great work was designed to investigate this system of general causes, though more often than not he selected his examples to illustrate theories whose basis was *a priori*, the primary assumption being that social phenomena were to be explained in terms of their complex interconnections with physical conditions and one another. That circumstances were relevant to sound political theories was no new contention. Aristotle himself always insisted on the importance of defining a constitution in terms both of its moral purpose and of its social circumstances. The effect of climatic and other natural conditions had been considered by Bodin in his *Republic* and at some length in his lesser-known essay on history. But it was easier to estimate the best possible polity when the scale was that of a classical Greek city; and the difficult moral and political problems which Montesquieu encountered did not arise when the natural order was believed to include the political. Aristotle had better grounds for drawing organic analogies from nature than had Montesquieu for attempting parallels from mechanics.

Montesquieu had inherited from the middle ages the triple distinction between the realms of God, man, and nature; and although he begins the *Esprit des lois* by saying that 'Laws, in their widest meaning, are the necessary relations which derive from the nature of things',[1] it is in their particular differences, according to whether the events were on the divine, human or natural level, that he is seriously interested. The moral law is apprehended by reason, as Locke held; but Montesquieu went on to claim that a further duty of reason was to distinguish the orders of laws one from another and to use this knowledge for the

[1] 1748 edition, vol. i, p. 2

understanding of events and the making of practical decisions.[1] He himself attempted to clarify the two confused realms of nature, the moral nature of man and the physical nature of the material universe. If he did not altogether succeed in bringing the judgments made in the two spheres into the harmony he desired, he brought clearly into the open what proved to be one of the most difficult problems with which eighteenth-century social thinkers had to grapple.

The difficulty was to decide whether in any given pattern of historical events, moral or physical causes were paramount, and what in fact were the relations between them. Montesquieu was aware that, according to the received theory, the claims of justice and equity under the decrees of natural law were perceived directly and intuitively, while the operation of physical causes was to be discovered by observation. The relationship between these two sets of laws was also a matter of observation. Montesquieu seems to have believed that he had himself shown how the required reconciliation could take place. For he is not prepared to retreat from the contention that both a political constitution and legislation ought to conform, or be trying to conform, to natural law and eternal justice. At the same time, however, legislators are equally bound to pay attention to the circumstances which, being no less inexorable, are no less liable, if ignored or flouted, to frustrate the best political design. For Montesquieu, as for other contemporary thinkers, the two systems of causes met together in the will of God ; but on earth it was, he thought, the business of human observers to assess each pattern and essay a practical reconciliation.

The most significant element in Montesquieu's own contribution to the production of this social harmony, in which the claims of justice shall not be rendered void by a failure to consider the social, economic and natural circumstances, is that he nearly always uses an analogy from mechanics or Newtonian cosmology to describe the political constitution nearest to his ideal. Moreover it is the analysis of political authority in terms of a balance of forces for which he is now chiefly remembered, and particularly in so far as this concept, among others, helped to mould the constitution of the United States. Apart from one passage in which the metaphor

[1] See vol. ii, p. 228

used is taken from musical harmony, his usual contention is that 'It is possible to have union in a state where it might be supposed there was nothing but disturbance, that is to say a harmony which results in that happiness which is alone true peace; it is like the parts of the universe linked together forever by the action of some of them, and the reaction of others.'[1]

Thus it is that we do not find in Montesquieu a strongly expressed preference for any particular constitution, for his primary concern is for the maintenance of the free moral life subject to law, and this depended more on the fitness of the political structure for its circumstances in the widest sense than on its precise arrangement of offices. What was to be avoided was a lack of balance within the constitution and a lack of governing moral purpose, whatever the constitution. A republic which proved indifferent to the common good might in the event be worse than tyranny. It was not enough to define a free state as one in which administration was honest and court favourites inoperative, if in practice it failed to provide those social advantages for which it was esteemed. Montesquieu is well aware that it is easier to decry despotism than to improve upon it. 'To form a moderate government, it is necessary to combine the powers, regulate them, temper them, make them function, give as it were a ballast to one to enable it to withstand another; this is a masterpiece of legislation, which chance produces rarely, and equally seldom prudence.'[2]

The political freedom which Montesquieu consistently upholds as the condition for the attainment of the good life is not noticeably different from Locke's own idea of life under the suzerainty of the law. Firstly, it is an absence of arbitrary interference, the demand that governments, like God, must act according to general laws. But it included freedom to conform to the moral norm, the special freedom of not behaving anti-socially. Political liberty does not at all consist, he tells us, in doing what we wish. 'In a State, that is to say, in a Society where there are laws, liberty can consist only in being able to do what one ought to wish, and in not being constrained in any way to do what one ought not to wish.'[3]

---

[1] *Considérations*, p. 98
[2] *Esprit des lois*, vol. i, p. 100
[3] *Esprit des lois*, vol. i, p. 241

The reference in this passage is moral; but Montesquieu thought of laws as a mode of adjusting the society to its circumstances as well as controlling the behaviour of the individuals within it. This view presented him with the implied conflict between the requirements of moral freedom and the social and economic demands of the situation. In what circumstances should the political power required to control the effects of the natural environment risk overstepping the limits of moral freedom? Slavery was plainly contrary to natural law; and yet in hot countries no one might work at all, were he not compelled. A moderate government might not be able effectively to control the prevailing conditions. A despotic government in any conditions jeopardized moral freedom.

It was these considerations which moved Montesquieu to seek a resolution of his paradox in the proposition that the abuse of power could only be avoided in constitutions in which no element in the constitution was strong enough to override the others and in which each was subject to the limitation of a balancing and opposing power. Locke had in general recommended the supremacy of the legislature and had sketched the theory behind English parliamentary procedure in his day. Montesquieu went further, partly due to his superficial misreading of political developments in England, and argued that the legislative, executive and judicial authorities in the state were themselves the prime constitutive factors in the political machine. Their theoretical separation must be matched by a practical balancing of their functions and authority, such that no one of them could override either of the others or exercise its characteristic duties without the concurrence of the others. The nature of things, Montesquieu tells us, demands this balance of power in the state; and on this mechanically conceived harmony the moral freedom of the citizens must depend.

Practice in England never conformed to this model, even in Locke's day; and when Montesquieu visited England, the close links between the executive and legislative branches of government were already being forged. But the influence of Montesquieu's theory has been very great, notably in the United States, where the doctrine of the separation of powers has received its most complete expression; and where the balance of institutional authority is specifically designed to safeguard the realm of natural rights, moral freedom and the pursuit of peace and happiness, which Locke and Montesquieu both desired for their rational citizens.

.   .   .   .   .

Political theories rarely have direct influence on historical events. This is true even in the case of Locke and Montesquieu, when we can trace the effect of their beliefs in the constitutional documents which illustrated the revolutionary changes in America and France. The reliance which these later generations placed on their theories appears greater than it was and the effect is distorted. It is, however, beyond argument that we find evidence both in 1776 and 1789 that those who framed the two famous declarations of those years not only turned to the doctrine of natural rights for a justification of their actions, but also to some extent attempted to construct their new political institutions in accordance with its tenets. Thomas Paine, the last great eighteenth-century protagonist of these beliefs, epitomized the common sentiment of the revolutionary movement in a single rhetorical sentence: 'What is government more than the management of the affairs of the Nation?'[1] Whether it was the attack on French bureaucracy or British imperialism, the critics agreed with Locke that government was a convenience and must be limited, either by the will of the people, an idea derived rather from Rousseau, or by a constitutional framework which embodied the fundamental natural law, according to which the governments must be judged. Both in theory and practice, there was a divergence between the American and French revolutions in regard to the political means which they supported and employed. About their final purposes, the two peoples were closely at one. Both wished to safeguard the inalienable rights and freedom of the citizens from the arbitrary intrusion of despotic governments, not answerable to the moral law.

It was the attempt to place legal limits on governmental authority which links both the American and French revolutions with the theoretical assumptions of eighteenth-century political thinkers. In *The Federalist*, a collection of papers almost wholly given up to precise criticism and consideration of the new con-

[1] *The Writings of Thomas Paine* (1894), vol. ii, p. 385. *Rights of Man*

stitution-making in America, we find two papers[1] concerned with Montesquieu's dictum regarding the separation of powers. But the author, having remarked that the British constitution was not an example of total separation, goes on to state that the government for which the colonies had fought was 'one which should not only be founded on free principles, but in which the powers of government should be so divided and balanced among several bodies of magistracy, as that no one could transcend their legal limits, without being effectually checked and restrained by the others'.[2] The doctrine was to be interpreted not as a magical constitutional device, but in order to prevent the whole power of one authority in the state falling into the hands of those responsible for one of the other two. For Paine, the so-called balance of power in Britain was meaningless, a mere device for preventing the commons, representing the democratic element, from exercising their authority freely. Already, towards the end of the century, we find a growing distrust both of the efficacy of constitutional machinery, except as a negative barrier, and even of the plain, incontestable clarity of the fundamental laws themselves. Richard Price, in a pamphlet contributed to the discussion about the secession of the colonies, remarks presciently that it is not enough to define freedom as 'a Government by LAWS and not by MEN', for it depends very much on which men make the laws.[3] To some extent, Locke himself was to blame for this development by the prominence which his theory of rights gave to the concept of property as a pre-political extension of the person. The safeguarding of the interests of the propertied classes played an important part in the framing of the American constitution; and Godwin was to remark later in his *Political Justice* that 'the poor man will be induced to regard the state of society as a state of war, an unjust combination, not for protecting every man in his rights and securing to him the means of existence, but for engrossing all its advantages to a few favoured individuals. . . .'[4] But

---

[1] Nos. XLVII and XLVIII, both by Maddison
[2] *The Federalist*, edited M. Beloff (Oxford, Basil Blackwell, 1948), pp. 254-55
[3] *Observations on the Nature of Civil Liberty, the Principles of Government, and the Justice and Policy of the War with America* (London and Philadelphia 1776), p. 6
[4] *Political Justice* (2nd ed., London 1796), vol. i, p. 17

for most observers these important economic issues, which in the
nineteenth century and in our own have come to the fore, were
shrouded in the unhistorical setting of the abstract theory of
rights.

The famous American declarations all draw their theoretical
content from Locke; and indeed the Declaration of Independence
contains perhaps the best-known statement of Locke's view of the
morally free individual. 'We hold these truths to be self-evident,
that all men are created equal, that they are endowed by their
Creator with certain unalienable Rights, that among these are
Life, Liberty and the pursuit of Happiness.' The substitution of
the 'pursuit of happiness' for Locke's 'estate' makes little difference to the intention of the assertion. Locke uses the term himself
to describe the achievement of satisfaction in this world; and the
Massachusetts Bill of Rights of 1780 specifically adds to life and
liberty the right of 'acquiring, possessing and protecting property;
in fine that of seeking and obtaining their safety and happiness'.
The Virginian Bill of Rights of 1776 includes a similar clause in
which happiness is added to property though not precisely linked
with it. For once, theory and practice appeared indissolubly
linked, for the very setting up of the new confederacy corresponded to the self-conscious decision of men in the state of nature
solemnly to contract with one another to form a political society.
A series of events which historically amounted to secession from
an already existing state, and which its ill-wishers called a rebellion,
was greeted by its supporters as the assumption of 'the separate
and equal station to which the Laws of Nature and of Nature's
God' entitled them. In presenting the *Rights of Man* to Washing-
ton, Paine described it as 'a small treatise in defence of those principles of freedom which your exemplary virtue hath so eminently
contributed to establish'.

It was in this treatise that Paine gave perhaps the best explanation we have of the relationship between individual rights and
social control. In one sense, it is a summary of the Lockian tradition, but the connection is defined more clearly; and Paine's
position foreshadows the transformation of the theory of rights
under the influence of other political theories already influential
when he was writing. He distinguishes the natural rights which
derive from the individual's presumed right to existence from his

civil rights as a member of society. The latter are all founded in the pre-existing examples of the former, but become civil by reason of the inability of the individual, relying on his own power, to ensure his enjoyment of them. Thus the individual retains all those rights which he has the power to execute, notably intellectual and religious rights. But he hands over to society the execution of those rights, notably security and protection, for which he cannot make personal provision. 'Society,' Paine concludes, '*grants* him nothing. Every man is a proprietor in society, and draws on the capital as a matter of right.'[1] It was in this last point that the theory of rights, particularly in the succeeding century, required amendment and development. Its predominantly unhistorical and abstract formulation prevented its exponents from understanding that to derive all political authority from the citizens is not identical with attributing all social advantages and benefits to the individuals who compose the society. Paine's use of the metaphor capital was ominous.

For the time being, however, the French revolutionaries were in substantial agreement with the Americans. France was a functioning great power changing its mode of government rather than a new colonial community beginning a separate political existence, and its problems were in many respects different. But Article II of the Declaration of the Rights of Man sets forth the same political purpose. 'The end of every political association is the preservation of the natural and imprescriptible rights of man. These rights are liberty, property, security and resistance to oppression.' These rights were reiterated in the later Declarations prefixed to the Constitutions of 1793 and 1795. Liberty was defined as the reciprocal right of doing whatever did no harm to others. Equality of rights was defined specifically as equality before the law. Property was defined in Lockian terms as the right to dispose of the fruits of one's labour and industry. The French doctrine of political authority had, however, been strongly influenced by Rousseau ; and in making the nation the source of sovereignty and, in 1795, declaring that the law is the general will, the sponsors of the revolution were no longer speaking the language of the natural rights' tradition.

All the radical thinkers of this period, with the possible

[1] *Rights of Man*, op. cit., vol. ii, pp. 306–7

exception of Godwin, concurred in agreeing that government of some kind was necessary. It was, as the 1789 Declaration said, the ignorance, neglect or contempt of human rights to which public misfortunes and corrupt government must be attributed. There was some uncertainty about the precise cause of this imperfection, but an optimistic belief that the promulgation of the fundamental rights in constitutional documents would go far to remedy the error. Paine had stated on the first page of his *Common Sense* that 'were the impulses of conscience clear, uniform and irresistibly obeyed, man would need no other law-giver'.[1] A similar sentiment is expressed in *The Federalist* where we read : 'But what is government itself, but the greatest of all reflections on human nature? If men were angels, no government would be necessary.'[2] By the end of the eighteenth century, despite the competing theory of natural goodness, there was a general tendency to attribute human imperfection to ignorance. 'Whatever is brought home to the conviction of the understanding, so long as it is present to the mind, possesses an undisputed empire over the conduct.'[3] These words of Godwin's, though quite general in the context in which they appear, describe very adequately the assumption behind the efforts of eighteenth-century revolutionaries to bring home to erring governments the political truths to which they ought to be subject.

Godwin believed that all positive acts of a government were evil in so far as they limited the scope of private decision which was the true seat of moral freedom. But Paine couples his support of natural rights with a lively sense of the services of a government to the people, if it be democratically directed. If the theory of natural rights, which began in the inviolability of the protestant conscience, developed into an extreme anarchistic individualism by the time we reach Godwin, we must remember also that in both the British and American constitutions it has affected the historical development of the western world ; and that, in our own day, the Preamble to the constitution of the Fourth French Republic solemnly reaffirmed the rights and freedoms of man and citizen which had been enshrined in the Declaration of Rights of 1789.

[1] Op. cit., vol. i, p. 69
[2] No. L1
[3] *Political Justice*, vol. i, p. 93

The opening words of the Preamble read : 'On the morn of the
victory gained by the free peoples over the regimes which have
attempted to subjugate and degrade the human person, the French
people proclaims anew that every human being, without distinction
of race, religion or creed, possesses inalienable and sacred rights.'

CHAPTER IV

FELICITY

'*Continual success,*' Hobbes tells us, 'in obtaining those things which a man from time to time desireth, that is to say, continual prospering, is that men call FELICITY; I mean the felicity of this life. For there is no such thing as perpetual tranquillity of mind, while we live here; because life itself is but motion, and can never be without desire, nor without fear, no more than without sense.'[1] This was no new description of the process of living; and that we should use the term felicity to designate the second main theme of the divergent political theories which developed after the Renaissance is to emphasize that Hobbes's sentiments had by that time come to have a political reference. His contention that the pattern of civil order and obligation must be correlated with the psychological attributes of human beings in restless pursuit of felicity has been increasingly and widely influential in the modern world. In certain important respects this philosophy, both in its earlier and later manifestations, has added new and challenging arguments to the traditional stock of political wisdom. Locke's attack on Hobbes's description of human character was guided by a fair estimate of the incompatibility of such premises with a theory of natural law and rights. But many of the characteristics of the theories grouped under the heading of Hobbesian felicity may be found in earlier thinkers and traditions. It is their new arrangement which is original and which renders Hobbes's own famous treatise, the *Leviathan*, one of the great masterpieces of political thought.

A much more thorough concern than Locke's with civil interests in this world is matched with a more subtle analysis than Montesquieu's of the interconnection between character, circumstances and institutions. This concentration on the immediate needs of humanity in the temporal flux has in general

[1] *Leviathan*, edited M. Oakeshott (Oxford, Basil Blackwell, no date), p. 39

117

given felicific theories an anti-religious bias, expressed in their emphasis on the power and sovereignty of the secular authority and a constant concern for the happiness of individual citizens. Neverthless, this pattern of thought owes more to Christian tradition and psychology than to the classical heritage and in some respects is a secular version of Augustine's view of man and society.

What Augustine would have called the uncertain and temporary peace of satisfied desire in this world, necessarily imperfect and only foreshadowing the joys to come, Hobbes calls felicity. The justice provided by the civil authorities, supreme in this world, as God's vice-regents, establishes the framework of civil peace within which every man may struggle for salvation. Correspondingly, the Hobbesian sovereign power, drawing its authority from the concurring wills of its subjects, provides for them that civil peace without which they seek to satisfy their desires in vain. The parallel is complete when we recall that it is the will of man, whether personal or imperial, which seeks these temporal manifestations of peace and order and which enthroned as the political authority, backed by force, is final in this world.

As we have seen, the disintegration of the western empire, the exclusive allegiance of all citizens to the catholic church, and the Thomist synthesis of Aristotelian rationalism with Christian revelation had rendered such views of the character of man and the organization of society either inapposite or unfashionable. Civil law was held to be open to testing either against the standards of natural law or of those of revelation as interpreted by the church. A return to a political theory much closer to that of Augustine than Thomas Aquinas in the new conditions of the renaissance world raises the question whether there was a logical connection, as Hobbes held, between his self-seeking men and his single, unconditional, civil authority or whether the new hedonists employed Augustinian imagery and arguments for historical reasons of which they were unaware.

There is evidence that the latter viewpoint may well be the better explanation. Other individualist thinkers, employing the language of contract and the myth of a state of nature, notably Locke and Rousseau, came to different conclusions from Hobbes and from each other. Moreover, one heterodox mediaeval theorist,

Marsilius of Padua, three centuries before Hobbes, stresses precisely the voluntarist argument that justice derives from the will of the lawgiver and that political authority is unitary, civil, and final in this world, without supposing his citizens to be other than good Christians and still believing the fashionable Aristotelian tenet that political society was natural, not artificial.

Marsilius was moved by the evident failure of the theory of the dual society and the balanced harmony of church and empire and even more by its abandonment in practice. His argument, in brief, was that if there was to be only one sovereign authority, it should not be ecclesiastical and theocratic. In this world, he noticed, effective sanctions were wielded by the civil power. The divine law, which he still recognized, had as wide a jurisdiction as expectation of its eventual effects hererafter might give it. Meanwhile, its claims were ideal and shadowy, limited indeed to strengthening the civil law by controlling the consciences of citizens beyond the latter's reach. For natural law, in its Thomist guise, Marsilius found no place at all. He maintained the general pattern of Augustinian emphasis on the maintenance of peace, but castigated the fourteenth-century papacy as the prime disturber of civil order. It was hardly surprising that his *Defensor Pacis*, completed in 1324, was condemned by the church.

It was the skeleton structure of this doctrine, no less Christian and mediaeval than Thomism itself, which was inherited by later hedonistic thinkers. The question left open for discussion was who or what were the principal threats to the peace and harmony of civil society. That a strong, central, absolute power was the proper means to achieve peace was not implicit in any particular answer to this enquiry ; it was, however, a tradition accepted and shared by thinkers as diverse in other respects as Augustine, Marsilius and Hobbes.

With the Reformation, the incipient division of the western church, heralded in the fifteenth century, became explicit. Ecclesiastical rivalries became increasingly a source of civil disturbance ; but the mediaeval pretensions of the papacy to theocratic sovereignty declined. Concurrently, the transformation of European cultural values, which in sum we call the Renaissance, engendered a new spirit of pagan concern for the joys and satisfactions of life in this world, a concentration on the Greek example of human living, untroubled by the metaphysical subtleties of Greek philosophy. The widespread economic and social changes of this period, of which sensitive observers were acutely aware, gave a fresh impetus to the unhampered development of individual experiment and at the same time strengthened the support for the new central powers of the nation-state, which were succeeding to the divided and contentious authority of feudal and ecclesiastical Europe.

The two movements conspired between them to produce conditions in which the theory of an absolute secular authority met the pragmatic needs of the new individuals and classes emerging from the chaotic disturbances of the fifteenth century. The pursuit of pleasure and success had had its devotees in pagan times, but they took for granted the political structure of the empire and influenced it little or not at all. It was the recrudescence and spread of such views in an age of political instability, religious disharmony and economic and social revolution which required a corresponding political theory. The advantages which natural law doctrines had for those who remained within the moral tradition of Christendom were not entirely suitable to the needs either of the new states or the new humanists. It was an open question, theoretically, how hedonists would behave when divorced from the ethical framework of an Aristotelian natural society. Whether the result would be social harmony or impossible confusion remained a principal item of speculation throughout three centuries of felicific calculation.

That we are using a new term to describe the desirable condition of satisfied individuals in a moving, changing world is more than linguistic substitution, for it is evidence of the transformation of the Christian concepts of peace and order. These, indeed, were still the ends of a well-regulated civil society. But they were to be obtained not as a defence for the church or for the faithful the better to pass through an alien world, but so that every man, intent on serving his own interests, might reach, under the aegis of the civil power, that condition of balanced desire and achievement which came nearest to successful living in a dangerous but rewarding society of similar men. This achievement was made possible where the law was the wilful decision of an absolute, unchallenged sovereign power; or, to put it the other way round, it was this echo from the old idea of imperial security and order which, of all Christian traditions, was most congruous with the needs of the new age.

It was an age, moreover, soon to be shaken by the development of mathematical studies in the seventeenth century, the impact of Cartesian philosophy, and, in Hobbes's case in particular, the fascination of geometrical reasoning as a model of valid argument. This revolution in the realm of knowledge undoubtedly discouraged the use of mediaeval organic metaphors and increased the tendency to think of communities as chance collections of individuals held together artificially, analogous to material atoms controlled by physical forces.

So much emotion and ill-feeling has been expended on this very important tradition of social thought, that it requires some effort to grasp its essential characteristics without distortion. Marsilius was denounced as a heretic; Hobbes did not escape the appellation of 'that father of atheists'; and Machiavelli, its best-known Renaissance expositor and in many ways one of the school's most penetrating writers, has become a by-word for cynical, worldly wickedness.

It is not difficult to see how, in this last case, the misunderstanding has been emphasized. Machiavelli, a prominent citizen of Florence at the turn of the fifteenth and sixteenth centuries, miscalculated his own chances in that turbulent age and spent the last fifteen years of his life out of office and rusticated. His meditations, during this period, on the best means for gaining and exercising power have proved more alluring than the political and psychological assumptions from which they arose. It is too often forgotten that, in principle, Machiavelli preferred a republic to a despotism and looked back with regret to the imagined excellence of the Roman republic. But he believed the times were out of joint, that too few citizens would genuinely co-operate for the common good, and that the distracted Italian cities of his day needed strong, ruthless, independent rulers. This was an imperfect, second-best arrangement in the prevailing circumstances. In the same way, Machiavelli maintains a moral estimate of men's behaviour. They are often too foolish to pursue their own interests successfully, but this is what they ought to be doing. For Hobbes, a century and a half later, these relative moral estimates became absolute and standard and morally neutral. This was the permanent human situation, a description of fact, not a tract for the times.

Machiavelli saw man as a creature of desire seeking, often unsuccessfully, to satisfy his appetites in this world. He needed for this purpose to be adjusted to his circumstances, whatever they might be, to have what Machiavelli called virtue, or the qualities of character needed for the enterprise in hand. He needed also power, the means to success as distinct from the disposition to win it. But all too often men were disappointed and frustrated. Desire was infinite; power limited; balance hard to achieve, more difficult still to maintain. This lack of balance, often the result of pride or some emotional disturbance upsetting the judgment, played the part of sin in this secular version of the good, or successful, life. Thus, parallel with Augustine, Machiavelli sees the necessity for a strong, central, political power to enable the restless and wilful citizens to find such satisfaction as they may in changing circumstances, protected by a firm system of public order.

Just as did Marsilius, Machiavelli blames the church and particularly the papacy for much of the contemporary discontent and political disorder. Indeed, he goes further and castigates Christianity itself for inducing meekness and the patient acceptance of injuries, and because it 'causes us to attach less value to the honours and possessions of this world'.

It is not that Machiavelli values worldly goods as ends in themselves, but rather as a means to the maintenance of that balance or adjustment between a man and his changing circumstances, the unknown complex of causes which he calls fortune. Socially, the setting up of a strong, central, secular power, able to control both unruly individuals and a church with political interests, was the most important single means to this same end. It would enable its citizens to master their circumstances more surely, more quickly and with greater hope for the future. To write maxims for a successful prince, even if they included advice contrary to the tenets of conventional moral standards, was for Machiavelli justified as a means to results which he considered both desirable and good in the circumstances of his time.

The classical statement of this theme was made by Hobbes in the middle of the seventeenth century. For Hobbes not only

universalized the situation which Machiavelli had seen as a
temporary necessity of a disturbed age, but by rigorously exposing
the assumptions implicit in Machiavellian psychology, he purged
it of all incongruous moral judgments and presented an un-
decorated picture of the natural man, for ever in pursuit of
fugitive satisfaction and of that precarious balance between
character and conditions which Hobbes himself called felicity.

.   .   .   .   .

There was an increasing tendency in post-mediaeval political
thought, despite the support enjoyed by the theory of the divine
right of kings, to argue that the exercise of political authority was
not justified from above, either by the native, aristocratic excellence of the rulers or by the inscrutable disposal of providence.
In some sense all government, whether by transference, delegation,
appointment or representation, derived its authority from the
citizens. It is this belief which distinguishes Hobbes's thought
from earlier arguments that the proper concern of the secular
power is to provide a framework of peace and order within which
the faithful may tranquilly proceed on their pilgrimage. It is,
indeed, this service which Hobbes's sovereign rulers are expected
to offer their subjects ; but the purpose of the arrangement is to
leave them individually free to live their natural lives and it is
out of their impelling need to do so as successfully as possible
that the political superstructure itself arises. The state is neither
the gift of God nor the secular arm of the church, much less the
reflection of a virtuous minority. But nor is it a convenient administrative expression of the common moral concern of the
citizens. The pursuit of felicity by the individual, Hobbes argues,
demands, as a necessary precondition of its success, the creation
of a political institution, for the maintenance of which the
citizens are continuously responsible. They can achieve nothing
directly by means of this organization, for it is not the business of
the government to make men successful or happy ; but they can do
nothing for themselves without it. The fear of death is the beginning
of politics.

Hobbes devotes the first book of the *Leviathan* to an analysis
of human psychology. It is like modern psychological studies in
the sense that he attempts to describe his subject without prejudice,

making no moral assumptions or, as we should now say, value judgments. He is concerned to discover how men react to their circumstances and how they themselves estimate these reactions for better or worse. But it is very unlike modern psychology in method; for Hobbes uses the old mediaeval system of looking for universal truth in an exhaustive analysis of an individual example. In the case of man, this involves introspection; and Hobbes's example, an example he assumes to be a type, is thus himself. 'He that is to govern a whole nation, must read in himself, not this or that particular man; but mankind. . . .'[1] This philosophical procedure, which is both unscientific and unhistorical, as we now understand these terms, subjects Hobbes's analysis to some obvious distortion and inaccuracy. These disadvantages, however, are slight compared with the originality of attempting for the first time in history to describe man's plight without attributing either some or even all of the blame for its imperfections to man himself. This statement requires qualification if we include the known classical thinkers, Lucretius, for example, who similarly saw man as part of a determined, natural, universal order and nothing more. But Hobbes alone set out from this premise to deduce a social philosophy which ends by deriving moral duties from political necessity, instead of following the customary tradition of arguing conversely.

When Hobbes analyses human defects, he discovers neither ignorance nor sin in the Greek or Christian meanings of those terms, but the inevitable contrariness of human nature, misfortune rather than misjudgment, frustration more than wickedness. The terms most often used to characterize this point of view, such as cynical, pessimistic, or low, are no credit to Hobbes's critics. His rigorous efforts to exclude all prejudice, particularly all moral prejudice, in his description of human behaviour ought rather to be emulated than denounced. But in some respects this otherwise careful writer has himself to blame. Like Milton's Satan, the description of the horrifying implications of an uncontrolled society steals the picture. It is the state of nature, according to Hobbes's whole argument an impossibility, which remains vividly before us in place of the ordered political rule created by the will of man in response to the advice of reason. Every student of

[1] *Leviathan*, Introduction

Hobbes, whether he has read him or not, will know that man's life is liable to be 'solitary, poor, nasty, brutish and short'. He may easily forget to conclude that this threat is rarely made good, for man is at all times at great pains to take political action to avoid it. The device of describing a supposedly non-political situation, whether communal as in Locke, individual and amoral as in Hobbes or something of each view as in Rousseau, is always confusing. The language of contract theory, by taking its principal metaphor from law, that is from the practice of an organized political society, never quite makes clear that the question at issue is whether politics itself is the essential precondition of human living or only one department thereof, subordinate finally to some other and separate end. Hobbes, who takes the first of these views, sets about proving his case as though he took the second, when in fact he holds that there is no felicity at all except under the protection of the political sovereign. Some light can be thrown on his method if we liken it to the stages of proving a geometrical theorem, in which the prime datum is human character; the effects of human behaviour in a mythically non-political state are construction lines, put in ostensibly to clarify the argument; and the conclusion, which allows these lines to be ignored, that only under a strong sovereign can man live at all, represents *quod erat demonstrandum.*

The important distinction between this tradition of thought and its principal rival up to the time of the French revolution lay in the qualities which its devotees attributed to the natural man. Was he a sinful creature who required to be kept in order, a moral creature who occasionally went astray, or was his general inclination, as Hobbes phrased it, 'a perpetual and restless desire of power after power, that ceaseth only in death'?[1] Hobbes was here making no moral judgment for or against this wilful pursuit of the means to satisfy desire, but he was by implication denying the doctrine that men were antecedently bound to each other by moral ties the maintenance of which must be their first political endeavour. On the contrary, he saw them as a natural element in the universal system of matter in motion, responding to the ceaseless flow of stimuli from without, by movement towards those

[1] *Leviathan*, p. 64

found desirable or away from those which provoked aversion. In these responses to circumstances, the decisions taken were the acts of the will, though it is not altogether clear from Hobbes's account what determined the interruption of the emotional reactions when a decision was made to act. The important conclusion was that there could be no final satisfaction, so that the process of acquiring various kinds of power, or means, to ensure present and future satisfaction was perpetual.

Nevertheless, Hobbes is not describing a machine or even a species of animal, undifferentiated by any traditional human characteristic. Man has the special gifts of speech and memory developed to a high degree and the outstanding aid of reason which enables him to argue from past experience of the causal system to expectation of its future behaviour. At the same time, he is prevented from acting imprudently by his consciousness that the character of many remote causes lies beyond his knowledge. This fear of the unknown, which for Hobbes is the proper characteristic of religion, is, together with reason, a factor which helps to prevent man in society from risking the perils of disobedience.

The final defeat of life's hopes and joys is death; and this fate must be postponed, as Hobbes himself successfully contrived for over ninety years, as long as possible. To avoid death and to acquire the means to do so and to maintain life in the interval is man's overriding concern. Within his circumstances he is free to take what steps reason recommends, that is as appropriate means, to achieve these aims. Nothing is based on moral grounds. In theory, a man is not answerable for his acts; and no intuitive values or revealed truths limit what Hobbes often calls his rights, by which he means the exercise of his power, to assure survival as effectively and as long as possible. Thus, virtue, in this amoral account of living, becomes, as it was for Machiavelli, a kind of fitness for survival, the superior adjustment to conditions which is tested by success. There are variations in this fitness, due to misjudgments, notably to wrong estimates of a man's strength or competence in a given situation, which Hobbes calls pride. But he does not suggest in general that ignorance or sin explains human imperfection.

The problem of social living is set by the very fact that other people of like character exist contemporaneously. The hazards of living at all in a difficult and dangerous universe are infinitely increased, so that insecurity becomes the rule and felicity minimal. But we must remember that this is all a hypothetical argument; and we must add that these are the results which would occur were men not united by common agreement with one another in a political bond. Left to his own resources, man for Hobbes, as for Augustine, is hopelessly lost, a fallen creature, condemned whether by sin or by nature to an impossible existence. But in company he may be saved; and even if the difficulties of living cannot be removed, they can be very greatly modified. For the fear which would degrade man to a condition of chaos, were it his only or dominant disposition, is balanced by reason which encourages the will to create order, or rather constantly to maintain it.

The relationship of man to his political institution, as described by Hobbes, is not unlike that of God to the universe in Christian thought. Both of them by creative acts of will bring into being and sustain from moment to moment a pattern of order, changing and moving it is true, but constant and sure; and, within this order, individuals are enabled freely to pursue their allotted purposes. We can thus see Hobbes's argument as a rigorous analysis of the political relationship, of the submission of most citizens to the control by force of a few of their number. His explanation of this phenomenon is that it represents the necessary precondition of their survival and satisfaction, of their being free to achieve that uncertain balance between self and environment, which is called felicity. But whether we seek to discover, with Hobbes, why the sovereign power has been set up or whether, assuming its existence, we ask why it is obeyed, the answer must be that all men being rational in Hobbes's sense, they all perceive such a political organization as the best, indeed the only, possible means to their natural ends. The pursuit of felicity, from which there is no escape, can, a rational man will tell himself, be effective only according to certain rules, which his equally rational neighbours will simultaneously be willing to accept. What is thus sacrificed is individual power; but it returns a hundredfold in the creation of tolerable conditions. 'The final cause, end, or design of men, who naturally love liberty, and dominion over others, in the introduction of that restraint upon themselves, in which we see

them live in commonwealths, is the foresight of their own preservation, and of a more contented life thereby.'[1]

Nevertheless, though Hobbes describes the setting up of a
sovereign government as the necessary effect of psychological
causes, he presents the process as the willed creation of the
individuals who then become the subjects of the new commonwealth. But this paradox is illusory, due to portraying as an
historical event the creation of a relationship which, properly
speaking for Hobbes, is implicit in the political situation. It is
a way of saying that all sovereign power is both derivative and
representative; and though he can still write that a government is
answerable for its behaviour to God, it is dependent for its
authority on the concurring wills of the citizens. It is true that
political control is exercised in the last resort by force, but not by
mere force, justified speciously and immorally as Marx would
have us believe. Hobbes's psychology may be amoral; his political
theory seeks to justify political power by holding, to use his own
term, that it is authorized. The covenant which, thus, unites the
disconnected individuals into a body politic is a constant, though
largely inarticulate, affirmation of concurring purpose, issuing in
the maintenance of the state and reflected in rational obedience
to the law. We must not modernize this concept and call it totali-
tarian. 'In cases where the sovereign has prescribed no rule, there
the subject hath the liberty to do, or forbear, according to his
own discretion.'[2] Authoritarian it may be, but the authority is
transferred from below. There is in Hobbes's theory a political
necessity which corresponds to the psychological necessity driving
the individual to pursue felicity. In both cases, he is happier
in submission to it than in revolt.

But the silence of the law, as Hobbes calls it, does not envelop
the church. There are not to be two realms of equal status, as in
Locke's argument. The only apparently extra-political sphere
comprises the undirected moments of the lives of individuals.
Any other arrangements made to institutionalize their responses
to the unknown, their fear of the unexperienced, must be controlled by the single sovereign to which all authority in this world
has been given. We may see here, perhaps, a reflection of Hobbes's

[1] *Leviathan*, p. 109
[2] *Leviathan*, p. 143

turbulent age or no more than a return to the civic deities of the classical world. Indeed Hobbes could have been excused if he had argued that religious discord was excessive in the seventeenth century and should be controlled in the interests of peace. His case, however, was a universal one. Uniformity can only effectively be enforced by the civil power. Even the divine revelation, therefore, must be countersigned by a responsible minister. God had become a constitutional monarch, who reigned, but no longer ruled.

Hobbes thus went much further than the natural law theorists in completely secularizing the dual society of church and state, though an important vestigial distinction remained in the two spheres of legal compulsion and individual freedom. The political emphasis was in one sense negative; it was the prevention of chaos not directly the production of felicity which was the duty of the government. But because Hobbes was concerned with the achievement of results in a situation containing an ever-present threat of chaos, and because results depended on effective sanctions in this world, the sovereign government which held the communal force in its sole guardianship became thereby the guardian, interpreter and promulgator of all moral values, whether secular or religious. We go too far if we argue simply that for Hobbes the law is morality, for what he is saying is that no moral rule or divine commandment can have any effect if it is not to be enforced.

It is this view which governs his treatment of what he misleadingly calls natural laws. These are not moral norms in the light of which political acts can be judged, but general rules of behaviour, discovered by reason in experience, which like the social covenant itself can only be relied upon when confirmed and enforced by the civil government. The typical example of these rules of expediency, *'that men perform their covenants made'*, which Hobbes believed impossible lacking coercion, may be compared with Locke's version of the same precept: 'For truth and keeping of faith belong to men as men, and not as members of society.'[1]

Two points may be noticed before we pass on to later variations on the felicific theme. Hobbes's method of descrying a universal pattern of political relationship in his analysis of an unchanging

[1] *Second Treatise*, II, 14

human nature allows no place for historical development or progress, or for the effects of continuity and tradition. This unhistorical approach also warps the views of some of the utilitarian thinkers who followed in Hobbes's footsteps. The notion that organized society is in perpetual tension between the centrifugal thrust of its participants and the centralizing pull of political power tends to overestimate the strength and authority required at the centre to keep an historical society in being. In particular, it disregards the part played by custom and habit and by the long continued life and influence of social institutions other than the government. This defect of Hobbesian theory was remedied in the following century by Hume and Burke. Hobbes himself saw that the possession of political power does not necessarily betoken its exercise any more than does the possession of wealth its spending. But he does not draw the conclusion that possibly much less power is required to achieve his ends.

Secondly, compared with Locke's version, Hobbes uses the metaphor of covenant or contract to suggest that men have naturally no interests in common, whereas the conclusion of the argument is that they have one overwhelmingly important common concern: the maintenance of civil society. Seeing that they are rationally united in pursuit of this purpose, it is pertinent to ask why they may not be considered similarly united in respect of other ends also. Later thinkers came to this conclusion, while still accepting the individual as the architect of the social structure. It is plain that different analyses of what pertains to the natural psychology of the individual will provide different answers regarding what steps he will take in company with his fellows to achieve his ideal felicity.

Against the changing historical pattern of political thinking, Hobbes adds an original new theme: that in addition to ignorance and sin, man is beset by the contrariness of his own nature and its social consequences, for which no one is strictly to blame, but which everyone must co-operate to remedy. 'All that is NECESSARY *to salvation*, is contained in two virtues, *faith in Christ*, and *obedience to laws*. The latter of these, if it were perfect, were enough to us.'[1]

[1] *Leviathan*, p. 385

Seventeenth-century England, beset with civil and religious conflict, provided an antipathetic setting for Hobbes's rational analysis of social motives and forces. It is easy to say that Hobbes was ahead of his time; more important than this, the men of his time were fighting battles which, within less than a century, had become largely irrelevant. Correspondingly, and particularly in England, the naturalistic and matter-of-fact approach to politics evoked increasing sympathy and support, despite the concurrent influence of Locke and the natural law school. Perhaps the most valuable restatement of Hobbes's position, though it could scarcely be described as influential, was that provided by the Scottish thinker, David Hume, whose *Treatise of Human Nature* came out in 1739–40. Hume himself was disappointed by the lack of public response to his work; yet, now, when Hume is being well compensated for the disregard of earlier generations, we can see that he is no whit less significant than Locke for an understanding of the movement of British political thought and practice during the last two centuries.

Hume reiterates the pattern of Hobbes's arguments, but alters the emphasis, disposes of the mythical, mathematical hypotheses and, without seriously modifying the conclusions, presents us with a description of human nature in which the moral attributes are not solely the reflection of political rule and the political relationship itself is seen in terms of historical growth. It might be thought that with these differences, the resulting theory scarcely remains in the same tradition; yet Hume rests his whole political thought on an analysis of human psychology, as he sees it, on the natural and necessary pattern of human living; he sees man as a creature at once driven and frustrated by passions which demand satisfaction; he believes that, while nothing can alter man's nature, reason can modify the conditions within which life must be lived and that these deliberate changes are artificial, conventional and political. Clothed in the language of an eighteenth-century sceptic, the voice is still demonstrably that of Hobbes.

If we are now disinclined to take the concept of the state of nature very seriously, it is probably because Hume remarked that 'philosophers may, if they please, extend their reasoning to the suppos'd *state of nature*, provided they allow it to be a mere philosophical fiction, which never had and never cou'd have any reality'.[1] Hume himself disposes of the implicit threat of social disorder in a very few sentences. He hints at the solitary and forlorn condition which violence and licentiousness would engender. He attributes violence and injustice to unrestrained self-love; and he describes the desire to acquire the means to satisfy needs, the avidity for goods and possessions, as 'insatiable, perpetual, universal, and directly destructive of society'.[2] Man is bent on immediate satisfaction in the present. Usually, he fails to take a long and sensible view of his requirements; and this defect in his nature cannot be radically cured. Men must palliate what they cannot cure; and, as Hobbes had also suggested, it is the redirection of the anti-social passions by reason trained in experience which offers the only sane path out of the impasse: 'nature provides a remedy in the judgment and understanding, for what is irregular and incommodious in the affections'.[3]

But Hume did not agree with Hobbes that only the sanctions of politically administered force would maintain the moral bonds of society, that moral obligation arose only in an efficiently ruled society in which the law alone embodied right behaviour. A moral sense was one of man's natural characteristics, enabling him to express approval and disapproval of his own and other men's actions; but Hume did not attempt to argue that social obligations and the content of the law reflected the insights of morally rational individuals, as Locke had done. He maintained, indeed, the preference which Hobbes had shown for describing social and political institutions as artificial arrangements to enable naturally selfish men to pursue their own best long-term interests. In this sense, Hume makes the adjustment in Hobbes's theory which is required as soon as we transpose Hobbes's mathematical model into an historical setting and allow for the effects of tradition, the social pressure of one generation on the next and the mere momentum of precedent and habit in any established and continuing social pattern.

Hume emphasizes these historical aspects of a society by

---

[1] *A Treatise of Human Nature*, edited L. A. Selby-Bigge (Oxford, Clarendon Press, 1896), p. 493
[2] *Treatise*, p. 492
[3] *Treatise*, p. 489

appending a moral theory to Hobbes's factual account of the social effects of human individual psychology. But Hume himself believed that he was being strictly empirical. He argued that we find all men in practice making moral judgments which, for the most part, agree with one another over periods of time. He did not attribute this concurrence to an intuitive knowledge of eternal standards, still less to revelation, but to subjective reactions to, or feelings about, our own and other people's actions. Admittedly, approval was accompanied by a sense of pleasure and disapproval by displeasure; but Hume was no simple hedonist and did not hold that we necessarily approve what we ourselves find pleasing. 'Morality, therefore, is more properly felt than judg'd of; . . .'[1] In the pursuit of moral ends as of any others, it is the feelings which guide us; reason tells us only about the most suitable means. But the effect of these feelings operating in a society over a period of time is to produce standard moral reactions. By a process of sympathetic adjustment to the opinions of others and by the operation of the association of ideas, a kind of constant social pressure, as we should now call it, is always at work establishing habits and behaviour which are socially valuable. This tendency is supported and encouraged by the political institutions which are at once its reflection and sustenance; but it does not, as in Hobbes, depend wholly upon the law for its maintenance; for, as Hume tells us, duty and obligation are not dependent on public knowledge of the actions in question.

Compared with Hobbes, Hume saw men united by interests more positive than their fear of one another and more precise than the imperative need to live at peace. They enjoy 'a general sense of the common interest' which may be likened to the motive which induces two men to co-operate in rowing a boat. This working in concert is not, Hume insists, a kind of contract or promise, for promises, apart from social rules, are not natural moral phenomena but governed by necessity and interest. Hume thus disposes of the somewhat barren discussion of the possible origin of political society and concentrates on analysing its present constitution. But in deriving social and political institutions from convention, he makes them artificial, as Hobbes had done, restraints upon human passions, which would otherwise

[1] *Treatise*, p. 470

destroy society, but nevertheless the offspring of the passions they
are restraining.

Hume used the term 'laws of nature' in much the same sense
as Hobbes had done to mean those rules of social expediency
which men found necessary to follow in order not to suffer from
the vagaries of their own character. Three of them were fundamentally important: stability of possession of goods and property;
the peaceful transference of such property by consent; and the
guarantee that promises and contracts would be fulfilled. Long
experience of the working and beneficial effects of these rules
would naturally promote feelings of moral approval towards
their maintenance and of disapprobation of their disregard. Thus,
though both the law and education would constantly support the
organization of social co-operation in this way, most members of
society would themselves be actively co-operating in its maintenance, not compelled to do so by fear of the penalties of the law
and contrary to their individual preferences.

This argument enabled Hume to modify Hobbes's contention
that government depended ultimately on force. The force, on the
contrary, was in the hands of the governed, and the rulers must
rely rather on the support of public opinion. Social stability was,
then, a matter of habit and in time political authority came to be
accepted as normal. Obedience to an established political authority
was so familiar, Hume asserted, that usually no one enquired
about it. Both politically and economically, established arrangements were to be preferred to revolutionary innovations; and the
sanctity of both political and property relations depended upon
the social conventions in which they originated and the moral
approval which upheld them remaining undisturbed. We might
also say that in this Hume agreed with Montesquieu that government was a legislative masterpiece, whereby men unable to change
their character could nevertheless adapt themselves to it socially.
'Men are not able radically to cure, either in themselves or others,
that narrowness of soul which makes them prefer the present to
the remote. They cannot change their natures. All they can do is
to change their situation, and render the observance of justice the
immediate interest of some particular persons, and its violation
more remote.'[1]

[1] *Treatise*, p. 537

We may find here an interesting secular echo of Augustine's theory of the major social institutions: that the very passions which selfishly threatened society with dissolution provided in an ordered setting the remedy for their own anti-social tendencies. Hume also thought of property, particularly its stability and peaceful transference, as the resolution of the scarcity of natural resources coupled with the selfishness of individuals. Government, similarly, was a contrivance to represent the public interest of which everybody approved, but nobody felt it his personal duty to promote. But it was not only the strong sword of the civil ruler which maintained these institutions. The constant and repeated moral approval of the citizens from generation to generation reinforced civil authority and greatly diminished its Hobbesian intensity and its Augustinian ruthlessness. Furthermore, this social phenomenon could ultimately be designated natural, for the passions from which it derived its force and persistence were themselves natural. But the political relationship was in another sense no less rational. Reason, learning from experience in time, slowly moulded the framework of a stable society which was maintained in being by the steady concern of its members to support the common interest and approve all those means, summed up by Hume in the term utility, which conduced towards this desired end.

Hume preferred to analyse the continuing source of political authority to laying bare the assumptions on which political society might originally be presumed to have been set up. In treating this latter problem as a question of history and of historical accident rather than principle, Hume also applied a historical analysis to the former question. 'Time and custom give authority to all forms of government, and all successions of princes; and that power, which at first was founded only on injustice and violence, becomes in time legal and obligatory.'[1]

This important development of Hobbes's thesis, which without contesting the unquestionable sovereignty of the executive power posited far less than the absolute power which Hobbes had believed necessary, was further supported by the eloquent advocacy of Edmund Burke. A Whig adopted by the latter-day Tories, an Irishman incorporated by his English admirers, Burke

[1] *Treatise*, p. 566

was a politician whose strong prejudices and emotional, imaginative pen have not prevented his being enrolled in the company of eminent social thinkers. On nearly every count, Burke was as different from Hume and Hobbes as was possible for one who also believed that tranquillity and happiness were the ends of government. A man of principles but not of theories, as he constantly tells us, Burke was persuaded that 'government was a practical thing, made for the happiness of mankind, and not to furnish out a spectacle of uniformity, to gratify the schemes of visionary politicians'.[1] In another passage, at a later date, he speaks of government as 'a contrivance of human wisdom to provide for human wants'.[2] That is to say that Burke so far agrees with Hume and Hobbes as to see political authority operating through an institutional device for a pragmatic purpose. Similarly, it is an empirical test whereby such authority is to be justified. 'Obedience is what makes government, and not the names by which it is called.'[3] The importance of tradition and established practice, the part played by habitual subservience and the support of public opinion in rendering any particular governmental authority legitimate are all facets of Burke's political thought of which we find evidence scattered throughout his speeches and writings.

Theories of social order which both see the business of government as the prevention of disturbance and hold that the absence of dissension and violence is itself the guarantee of stable political authority are characteristically anti-revolutionary. But this conservative tendency entails the danger of supporting the establishment, regardless of its moral status and the demands of social justice. The problem of what price is worth paying for order and stability is a perennial political conundrum. Hobbes evaded this historical issue; Hume trusted in the good sense of an organized community having traditional, time-honoured values and Burke agreed in general with this view. But Burke was not unaware of the need for reform and change and of the injustices embedded in current practices. His tirades against the French revolutionaries

---

[1] *The Works of the Right Honourable Edmund Burke* (London 1826), vol. iii, p. 182. Letter to the Sheriffs of Bristol
[2] *Works*, vol. v, p. 122. *Reflections on the Revolution in France*
[3] *Works*, vol. iii, p. 60. Speech on Conciliation with the American Colonies

have sometimes led his admirers to forget his sympathetic understanding of the case for the American colonists and his denunciation of Warren Hastings. It is true that he thought the French
revolution a disaster, but he regretted the American revolution
as unnecessary. Reforms and even constitutional change, when
the circumstances warrant them, are among the measures likely
to preserve historical continuity and stable government. Politics
ought to be adjusted 'not to human reasonings, but to human
nature ; of which reason is but a part, and by no means the greatest
part'.[1] Burke, indeed, nowhere gives a formal account of what his
view of human nature is, but we can gather that he thought men
neither wholly corrupt nor altogether virtuous ; and he consistently recommends that the policy and behaviour both of
rulers and subjects must be wisely tempered according to circumstances. He displays something of Montesquieu's awareness
of the relevance of changing conditions to political decisions ; but he favours slow, unhurried and carefully considered
change.

These were the grounds for Burke's rejection of the contentions
of the revolutionaries in France. 'Time is required,' he writes in
the *Reflections*, 'to produce that union of minds which alone can
produce all the good we aim at. Our patience will achieve more
than our force.'[2] He supported, therefore, the 'old, cool-headed,
general law' and was against 'hot reformations'. This attitude,
however, must not be seen, whatever our own views of the need
for constitutional reform of the *ancien régime* in France, as insen-
sitivity to the central paradox of politics, the need to reconcile
restraint and liberty. Burke was arguing that it was idle to discuss
the relation of freedom to law as an abstract problem, without
'considering what are the laws and who are the makers'.[3] It was
his conviction that the leaders of the French National Assembly
lacked the ability to strike the proper balance which underpinned
his denunciation of French revolutionary politics. 'To make a
government requires no great prudence. Settle the seat of power ;
teach obedience : and the work is done. To give freedom is still
more easy. It is not necessary to guide ; it only requires to let go

---

[1] *Works*, vol. ii, p. 170. *Observations on the Present State of the Nation*
[2] *Works*, vol. v, p. 305
[3] *Works*, vol. iii, p. 84. **Letter to the Sheriffs of Bristol**

the rein. But to form a *free government*; that is, to temper together these opposite elements of liberty and restraint in one consistent work, requires much thought, deep reflection, a sagacious, powerful, and combining mind.'[1]

The conditions of what Burke would have described as a free society, by which he meant something closely approaching the England of his time, included, indeed, more than the stable government and the recognized system of established laws. The interrelationship of custom, language, political constitution and social habit together with the other social institutions which expressed the common purposes of the community, such as the class structure and the established church, came, for Burke, to possess an almost mystical unity. It was a stable social order for which he contended, persisting from one generation to the next and adjusting itself slowly and gently to what were at that date presumed to be only slowly changing conditions. This apotheosis of the nation-state and the naive assumption that it was a permanently valid political form had been building up from the European experience of the previous two centuries and was to play an increasingly influential part in the politics of the succeeding hundred and fifty years. The people of England well know, wrote Burke, 'that the idea of inheritance furnishes a sure principle of conservation and a sure principle of transmission; without at all excluding a principle of improvement. . . . Whatever advantages are obtained by a state proceeding on these maxims, are locked fast as in a sort of family settlement; grasped as in a kind of mortmain for ever.'[2]

It was this same spirit which characterized what is by now doubtless the most widely quoted passage from the *Reflections* in which Burke denied that the state, by which he usually meant not the government but the community, was nothing better than a trading agreement in 'pepper and coffee, calico or tobacco, or some other such low concern'. On the contrary: 'It is a partnership in all science; a partnership in all art; a partnership in every virtue and all perfection. As the ends of such a partnership cannot be obtained in many generations, it becomes a partnership not only between those who are living, but between those

---

[1] *Works*, vol. v, p. 434. *Reflections on the Revolution in France*
[2] *Works*, vol. v, p. 78. *Reflections on the Revolution in France*

who are living, those who are dead, and those who are to be born.'[1]

This theme of communal unity and continuity was developed more fully by continental thinkers than in the English utilitarian tradition in which Burke also shared. Indeed, it was Rousseau, whom Burke roundly denounced, who may be said to have provided the political theory of the modern nation-state. Burke had a fine disregard for the ravings of foreigners and his nationalism was perhaps in some respects ahead of his time. The main stream of British social thought continued for over half a century after the French revolution to be individualist and to see the structure and exercise of political authority in artificial terms. Moreover, this tradition was less free from continental influence than Burke cared to suppose. 'We are not the converts of Rousseau;' Burke declaimed; 'we are not the disciples of Voltaire; Helvetius has made no progress amongst us. Atheists are not our preachers; madmen are not our lawgivers.'[2] But these assertions were not altogether true. Helvetius had made some notable progress; and in the succeeding century his disciple Bentham was to be more influential, both in theory and practice, than Burke himself.

.   .   .   .   .

The extreme individualism of Hobbes's theory had been balanced by an extreme concentration of power at the centre. The modifications of this theory in the eighteenth century suggested that something at least of the political coherence of a society could be attributed either to its historical continuity and traditional institutions or to the moral interdependence of the citizens' interests, despite their assumed self-concern. In France, where these questions were constantly discussed by social reformers inclined to be covertly critical if not overtly antagonistic towards the established constitution, we find evidence of both the more important speculations which were to influence the theory and practice of later generations. The first laid emphasis on the natural concurrence of interest and purpose among the members of a community and tended to suggest that historical governments

---

[1] *Works*, vol. v, p. 184
[2] *Works*, vol. v, p. 166. *Reflections*

impeded the free agreement either of the wills or the social feelings of their subjects. This view received its classical exposition in the writings of Rousseau and was one of the influences which shaped the French revolution. We shall consider this theme in the last chapter. The second theory remained much closer to the trend we have considered in English thought and laid its emphasis on the cardinal role of the laws in promoting harmonious co-operation between citizens confronted by the contrary demands of satisfying their own impulses at each other's expense and of relying on communal support and co-operation in order to attain their private happiness satisfactorily.

Social interdependence is involved in both points of view, but it requires to be differently defined. Many of the French social thinkers saw the individual as dependent upon a greater whole of which he was in a sense a part. But his partnership was often thought of in the mechanistic terms fashionable at the time. For Helvetius, the laws were only the most significant of the external circumstances which moulded the lives of the citizens. This view was not incompatible with the belief held, for instance, by Holbach that society was a collection of reciprocally needy individuals. The concept of community included both these views current among the French reformers. It was a whole, but as often an artificial as a natural unity. Holbach, a German long domicled in France, belonged to the atheistic wing of the advanced critics of the regime. His *Système de la Nature* came out in 1770 and its social thought echoes that of Hobbes in several ways. Man is weak alone, but strong in society in which reciprocal support is possible. Organized society is thus seen as part of a necessary system of causes and effects, for man 'cannot all alone procure for himself everything necessary to his felicity'. This contention that man's very weakness demanded a social milieu, if he were to 'obtain real and true happiness', had already found a place in the great French *Encyclopaedia* in the article on 'Society', written by Diderot. All the reformers assumed that happiness was man's due. The paradox of the apparent conflict of individual and social claims was resolved succinctly by Holbach who wrote 'that it is man who is most necessary to the well-being of man'.

This thesis was a positive edition of Hobbes's theory; it was also in a restricted sense a moralization of it. Society became a repository for lasting moral values, only fitfully represented in the individual. Diderot's statement that 'the individual passes but the species has no end' carried with it a sense similar to Burke's famous declaration in his speech on the reform of representation that 'the species is wise, and when time is given to it, as a species, it almost always acts right'.[1] Diderot's article on 'Society' was significantly subsumed under the general heading of 'Morals'; and the close connection between moral and social theory was characteristic of the French reformers. Diderot's co-editor of the *Encyclopaedia*, the mathematician d'Alembert, expressed the general conviction when he wrote that morality 'is founded on a single but incontestable truth of fact, on the mutual need which men have for one another, and on the reciprocal duties which this need imposes upon them'. This was an apprehension of natural law in Hobbes's sense, not Locke's. It was empirically observed rather than intuitively grasped.

Men necessarily pursued their own happiness. The problem was to canalize this tendency along socially desirable paths by linking individual interest to the general advantage. It was essential, therefore, for moral valuation to go hand in hand with politics and legislation. In Helvetius's words, were this not to be the case, ethics was only 'a frivolous kind of knowledge'. He himself recommended that all laws should be framed according to a single, simple principle which he called public utility and defined as the utility 'of the greatest number of men subject to the same form of government'.[2] His argument was that individuals would always prefer self-interest to the common interest, unless a system of legal penalities and recompenses moved them to behave in a socially virtuous manner. The virtuous man, says Helvetius, is not the one who sacrifices his personal pleasure to the public interest, but whose passions conform so closely to that interest that he may be said to be virtuous by necessity.

Individuals were open to this kind of social influence because they responded to pain and pleasure with fear and desire. A man had no innate moral disposition, a view more akin to that of Hobbes than Hume, but was judged good or bad according to the

[1] *Works* (1826), vol. x, p. 97
[2] *De L'Esprit* (Paris 1758), p. 175. The book appeared anonymously with royal permission, doubtless because its author was a wealthy tax official.

quality and social effects of the passions which moved him. He had a power of response rather than of choice and his attainment of felicity or happiness depended on the outside causes necessarily affecting his will. In Helvetius, we can see how the system of self-interest, without being either divinely or naturally arranged to issue in social harmony, could nevertheless be assumed to support a scheme of society and government believed to promote general virtue and happiness.

Further support for the application of a single impartial principle to the framing of the laws came in the seventeen-sixties from an Italian social thinker, Beccaria. His short but widely influential essay on *Crimes and Punishments* was indebted to Helvetius and through Priestley in England helped to form Bentham's opinions as a young man. It is at the beginning of this essay that he defines public utility in memorable terms as the greatest happiness of the greatest number. Interested in the reform of the law, as was Bentham later, Beccaria suggested that the proportion to be established between punishments and crimes in a society ought to be worked out with 'geometrical precision'. His intention was to obtain the most efficacious and lasting results at the cost of the least cruel and painful effects. It was important also. he argued, that punishment should follow closely enough upon the crime to seem like the necessary effect of its commission.

Beccaria followed Helvetius in emphasizing the positive purpose of the laws in promoting socially desirable behaviour in addition to curtailing anti-social activities. Laws must not only themselves be rational, but must be seen to be so, and this freedom from arbitrary control would itself guide the citizens in the path of public utility.

Between them, Helvetius and Beccaria raised the principle of utility from an egoistic, neutral and amoral concept to the level of a political and legal criterion on which good hopes of future happiness and virtue might be built by social reformers. The most famous of their English adherents was Jeremy Bentham; in his hands these hopes began to be embodied in some of the reforms which eighteenth-century thinkers demanded.

Bentham tells us that he learned of the principle of the greatest happiness of the greatest number from reading Joseph Priestley's pamphlet, *An Essay on the First Principles of Government*, which came out in 1768. Priestley, famous as both a natural scientist and a unitarian divine, saw society and government as instruments in the hands of providence to lead men along a predestined path to perfection. The test of a good government was the extent to which it promoted 'the good and happiness of the members, that is the majority of the members of any state'.[1] The authority of the magistrates, for Priestley, was directly limited to their promotion of the public good.

It was by results in terms of happiness that Priestley wished to settle the vexed question of interference in the lives of citizens. Individuals retained their freedom only where it could be shown that the political authorities could not conduct the business better, that is more to the advantage of society as a whole. This incipient despotism is limited, as indeed it is in Hobbes, by Priestley's belief that in practice 'the greater part of human actions are of such a nature that more inconveniences would follow from their being fixed by laws, than from being left to every man's arbitrary will'.[2]

Despite this allowance for varying individual responses, the total system of experienced pains and pleasures was as determined within a necessary system of causes and effects as in Hobbes's description of human psychology. In Priestley's view, God was responsible for this system and had deliberately designed it. Only if men can be influenced in what he describes as a mechanical manner by hopes and fears can they attain a state of moral discipline, in which rewards and punishments are distributed according to the quality of characters and actions. Only thus can God secure his great object, the happiness of his intelligent offspring.

There is no very clear difference between this heavenly kind of utilitarianism, as this tradition of thought came later to be called, and its less fanciful secular counterpart. The origin of the system is, in any case, irrelevant to its political consequences.

The idea that man is a self-concerned creature, pursuing always his own interests, and that his public behaviour can be organized by a sovereign power sufficiently strong to prevent the clash of these individual interests or sufficiently wise to harmonize them

[1] *Essay*, p. 17
[2] *Essay*, p. 54

remains a recurrent theme in the thought of this school. In Hobbes the purpose of government is to prevent an inherently unstable situation deteriorating. But the concept of utility loses its neutral character the moment it is suggested that men are so clear-headed that they can successfully calculate their greatest advantage in any given situation and that their rulers are able, and indeed obliged, to order conditions so that this advantage is seen exclusively in virtuous, co-operative and socially useful actions. The geometrical precision for which Beccaria asked, the conviction that men could and did make such calculations, was the special contribution of Jeremy Bentham.

.   .   .   .   .

Bentham, like Beccaria, was primarily interested in reforming the law; and when the ideas of utility and of the principle of the greatest happiness of the greatest number became part of his social thought, he used them as weapons to effect the reforms which he wished to initiate. In this process they suffered some decline as possible moral principles. Utilitarianism was an influential creed in social affairs throughout the nineteenth century and still plays a part in our modern social service state; but as a moral philosophy it scarcely survived the confusion in which Bentham involved its leading ideas. As a political theorist, Bentham is inferior to Hobbes; as a moralist, he handles the concept of utility far less competently than Hume. Neither original nor outstanding, Bentham nevertheless served to canalize the hedonistic ideas of his French predecessors, which Burke was at such pains to discount, and to spread their influence widely through the succeeding century.

'The age we live in is a busy age; in which knowledge is rapidly advancing towards perfection.'[1] These opening words of the Preface to Bentham's criticism of the traditional natural law theory, as he found it expressed in the Introduction to Blackstone's *Commentaries on the Laws of England*, bespeak his confidence in the spread of rational enlightenment and in the prospects for reform. It was not difficult to criticize natural law in Blackstone's

[1] Bentham: *A Fragment on Government*, edited F. C. Montague (Oxford, Clarendon Press, 1891), p. 93. First published in 1776.

confused presentation of the theory. It is the grounds of Bentham's attack which are important. The law of nature, he argued, was only a cloak, 'nothing but a phrase' he calls it, to cover those rules of expediency whereby men in fact lived and according to which the laws ought to be judged. In another sense, Bentham accepted a law of nature, as Hobbes had done, for he believed that human nature was everywhere expressed in the same psychological constitution and that therefore a universal criterion might be applied to laws in different countries. Law ought everywhere to be to a great degree the same; for the rules of jurisprudence could be codified in a natural manner, in so far as they were made simple and obvious in terms of their felicific effects and could thus be easily understood by all men.

If the happiness of the agent were the end of all actions, as Bentham believed, then the tendency of the actions to achieve or frustrate this end could be rationally assessed and made plain equally to all men. Bentham uses the term utility to describe the felicific quality of an action and mischievousness, which has never achieved the same popularity, to designate its failure to bring happiness. 'With respect then to such actions in particular as are among the objects of the Law, to point out to a man the *utility* of them or the mischievousness, is the only way to make him see *clearly* that property of them which every man is in search of; the only way, in short, to give him *satisfaction*.'[1]

It would be true to say that the pursuit of happiness as the end of man and the promotion of the happiness of the people as the proper end of government were commonplaces of eighteenth-century speculation. Bentham's special contribution to hedonistic thought lay in his acceptance and propagation of the idea that the means to happiness, the felicific quality of actions, could be measured, calculated, compared, and easily demonstrated. The principle of utility would enable all debatable questions in the realm of jurisprudence to be settled on the basis of matter of fact. Bentham rather oddly calls this 'future fact—the probability of certain future contingencies'.[2] If the consequences of any law could be estimated in terms of expected pleasure and pain, no one need consult a lawyer to discover what such terms meant.

[1] *Fragment on Government*, pp. 118–19
[2] *Fragment on Government*, p. 226

Bentham demanded reasons for all actions ; his ethical theory, however confused, is always teleological. Like Hobbes, he saw men moved always by desires which required satisfaction. It was a view which necessarily rejected any theory of an intuitive moral sense or right reason, and any system of ends which apparently, like asceticism, denied the value of pleasure. It was characteristic of Bentham that he rejected revelation as a guide on the grounds that the moral principles revealed were too complicated when worked out in practice. The happiness for which men seek could, however, readily be obtained through their capacity to respond to social guidance, in which the law, administered indeed by wise rulers, could achieve for the people what they could not do for themselves.

If men are necessarily driven to act and forbear in a prescribed manner, the government through the medium of the law is able to aid or frustrate the aims of individuals, according as its political practice conforms or not with the simple rules of calculation implicit in the principle of utility. The law, operating a system of rewards and punishments, but primarily the latter, not only prevents each man's prosecution of happiness from interfering unduly with that of his neighbours, which was the office of Hobbes's sovereign power, but positively induces men to achieve a greater common fund of happiness than would be possible without such an institution.

It is important not to interpret Bentham's theory of law despotically. Not only, as in a Hobbesian state, are the citizens free where the law is silent, they are also free rationally in the sense of enjoying 'the right which a subject has of having the reasons publicly assigned and canvassed of every act of power which is exerted over him'.[1] It is the alleged ability of the government to provide these reasons and to act upon them, the competence of the subject to understand them and respond to their influence, which constitute Bentham's peculiar contribution to utilitarian politics.

Pleasures and pains were not only the final causes of all actions but, as instruments of the government, efficient causes also, means whereby the citizens could be influenced to behave in desirable ways. Bentham followed Helvetius in arguing that it was the business of the legislator to arrange artificially a harmony of

[1] *Fragment on Government*, p. 217

interests not provided in nature. In his *Principles of Morals and Legislation*, he describes pleasures and the avoidance of pains as both 'the *ends* which the legislator has in view' and 'the *instruments* he has to work with'.[1] He must, therefore, appreciate their value in both these senses, as ends and as means.

Bentham listed the conditions which determined in his view the relative value, or measurement, of pains and pleasures. Each unit is called a 'lot', but the concept is vague because the consequential effects of any action can only be surmised. The tests to be used were intensity, duration, certainty or uncertainty, propinquity or remoteness, and in the case of actions as distinct from states, the likelihood of their being followed by similar sensations. This was the process of estimation which should normally, though not always strictly, precede a moral judgment. Governments must further take into consideration the number of persons likely to be affected. It is scarcely credible to suppose that Bentham made such calculations himself, and yet his character lent itself to such an exercise more closely than that of most men. Yet, it was his contention that men not only pursued their own happiness but did so by a comparison of their experienced and expected pleasures and pains in this quasi-mathematical manner which supported his belief that the manipulation of the laws by the government was an essential and important factor in the achievement of happiness.

'The business of government is to promote the happiness of society, by punishing and rewarding.'[2] The social effect of a political act was to be estimated by a comparison of the sum totals of its good and bad consequences. They would be infinite, of course, so that only the resulting pains and pleasures, the material consequences, need concern the legislator. The subject, it was assumed, could make similar calculations. Bentham's discussion of the need to make the punishment proportionate to the crime is much longer and rather less clear than Beccaria's, but he reaches a similar conclusion. The expectation of pain from the punishment must be just greater than the pleasure of the

[1] *An Introduction to the Principles of Morals and Legislation*, edited W. Harrison (Oxford, Basil Blackwell, 1948), p. 151. First printed in 1780, it was not published until 1789.
[2] *Principles*, p. 189

intended crime and the proportions must be rationally obvious to the would-be offender. Furthermore, punishment, being itself painful, must be kept to a minimum consistent with its achieving its aim of the augmenting of general happiness. The question of rewarding the socially virtuous might develop, Bentham hoped, into a new branch of law, which he called remuneratory. It was little cultivated, as he remarked, and he did little to remedy this disregard.

Compared with Hobbes's sovereign, Bentham's legislator could count on a certain amount of socially advantageous behaviour in making his calculations. Men were largely self-regarding but sometimes benevolent. The legislator should direct his subjects' hopes and fears in the character of a tutor, bending their reactions in a morally desirable direction. Bentham emphasized the close unity between morals and politics favoured by his French predecessors and supported by Hume. It would, indeed, be difficult to deny on grounds of expediency alone that political government is a desirable means to commonly accepted social ends. When this agreement is raised to a moral level and the pursuit of happiness becomes, at any rate for the government, a political obligation, the facts remain the same but the interpretation is confused.

Bentham himself had no hesitation in defining ethics in general as 'the art of directing men's actions to the production of the greatest possible quantity of happiness, on the part of those whose interest is in view'.[1] For the individual, morality was the art of self-government. Political government and administration was this art practised on behalf of the happiness of other people. It is plainly open to argument, when we say that such a practice ought to be undertaken, whether the obligation is one of expediency or of moral value. Bentham's particular contribution to utilitarian politics consisted in his conviction that governments both could and should promote the happiness of their subjects and that this happiness was adequately defined in terms of pleasures in their sundry Benthamite characteristics. At bottom, Bentham, like Hobbes, relied on man's rational ability to profit from his knowledge of causal systems to effect his salvation in terms of this world's felicity.

[1] *Principles*, p. 411

The weakness in Bentham's political principles was a moral one. In so far as he was asserting the contention that governments were able to 'rear the fabric of felicity by the hands of reason and law', or even that no such fabric could be otherwise erected, the argument is little different from Hobbes's. In suggesting a convenient and simple principle according to which this task might be undertaken, Bentham had refined the political principle involved. But in holding that there was a moral obligation to govern in such an enlightened manner, Bentham assumed an unwarranted benevolence on the part of the rulers without accepting Hobbes's conclusion that in any case no price, except death, was too high to pay for orderly government.

It was no accident that the last phase of utilitarian thought was democratic, in the peculiarly English sense of advocating representative government. Abstracted from its unhistorical and non-institutional setting, Bentham's enlightened despotism was transmuted by his collaborator, James Mill, into a plea for the need of the governed at least to choose if not to control their rulers. In the hands of the latter's son, John Stuart Mill, the ends of political organization as well as the means to regulate it, though still nominally utilitarian,[1] were described in terms which could neither be subsumed under the single, simple head of utility, nor described as facets of an undifferentiated happiness, confined to the satisfactions of individual citizens alone, without regard to the needs of a developing, historical community.

Undoubtedly, the convulsion of the French revolution, the social changes which accompanied the prolonged wars and the repressive measures of British governments during the period after Waterloo all contrived to draw the attention of social reformers such as Bentham and the elder Mill to the pressing problem, masked by Bentham's moralizing, of how to prevent political power being used despotically. James Mill's *Essay on Government*, in which this issue is faced, was contributed as an article to the *Encyclopaedia Britannica* in 1820. His answer to the threat of a ruling class governing in its own interests in default of its political obligations was to enfranchise the citizens and to extend their political awareness by education.

[1] J. S. Mill wrote an essay *Utilitarianism* (1861) in defence of Bentham's views.

The government still filled its Hobbesian role of preventing its subjects from interfering with each other's pursuit of felicity, but the moral control was to be exercised in the last resort by the citizens. Only the greatest number knew what measures would achieve the greatest happiness.

Mill's more famous son carried the criticism of the received doctrine yet further when he questioned the competence even of a majority to refrain from the perils of despotism. For John Stuart Mill, the happiness of the individual was no longer easily calculated, no longer equivalent to that of any other individual, ought in certain circumstances to be sacrificed, and might not be guaranteed, as he tells us in his *Autobiography*, by the realization of the public good. The twin convictions that personal happiness was not achieved by aiming at it and that men were not to be recruited for the public service solely by an appeal to their self-interest transform Hobbesian individualism into a more complex and more subtle political doctrine. Furthermore, in Mill himself, representative as he was of mid-Victorian England, they are accompanied by an acute awareness of the special problems of the new industrial age and the immense social changes which were accompanying the growth of knowledge and power.

In his positive political views, J. S. Mill may be better seen as a representative of the school of thought which we shall consider in the next chapter under the theme of progress. But its origins go back over a century before Mill and its influence outlived him. Mill himself realized that he was breaking with the past. In his *Autobiography*, he tells us frankly : 'If I am asked what system of political philosophy I substituted for that which as a philosophy I had abandoned, I answer : No system, only a conviction that the true system was something much more complex and many-sided than I had previously had any idea of, and that its office was to supply, not a set of model institutions, but principles from which the institutions suitable to any given circumstances might be deduced.'[1]

---

[1] 5th edition (London 1875), p. 161

CHAPTER V

PROGRESS

IT IS only a single generation back since J. B. Bury described the doctrine of progress as 'the animating and controlling idea of western civilisation' and the earthly progress of humanity as 'the general test to which social aims and theories are submitted as a matter of course'. There was, he averred, and the date was 1920, a 'prevalent feeling that a social or political theory or programme is hardly tenable if it cannot claim that it harmonises with this controlling idea'.[1] In the middle of the twentieth century, we are already conscious of the marked loss of prestige suffered by this way of thinking in the face of contemporary catastrophe and a threatening future; and it is interesting to recall that it is hardly two centuries since this influential doctrine was little more than an aspiration, a minority reformist cult, supported principally in France. Voltaire expressed the point of view of progressive thinkers in a single sentence penned in 1764. 'The first places will one day be filled by philosophers; the reign of reason is being made ready.'[2]

There are senses in which the reign of reason might be taken to mean the fulfilment of the types of rational society described in the last two chapters, with the emphasis placed either on the defence of the rights of man against despotic governments or on the achievement of the greatest happiness of the greatest number by the rational reform of the legislative system. Devotees of the doctrine of progress have at different times included such aims among their objectives. But their claim to separate consideration rests upon the sponsoring of a variety of social thinking which, while it agreed that happiness described the ideal end of society, was generally less concerned with the fate of individuals than of groups or even of the race itself; and, while usually concerned with moral purposes, expected the knowledge of social values to

[1] J. B. Bury: *The Idea of Progress* (London 1920), Preface, pp. vii–viii
[2] From a letter to d'Alembert.

151

emerge gradually, but progressively, rather than to be intuited or revealed once and for all time.

This emphasis on the historical development and the methodical discovery of what came to be designated social laws justifies the use of the term progress to differentiate this pattern of social thought. It was a theory, however, in other respects no less concerned with felicity than Hobbes and as forward as Locke to demand that governments be responsive to moral rules. But its method was not an analytical interpretation of the structure of a permanently valid political relationship. It was rather an attempt, or a series of attempts, often beginning from assumptions which were indistinguishable from acts of faith, to decipher a meaningful pattern in recorded history which gave grounds for holding that future changes could be plotted with more or less accuracy and, of capital importance, that these developments would be increasingly beneficial to men or mankind. In these respects, we can see that this movement of thought was one more effort to find a secular alternative to Christian social theory in the post-mediaeval world. In practice, it was one of the most successful alternatives.

Compared with Burke's support of custom and established institutions, the progressive theorists emphasized that the generations, standing on the shoulders of their predecessors, followed each other cumulatively rather than repetitively. This belief had already been mentioned by the French reformist statesman, Turgot, in the middle of the eighteenth century, when he characterized the successive stages of man's ascent as religious, metaphysical and scientific, and was repeated by Comte in the early nineteenth century. This distinction is in terms of increasingly superior, because more accurate and valid, modes of knowledge.

At this stage, it would be too early to call this theory of social change evolutionary; but it was the intelligible development of human society through successive periods of history which these observers were seeking to describe. The doctrine of progress owes some of its inspiration to the Christian view of providential history and shares with revolutionary reformers, like Rousseau and Marx, their moral zeal to improve or supersede the political constitutions and practice of contemporary society. But its spirit was wholly secular and looked for perfection as an attribute of posterity; and the coming social revolution was not to be the creation of the rational will so much as the by-product of the enlightened intellect.

The idea that historical events could be interpreted to display a meaning and purpose other than mere successiveness was familiar to Europeans from their Christian heritage. Augustine had already provided what Voltaire called a philosophy of history. But in practice it had issued either in the more or less passive acceptance of the established order as divinely ordained and beyond criticism or, in protestant circles, in the belief that worldly success was one of the criteria of divine election. Both attitudes enabled some social groups to exploit or ignore the condition of others with a light conscience. Eighteenth-century historians, however, many of them busy reflecting on the tragic fate of the Roman empire, were inclined to moralize their historical studies, seeking in the past for lessons in social living which would enable them to improve the lot of their successors. Montesquieu, as we have seen, sought to delineate the permanent characteristics of healthy social adaptation. Voltaire himself depicted the panorama of events to underline the prevalence of human failure and misery and the need to build a rational society. But one of the first clearly progressive historical surveys we know was provided by the French reformer Turgot in 1750, when still a young man of twenty-five.

Turgot accepted from Voltaire that many errors had been made in the past, but he saw them as necessary factors in progressive improvement. Setbacks were part of a necessary rhythm of moral advance. To discover the general laws, the causal system according to which this advance was taking place was the purpose of the study of history. If there were general laws, they applied generally in the first instance; and both in Turgot and many later writers we find a tendency to prophesy the future of the human race and to consider the history of its generic character. This concept corresponded to the ideas of man and human nature which we find in the unhistorical writers, with the difference that the fortunes of the race are changing and improving. Correlative with this view was the dependence and, in some cases, the unimportance of the individual. It was mankind's lot on earth which interested the progressive thinkers and they substituted the achievements of posterity in this world for the traditional concern for the church triumphant in the next. Diderot dedicated the *Encyclopaedia* to posterity, which he described as 'THE BEING THAT DIES NOT AT ALL'.

Behind this new hope in the possibilities of understanding the developing pattern of human society lay the growing prestige of the natural sciences and the conviction that the methods of empirical observation which by the middle of the eighteenth century had already proved their worth would reveal similarly dependable truths when applied to society. Condorcet, perhaps the most famous of the French believers in progress, tells us how d'Alembert believed that man would come to 'see ethics and metaphysics born of his observations of himself; the science of governments, and that of laws, of his observations of society'.[1] These truths would be naturally, not divinely or only remotely divinely, revealed; and the information collected would be progressively beneficial. Meanwhile, as reform waited upon the spread of enlightenment, current abuses and imperfections in the political sphere must be attributed to ignorance.

This curious marriage of the Greek theory that society is natural with the Christian conviction that history is dramatic is itself an interesting historical occurrence. It presented immediately two grave difficulties, closely connected with the employment of the term natural. The first was its use to describe events as they were known or believed to have occurred, regardless of their conformity with or divergence from any universal standards, abstract principles or imagined, non-political social states. In this sense, as some perspicacious observers remarked, everything which in fact occurred was natural, whether customarily reckoned good or bad. Secondly, the overt modelling of the observation of social events on the methods pursued in the physical sciences encouraged historians and social thinkers to discover regularities and repetitions in social behaviour, but in fact gave no guarantee that such laws, if they were laws, were either beneficial to man or morally acceptable. These dilemmas were disguised to some extent in the eighteenth century, so long as nature was widely used as a synonym for God with the implied assumption that its laws were good. In the nineteenth century, the growth of the biological and

---

[1] From Condorcet's obituary eulogy of d'Alembert.

psychological sciences rendered this easy assumption seriously suspect.

The possibilities of investigating the natural causes of social change were noticed as early as the sixteenth century by Bodin, who remarked that of the three explanations of change, the natural did not have the disadvantage of the inscrutability of divine providence nor of the uncertainty of human decisions. Montesquieu, two centuries later, similarly rejected chance, or fortune, as the explanation of the developing pattern of events, though in common with other eighteenth-century observers he was at pains to correlate the moral and physical orders. This was the crux of the problem at that date. Reformers, particularly in France, were aware of the social imperfection of the time. They had outgrown the fashionable Leibnizian optimism of the first half of the century and replaced it by hope for amelioration in the future, relying upon their conviction that the natural order was regular and that society was part of it, so that with increasing knowledge would come closer harmony. But this latter expectation depended on the belief that the observed order was also good. This uneasy alliance was never very secure. Doubts were continually expressed, even by those who, like Diderot, most wished to believe in the future to be enjoyed by posterity. Those thinkers who, like Holbach, were dogmatic atheists, accepted that if nature were a system of necessary causes and effects, increasing knowledge would produce in practice an ever closer adaptation to necessity. This idea, that progress meant better adjustment to circumstances, was, however, not popular at the time. The most rigorous thinkers were the least influential. It was not until the following century that the disharmony between what happens and what ought to happen in the moral sense was openly accepted as a corollary of the scientific observation of social change.

In the process of reaching this conclusion, all the traditional explanations of the gulf between practice and ideal aim had been discarded. Greeks and modern natural lawyers had held that some or most men had sufficient rational insight into moral norms to provide a stable political framework for those of their fellows who lacked it. Christians, using the fecund concept of sin, could explain how men who knew what they ought to do failed in the performance and were properly punished. Hobbes and later utilitarian thinkers expected difficulty and disharmony anyway in the chance confrontation between man and his indifferent circumstances and argued that, because of this, deliberate arrangements must be made to minimize the risks. Having rejected these possible explanations, progressive thinkers had either to substitute a theory of adaptation to changing circumstances for the traditional normative theory of social ends or to hold, as an act of faith, that history itself revealed a moral progress in man's understanding of his social affairs and that its end was perfection. This perfection was sometimes guaranteed by God, sometimes by nature. It lay in the future and to work for posterity was the final cause of present effort, the justification for present suffering.

There were two possible interpretations of the need to adjust to circumstances. One, assuming the passivity of individuals, was to argue that, given an enlightened government, social conditions could be planned to promote the growth of a harmonious society in which justice, equality and honest behaviour flourished. This argument had much in common with the enlightened despotism of early utilitarian thinkers, but we hear much less about individual self-interest and the emphasis is placed on teaching citizens to develop their social interests, to give rein to the characteristic which the French thinkers called sociability. The second answer was to argue that the most important social freedom was freedom to profit from experience and that as many citizens as possible should be educated to do this. These two views were not exclusive of one another and in the nineteenth century in England we find in John Stuart Mill a classical example of their uneasy alliance.

The importance of education was emphasized by all the believers in progress: not a limited Platonic education aimed to develop specific social functions, but the general enlightening of the minds of the citizens so that all the sources of ignorance, and therefore social disharmony, might progressively diminish and disappear. Holbach argued it was better to educate citizens than to punish them. But he thought of education as a conditioning process: 'the art of making men contract early . . . the practices, opinions and ways of life adopted by the society in which they will live.'[1]

[1] *Système de la Nature* (London 1770), vol. i, p. 140

But because the educated citizens of the future would in turn help to build better societies, there was a sense in which the freedom to profit from experience took precedence even of the freedom to be happy. This latter condition was not forsaken as a proper social end, but was seen to be implicit in the former achievement.

'The science of government is perhaps only the science of education applied to the establishment of an entire society.'[1] Behind this and similar comments was the belief that the moral system was the same sort of causal whole as the physical and that the possibility of progress lay in using political means to inculcate moral virtue. By modelling social laws on natural laws, in the physical sense, control could be established over human vice and misery. This was the only means of promoting general and lasting happiness. To do this, men must learn to make civil society their sole allegiance, a divinity Diderot calls it, undistracted by other loyalties in this world or the next. Temporal salvation required time for its fulfilment ; ignorance was entrenched ; knowledge grew only slowly. Natural truth could be acquired only by observation, shared by many observers over generations ; and the corollary of this conviction was that the individual could never be freed from his impediments by his own efforts. He must depend, not, as the theologians had argued, on the grace of God mediated by the church or his own right reason, but on progressive awareness of nature's laws reflected through the institutions of civil society.

Although most of the French supporters of this point of view had died before the great revolution began, they were represented by one of the most distinguished minds, and by common consent one of the most virtuous characters, of the period in the person of Condorcet, at once a sponsor and a victim of revolutionary zeal. For Condorcet, the perfectibility of man was 'a general law of nature'.

.   .   .   .   .

The biographer and friend of Voltaire and Turgot, Condorcet represents for us better than any other single social thinker the common concerns of enlightened eighteenth-century thought,

[1] *Correspondence inédite de Grimm et de Diderot* (Paris 1829), p. 394

with its dominant belief in the alliance of progress and virtue with increasing knowledge of the constant laws of nature. This was the initial act of faith ; but it was supplemented by the quasi-empirical statement that evidence for social truths of this character was to be found in history. Finally, it was held that such truths were either indistinguishable from, founded upon, or at least analogous to the truths of mathematics or physics.

The conviction that there is a social wisdom which can be known, with the correlative idea that social disharmony or imperfection is the effect of ignorance, appears at first sight very like the Platonic analysis of the polis. But although the duty of the enlightened to rescue the ignorant has much in common with the moral status of the Platonic guardians, there are important differences between the two theories. The new task is less to rule and guide than to instruct and reform the unenlightened classes. The intrinsic clarity and simplicity of empirical social truths are such that all or most men could be expected in due course to grasp them. The citizens would, therefore, be able to take an increasing part in building the progressive society and, above all, in helping to modify or alter those established institutions no longer in harmony with the new and ever-changing social conditions. There was in this movement of thought a close reunion between politics and ethics, cemented and strengthened by the unifying method and achievement of natural science.

In the sketch for the history of progress which he never lived to write, and which he penned in hiding during the winter of 1793–94, Condorcet declared that a study of history provided 'the strongest motives for believing that nature has set no bounds to our hopes'.[1] Hope, not in the world to come, but in the indefinite amelioration of conditions in this world, was the hall-mark of progressive thought. It was no idle hope, for nature provided also its foundation. Teaching always the same lessons of virtue, justice and benevolence, nature required only to be freely and progressively consulted to induce in all men a profound knowledge of this moral constitution which must necessarily result in ever-increasing social harmony. The progress of the moral and political sciences was to be reckoned, indeed, in terms of the habitual

---

[1] *Esquisse d'un tableau historique des progrès de l'esprit humain,* edited O. H. Prior (Paris 1933), p. 217

virtue and ease of the practice of the good life which resulted from their teaching with reference to human feelings and behaviour. In these aspirations, Condorcet was supported by a belief that acquired characteristics, even those inculcated by education, were inheritable, a view which falsely over-simplified the perennial social problem of an inharmonious social and political environment.

Knowledge, and the conditions in which knowledge could be freely acquired and transmitted, was the prime factor in a progressive society; and the freedom to observe, think and learn one of the surest tests that a society was progressing. When Condorcet applied this test to the past, he saw evidence of this progressive law of advancing knowledge; and by analogy with the empirical sciences believed that he could rationally predict the future series of social events in conformity with this historical pattern. 'The sole basis for belief in the natural sciences, is this idea, that the general laws, known or unknown, which regulate the phenomena of the universe, are necessary and constant; and what reason is there that this principle should be less true for the development of man's intellectual and moral faculties, than for the other operations of nature?'[1] Condorcet did not think it necessary to answer this rhetorical question; yet it remains one of the most challenging questions in social theory.

In its moral and political sense, the idea of progress implied that each new era was not only more successful in its adjustment to and control of environment, but morally superior to earlier times. Condorcet, while accepting that in the past the lack of scientific knowledge and the means to spread its truths had hindered continuous progress, saw the next advance, in the current terminology of the eighteenth century, as the gradual supercession of arbitrary authority. In political terms, arbitrariness meant rule by men rather than by rational principles; and rational principles in the sense of the public recognition of discoverable social laws had long been resisted, he held, by those in power. Arbitrary government in the political realm corresponded to the idea of chance in the natural; but as chance occurrences were subject in time to rational explanation, being not accidental but due to what Condorcet called unknown causes, so could the vagaries of

[1] *Esquisse*, p. 203

irresponsible or self-interested ruling groups be brought within the limits of intelligible law.

This process inevitably took time. The ignorance and superstition of the past necessarily had evil consequences, notably the division of society into the possessors of special knowledge and the untutored subjects who could only believe what they were told. Condorcet tends to support the view that the superior classes, particularly the priests, deliberately exploited their advantages and deceived the people in order to dominate them. We find this view in early eighteenth-century communist theory and it has persisted to our own day. It will be considered more fully in the next chapter.

Even when the laws were not being used to exploit the citizens, they failed in their principal purpose, in Condorcet's view, of eradicating evil by concentrating on controlling its effects rather than on removing its cause. He notes that this is a general historical tendency and evident already among the Greeks. It is, indeed, a valid criticism both of Christian and utilitarian theory also ; for the view which Condorcet upheld is clearly opposed to all those who conclude that human wickedness, ignorance or self-interest can only be palliated, but never cured. This divergence of emphasis marks one of the key divisions of social theory in the modern world.

Condorcet stood with those who believed in remedies and is among the most eminent of those who thought that in time man could contrive his own emergence from the social and political imperfection of his traditional institutions.

His social ideal was epitomized in the concept of equality. It was a term not unlike freedom as used by Rousseau, implying a condition of independence from others which thereby facilitated co-operation with them. Too many people were still dependent in society, due in the first place to ignorance. All cliques of wise men were suspect to Condorcet ; and his distrust extended to lawyers and universities. Both justice and rights were vain ideals so long as 'inequality of the moral faculties prevents most people enjoying these rights to their full extent'. The remedy was to make an agreed, objective truth available to all men (and women he insisted) so that none should be dependent on another or his superiors but all freed through knowledge.

Condorcet's hopes were sustained by his belief in the application of mathematical techniques to the measurement and prediction of social phenomena : 'social mathematics' he called it. Thus laws could conform with reason as the result of being in conformity with a valid conclusion drawn from true propositions. That such a process was also morally good was accepted by Condorcet because he believed that all judgments of conduct were formed on estimates of probability; and probabilities were subject to statistical calculation. This process could be applied, he argued in a learned mathematical treatise, even to assessing the degree of justice in the decision of a legislature or similar body, in which the greater the majority in favour, the closer would the decision be to the moral truth. But this would occur only in an assembly of enlightened persons. Where the intelligence was low, it would be the probability of error which would increase with the size of the majority.

Education, then, was necessary to progress; but the instruction must be in terms of those known facts and statistical data of high probability in which consisted truth. There were to be no imposed or doctrinal moral and political views. The objective truths were to be made available to all, for only thus could inequality be removed and independence established. No longer a slave to political and priestly superiors, rational man would become his own master. But because all men would be conducting their moral lives according to observed natural laws, an unprecedented social harmony would ensue.

Meanwhile, several important political conclusions followed from Condorcet's analysis. A democratic constitution could not be operated by an unenlightened people. Secondly, it was the intelligence of a legislative assembly which was important rather than its form or procedure. Finally, the more enlightened the members, and therefore the greater the probability of their decisions being right, the better it would be for the less enlightened to submit.

The ideal of equality found no support among his progressive successors more fervent than that which Condorcet accorded it ; and in the inchoate writings of another intellectual French nobleman, Saint-Simon, it is rather the duties of enlightened leaders which we find emphasized. 'Remember,' he wrote in 1803, 'that, in the general interest, domination should be proportionate to enlightenment.'[1] Saint-Simon is in general agreement with his fellow-enthusiast in the principal assertions of enlightened progressive theory, as they came to be stated at the end of the eighteenth century. But he both developed and supplemented the theory of society built on these premises, as well as providing an important link with the somewhat different, but even more widely influential, doctrines of Marx.

For Saint-Simon it was primarily the *savants*, a group which included all who worked with their minds and notably the scientists, who stood for progress. The property-owners represented stability and the representation of equality belonged to the rest. These groups should be functionally interdependent and had, he argued, a single overriding common interest in the progress of the sciences on which their increasing welfare depended. Saint-Simon was impressed by the coming possibilities of the new industrialism, which was the fruit of the applied scientific theory of the previous century and a half; and he saw that any development of this potential source of wealth and plenty must depend on the economic and social organization of the new industrial bankers and business men in co-operation with the workers. Artists, scientists and industrial leaders had common interests with the mass of men, but were naturally called upon to guide and organize them, in their role of the new aristocracy of talent and knowledge.

It would be less than the truth to simplify this theory by calling it organic, but it plainly had themes in common with the Greek view of politics as the interdependence of specialized groups. More striking, however, were its divergences, for the common concerns and shared values of the citizens were not only to take precedence of the particular interests of the distinct classes, but through common education and ethical standards to provide what Saint-Simon calls 'the essential bonds in any political association'. Moreover, the society's principal purpose would be not so much its maintenance as its transformation through the ever-rising standard of material welfare of its poorest classes.

---

[1] *Henri Comte de Saint-Simon (1760–1825): Selected Writings*, edited F. M. H. Markham (Oxford, Basil Blackwell, 1952), p. 9. *Lettres d'un habitant de Genève*

Saint-Simon's insistence on welfare as the test of progress, and the work necessary to provide it as the first duty of the citizens, brings his thought very close to modern times. A further important insight into historical development, which prefigures Marx, was Saint-Simon's understanding of the relationship between social institutions and the purposes they were designed to serve and the persons who manned them. This relationship was not always one of harmony and equilibrium; and the functioning of institutions designed to express beliefs no longer widely held was, he thought, a serious impediment to progress. 'Any institution founded on a belief ought not to outlive this belief.'[1] This was a more subtle and truer analysis of the political situation at the time of the revolution than the straightforward rejection of arbitrary government common among earlier reformers.

The early nineteenth century called for institutions suited to the changing economic and scientific demands of a new era and consequently for new men to run them. Saint-Simon remarked that the traditional governing class of a military, landowning nobility was wedded not only to the *ancien régime* but to its theory, symbols and language. The foundation of their social and political knowledge was what he called conjecture; whereas now an age of positive knowledge was coming into being, a world of applied science and industrial techniques, in which he had the prescience to see the renaissance pattern of warring nation-states was out of date. Conjecture was transmuted into positive knowledge by the application of scientific method; and those who were able to do this should, therefore, enjoy the power and authority of the former governing groups who in this respect were mere collections of amateurs.

The required constitution must be discovered by reason based on experience. There would not need to be any argument about its form among those who accepted this method. As there was only one form of right reasoning, so could there be only one kind of good government. It might have local variations according to the needs of different peoples; but Saint-Simon would not accept Montesquieu's contention that its principle should vary with social conditions. The change in the principle of government was from the past; for progress demanded radical readjustment to

[1] *Selected Writings*, p. 30. *De la réorganization de la société européenne*

wholly new conditions. Saint-Simon himself sees the new principle as the supersession of the old concept of ruling by an idea which comes closer to organization in its business sense and reminds us a little of Engels's later phrase, the administration of things. Society would be concerned with productive work in order to raise standards and the government's first concern would be to facilitate this activity. 'Governments will no longer order men about; their function will be limited to ensuring that useful work will not be hindered.'[1]

In a sense, the directing authority in the community was to pass to the new élite of *savants*: 'The spiritual power in the hands of the scientists.' It was a return to some of the theocratic pretensions of the middle ages, a period whose presumed social and spiritual unity Saint-Simon much admired. But the ends pursued by these latter-day priests were firmly located in this world and included, as a primary objective, the eradication of poverty and the incorporation of the subject classes in what might not inaptly be called a welfare state. Temporal institutions were to become positive as against their negative character in traditional Christian theory of limiting the effects of sin. Thus could the formerly partial and incomplete organization of church and state be united in a common purpose in this world, standing together on the principle of treating all men as brothers and directing 'all institutions of whatever kind towards the improvement of the well-being of the poorest class'.[2]

Of the three catchwords of the French revolution, it is *fraternité* which Saint-Simon most obviously represents; and he presages the attitude and fervour of later socialist doctrine and the organization of welfare economics. Saint-Simon had no doubt that the new world was coming; but he believed it was better consciously to prepare to meet it and adjust to it than, as he puts it, 'to let ourselves be dragged there'. 'The Golden Age of the human race is not behind us but before us; it lies in the perfection of the social order. Our ancestors never saw it; our children will one day arrive there; it is for us to clear the way.'[3]

·   ·   ·   ·   ·

[1] *Selected Writings*, p. 71
[2] *Selected Writings*, p. 85. *Nouveau Christianisme*
[3] *Selected Writings*, p. 68. *De la réorganisation de la société européenne*

Of those who dedicated their lives to the missionary enterprise of clearing the way for the new social order, Auguste Comte, sometime Saint-Simon's secretary, was probably the most considerable and certainly the most voluminous. This 'morality-intoxicated man', as J. S. Mill called him, represented the high-water mark of French progressive thought, which had been flowing steadily since Turgot's critical essays in the seventeen-fifties. Comte built consciously on Saint-Simon's foundations, and indeed claimed many of the ideas they shared as originally his own. There is the reiteration of the contention that political authority should be vested in a new aristocracy of scientists and industrialists; and the repetition of the belief that the new social order was to be uniform, organized, and devoted to raising standards of material living. But Comte went further in his desire to bring all aspects of social life within the scrutiny of positive thought, and to reform all outdated institutions in accordance with its principles.

Comte published his six large volumes of the *Cours de philosophie positive* from 1830–42 and the four volumes of the *Système de politique positive* ten years later; but it is by no means easy to assess the significance of positivist thinking for political principles and practice. J. S. Mill began his study of Comte's ideas by remarking of the tenets of positivist philosophy that 'It is not very widely known what they represent, but it is understood that they represent something.'[1] The progress of a further century scarcely requires this comment to be modified. Certainly, they represented the rejection of what Saint-Simon had called conjecture in favour of the scientific study of all social phenomena. Certainly, too, Comte accepted that this study was made possible only because such phenomena or events could be described, he believed, in terms of invariable natural laws, as Turgot had said a hundred years before.

Turgot's triple division of progressive human knowledge was indeed one of Comte's starting points. But he went further. The designations theological, metaphysical and scientific, which, for Turgot, had characterized changing modes of knowledge or approaches to the truth, were used by Comte almost metaphorically. They described social relationships, class structure, the

[1] J. S. Mill: *Auguste Comte and Positivism* (London 1865), p. 1

institutions through which public affairs were prosecuted, economic organization, political principles and, even, religious beliefs. To employ a term of which Comte is credited with the authorship, they were used sociologically. Comte thus saw the theoretical assumptions of any given society intimately bound up with its whole social and political organization and way of life. But he maintained the progressive character of the changing pattern. If a positivist age required a positive religion, then this system of belief was superior to the earlier religious manifestation which we call theological. It was theological speculation which made certain religious practices primitive and properly superseded. A scientific age should have a scientific religion to match it and social institutions to express it.

The form of social and economic organization proper to an era of positive knowledge was industrial. Comte contrasted this with the military organization of less advanced communities in the past. This judgment was, in effect, historical and, fallaciously as it turned out, correlated militarist social order with an agricultural economy. But he would hardly have accepted the term order to describe a network of social relations which he sometimes called anarchy. The previous four centuries, the age of the nation-state, seemed to Comte given over to uncertain authority, instability and a chaos of competing opinions. It was a period of transition, a favourite phrase for all historians who become aware of the relative rate of change in certain periods of history.

Saint-Simon had also characterized successive historical periods as alternately organic, which is to say concentrated, stable, orthodox and homogeneous, and then by contrast critical, by which he meant diffuse, inconsistent, heterodox and heterogeneous. Both men shared something of the romantic revival of Gothic charm and, without our modern knowledge of mediaeval history, idealized the mediaeval church and empire by contrast with the intervening period. They both agreed that a new constructive, unitary and organized social order was in the throes of coming to birth. Sociology, the midwife of this new social order, represented an accumulation of scientific social knowledge about human relations and the working of institutions which would once again make possible, but on a higher plane, a coherent and progressive community.

The creators and sustainers of this new society were to be endowed with the combined power of spiritual and temporal authority, resting upon a body of unassailable, because wholly objective, social truth. Critics have not been slow to assail Comte for suggesting that such an authoritarian government could be compatible with the advance of scientific knowledge, on which its own authority would ultimately rest. But Comte's argument was scarcely an innovation. Indeed, it was implicit in what many of his predecessors among French social reformers had been saying for a century. Despotism which was enlightened had never been reckoned as tyranny proper. If the ruling group were benevolent, responsive to the demands of the prevailing conditions, and loyal to the truth, their authority, however unquestionable, was to be preferred to arbitrary decisions, however freely reached. Freedom of thought, belief, and spirit was no sure ground on which to build a stable society. For Comte, in Faguet's words, 'Freedom is the right not to accept the moral and social conditions in which we are placed; it is not a force capable of creating any moral or social condition whatsoever.'[1] It was neither the origin nor the form of political decision which concerned Comte, but the social truth enshrined in it. Persons or bodies likely to detract from the purity and objectivity of such decisions had no authority to make them. It was thus that Comte rejected the individualist arguments put forward by some radical thinkers. Nor would he accept Condorcet's plea for equality. Democratic popular sovereignty was no more than the theory of divine right mistakenly transposed from ruler to people, in which contention there was, historically at least, a grain of truth.

The significant social unit, for Comte, was not the individual but the group; for the primary affirmation of scientific sociology was the interdependence of all aspects of social life. He did not view this complex intercausal relationship with a bias in favour of any one particular group of social forces. We do not, for example, find him claiming the primacy for the predominating influence of economic causation. Comte remained in the eighteenth-century tradition by suggesting that progress depended in the first instance on the changing modes of advancing know-

[1] E. Faguet: *Politiques et moralistes du dix-neuvième siècle*, deuxième série (Paris 1898), p. 296

ledge; but these changes were themselves correlated with the progressive pattern of history. Comte allegedly found in this forward movement a guarantee that intellectual and material progress would promote each other, not that they would always be in step, but that they would ensure each other's steady advance.

It was in the field of moral and political agreement that Comte's proposals were most obviously authoritarian. The positivist ruling class, deriving its authority from its special knowledge of society, was to be empowered to impose a uniform pattern of ethical values on all the citizens. It was idle to discuss and debate true propositions which were scientifically demonstrable; and Comte consistently castigates divergence of private judgment as anarchical. He found a model for this enforced orthodoxy in the catholic doctrinal unity of mediaeval Christendom, whose form though hardly its content met with his enthusiastic approval. By contrast, the Reformation with its long train of sectarian divergence was the beginning of that period of transition and instability, which was, he believed, in his own lifetime, happily drawing to a close. The very progress of knowledge, however, precluded Comte from making use of any of the theological content of the last great period of doctrinal unity; and it was this impossibility which drove him, in his later writings, to undertake the bizarre construction of a new religion, supposedly founded on the positivist principles proper to the new age, suitable to serve the spiritual needs of a scientifically organized society.

In this development of his thought, as Mill critically remarked, Comte had ceased to apply the three stages of progress as modes of knowledge of an observed causal system, with no reference to its origin or purpose, in order to use the same analysis in the appraisal of moral values. This was to use the law of progress as the guarantee of its own validity. Many grounds had been suggested in the past for holding that social co-operation, an orderly institutional life, increasing welfare and political stability were worth-while ends to pursue. But the argument that a scientific, positive and objective knowledge of developing social processes disclosed these ends as the incontrovertibly true purpose of politics had no grounds apart from Comte's personal predilections.

The paradox at the heart of Comte's philosophy is not simplified by his extension of the realm of political thought from its traditional concern with problems of civil authority to include the whole field of social phenomena. In respect of the scope of the subject, this is to return to Greek usage and to say that all the affairs of the polis are the concern of the philosopher. But the moral assumptions of Greek political thinkers were in certain respects quite unlike those of Comte. For he was all along contending that what ought to happen could be discovered from the observation of successive events, as though there were a political and social reality comparable to the natural order. This reality, he thought, could be inspected, appraised and, finally, delineated in terms of an organized series of interacting laws, the full description of which would constitute social truth.

This contention, which will concern us again in another form in the next chapter, has provided our present century with one of its gravest political challenges. 'Infallibility,' wrote Sir James Stephen, 'if credible, supplies an unassailable ground for persecution.' But Comte's attempt to build a religion of humanity on positivist principles was supported by fewer marks of incontestable truth than the religion he was trying to displace. Moreover, his propaganda in its favour had all the intensity and pretensions of a missionary campaign and little of that appeal to demonstrable truth which has come to be associated with natural science.

Progress in this moral sense signifies something more than continuous and indefinite change and leads to the belief that society will sooner or later achieve a perfect equilibrium. Neither Christian nor utilitarian thought envisaged a closed society in this sense. But, as Mill, who was nevertheless himself influenced by reading Comte, mildly observed: 'It is one of M. Comte's mistakes that he never allows of open questions.'[1]

.   .   .   .   .

The question which should have been an open issue for progressive thinkers was whether they had any evidence that human society was developing historically for the better in compliance with a universal and necessary law of progress. Mill justly criticized this alleged law on the grounds that it might be true of a

[1] *Auguste Comte and Positivism*, pp. 15–16

particular series of observed events, but, if this were so, it would enjoy no more than the status of an empirical law. It was in this situation that the hypothesis of evolutionary development, having the more exalted provenance of a natural scientific law, became particularly valuable for supporters of progress. Evolution, however, was not in itself a more satisfactory basis for a progressive social theory. Equated generally with Darwinianism from its connection with its most famous expositor, evolutionary theory covers more than one interpretation of events in time. Moreover, it was not on Darwinian assumptions that its principal influence on social thought made itself felt.

The facets of evolutionary theory which were most revolutionary in the mid-Victorian age were the possibility that the traditional distinction between man and nature was not justified, that man derived from no special act of creation but was continuous with the rest of biological phenomena, and secondly that earlier eras of change and development stretched, perhaps endlessly, into the past and would similarly last on into the future. These shocks to established thought provoked much resistance and were only slowly absorbed into the general consciousness of the time.

Darwin provided in his theory of natural selection an intelligible and precise description of the principle according to which development took place. It was a neutral principle not framed in ethical terms and establishing no more than the character of the relationship between a species and its environment. 'The theory of evolution,' as T. H. Huxley was to say later, 'encourages no millennial anticipations.' For Darwin, the variations selected for survival were accidental and not the result of any conscious adaptation. But the climate of opinion was so altered by this new view of the biological universe that ideas such as the importance of the environment, the possibility of deliberately altering conditions, and the ever-changing and moving interrelations of man and the universe, though not wholly ignored in the past, came to the fore as factors of the first importance in the discussion of social problems and the character of political development.

The spread of this new attitude of mind was promoted in England from the eighteen-fifties to the eighteen-eighties largely by the constant and voluminous publications of Herbert Spencer. Spencer, understandably, is not often read to-day and it is true that he was frequently contradictory and inconclusive in his social thinking. Yet, he was a nineteenth-century phenomenon of some significance and the foremost English exponent of progressive thought of the Victorian era. But both his assumptions and conclusions were strikingly different from those of Comte, characteristics which must to some extent be attributed to the use Spencer made of evolutionary arguments.

He did not set out from Darwinian premises and published his *Social Statics* in 1851, while Darwin's *Origin of Species* did not come out until 1859. Evolution, for Spencer, was a law of development of the cosmic order and everything in it. He assumed that it consisted in a necessity, decreed by providence, whereby adaptation to conditions not only ensured survival but in the case of sentient beings a state of satisfaction which he calls happiness. Not to be adapted was evil; it was also self-destructive, so that evil necessarily and continuously diminished. Spencer, however, unlike earlier French thinkers who envisaged an inevitable progress towards a state of perfect equilibrium, did not pursue his analysis in terms of social groups but, like Hobbes, by seeing society as a conglomeration of individual units. Only if these individuals were free could they successfully exploit their conditions and adjust themselves satisfactorily. Unfortunately, the conditions included other persons like themselves. It was, therefore, self-evident that each man's freedom must not be permitted to infringe on the next man's, that we must 'apportion out the unavoidable restraint equally'. Thus Spencer deduces his law of equal freedom: 'that every man may claim the fullest liberty to exercise his faculties compatible with the possession of like liberty by every other man.'[1] But this otherwise Hobbesian picture is modified by the possibility of change. 'The social state is a necessity. The conditions of greatest happiness under that state are fixed. Our characters are the only things not fixed. They, then, must be moulded into fitness for the conditions. And all moral teaching and discipline must have for its object, to hasten this process.'[2]

[1] *Social Statics* (London 1851), p. 78
[2] *Social Statics*, p. 70

It is in the mode of the application of this discipline to developing human character that Spencer differs most obviously from earlier supporters of progress. Among the qualities making for the survival of a successful species might well be included, on the Darwinian hypothesis, its ability to organize and sustain a co-operative group life. The adaptation of the more ignorant members of the group might then depend on the foresight and control of those better fitted to understand the conditions. Such an argument could have harmonized with a Comtian view of progressive development. But at this point Spencer introduces a contrary theme for which there was little biological evidence and which in origin was part of the traditional distrust of central organization and an insistence on the sanctity of private rights against the state. The subjects of successful adjustment to conditions are always individuals and Spencer sees the political functions of the institutions of the group as increasingly frustrating. They tend rather to inhibit the requisite freedom of individuals to obey the evolutionary law of nature which compels them to adapt or perish.

The case for individual rights against the state had, as we have seen, a historical origin and serious moral arguments in its favour. It was particularly popular in nonconformist protestant circles as a weapon to diminish allegiance to Hooker's state-church. Spencer certainly took over these ideas with his inherited dissenter's background. The traditional rights, however, which Spencer lists in their familiar nomenclature : life, liberty, property, exchange, free speech, and what he calls the right to ignore the state, or secede from it, are now defended on the grounds of natural necessity, the cosmic law of adjustment to conditions as the first law of living. This is Locke's moral law defended with Hobbes's arguments in terms of an evolutionary process for whose character and validity we have nothing but Spencer's word. That such an ingrained and popular theory should apparently have the backing of the latest scientific knowledge doubtless accounted for Spencer's wide influence and popularity. With his demise there was nothing to hold its disparate premises together.

Spencer does not deny that the state, by which he nearly always means the government, once possessed a social use at a more primitive stage of development in the past. When Spencer is thinking primarily of society and less of its members, he uses the language of organic metaphor. As the organization of society progressively advances, the relationships best suited to survival at an earlier stage, of which Spencer like Comte instances a military hierarchy, must give place to a superior social structure, to wit industrialism. But this advance is assumed to be according to a principle of increasing individuation; and the government, which always figures in Spencer's thought as an oppressive agency, however necessary in existing social conditions, is an imperfection steadily to be diminished with progressively more perfect adaptation of individuals to their conditions. There is an odd parallel between the Marxian conviction, expressed by Engels, that the state is destined to wither away and enjoys only a limited, historical significance and Spencer's belief that the moral sense supporting each man's assertion of his freedom will eventually deter all coercion, even by a majority, and render government impossible. 'Progress towards a condition of social health—a condition, that is, in which the remedial measures of legislation will no longer be needed, is progress towards a condition in which those remedial measures will be cast aside, and the authority prescribing them disregarded.'[1]

In his later sociological writings, Spencer worked out the parallel between the social and the individual organism in very great detail. But his social organism was never complete; it required to be retranslated in terms of the interests of its members. In so far as a human social unit was organic, it was uniquely so: 'the welfare of the aggregate, considered apart from that of the units, is not an end to be sought. The society exists for the benefit of its members; not its members for the benefit of the society . . . the claims of the body politic are nothing in themselves, and become something only in so far as they embody the claims of its component individuals.'[2]

Spencer succeeded more than once in stating the central problem of politics, but apart from a simple optimistic faith that it would naturally and eventually cease to be significant, he never came to grips with the conflict presented by self-conscious and sometimes self-seeking individuals having to live together. Nor

[1] *Social Statics*, p. 215
[2] *The Principles of Sociology* (3rd edition, London 1893), vol. 1, pp. 449–50

did he present any convincing case for holding that evolutionary arguments could be advanced in favour of a theory of individual rights, whether moral or natural.

As an example of a less confused, but not dissimilar, application of evolutionary theory to social problems among progressive thinkers, we may instance T. H. Huxley. Huxley, accepting in general the Darwinian argument regarding the survival of the fittest in relation to natural conditions, was not tempted to ground extravagant hopes, as had Spencer and Condorcet before him, on the discredited theory of the inheritance of acquired characteristics. A Darwinian account of natural processes did not lead him, therefore, to support what he called 'the fanatical individualism of our times' or to approve of attempts to apply the analogy of cosmic nature to society. Modes of behaviour which might represent the successful self-assertion of the individual should, on the contrary, be constrained on behalf of the group; and Huxley correctly estimates, though not by name, Spencer's evolutionary theory, when he says that 'the duties of the individual to the state are forgotten and his tendencies to self assertion are dignified by the name of rights'.[1]

Huxley is nearer Hobbes in his acceptance of the disintegrating but natural selfishness of individuals, and he makes no attempt to moralize this situation, as had Spencer. It is the interest of the group from which arises the possibility of a social process in origin natural but in the event conflicting with the characteristics of natural selection. Nature supports those best adapted in any given situation. To alter the conditions is therefore no less important than adjusting those living in them; and it is the power of an organized group to do this which enables it to pursue a moral end, the survival of the best, instead of passively responding to the changes and chances of external stimuli. The conscious ethical mind which can substitute a self-restraining purpose in concert with other similar minds for the blind aggression of nature represents a new force in the cosmos. But this force had itself evolved. Huxley was an untiring expositor of the intimate relationship between man and other forms of life; and he saw 'no excuse for doubting that all are co-ordinated terms of Nature's great progression, from the formless to the formed—

[1] *Evolution and Ethics* (London 1893), p. 34

from the inorganic to the organic—from blind force to conscious intellect and will'.[1]

Huxley himself inverts the fashionable formulation of his problem. He is concerned not with the ethics of evolution but with the evolution of ethics and he sees 'no limit to the extent to which intelligence and will, guided by sound principles of investigation, and organized in common effort, may modify the conditions of existence, for a period longer than that now covered by history'. But to match this encouraging outlook 'Ethical nature may count upon having to reckon with a tenacious and powerful enemy as long as the world lasts.'[2] This identification of the sinful or natural self is substantially the same in Augustine, Hobbes and Huxley. The function of the political power is to control it, school it, and punish it when necessary in the interests of the maintenance of a common understanding with regard to the general interest. In its simplest form, this understanding, for Huxley, is that of the pack: that its members should not attack one another. Human society has made the great advance of agreeing to use the force of the whole body against individuals who violate this, possibly unexpressed, understanding in favour of those who observe it.

Plainly these views constitute a restatement of traditional theory; but in addition Huxley held that progress in the doctrine of evolution was competent to help us in the great work of helping one another. The possibility of doing so involved, self-evidently, the duty to prosecute this communal end. 'Finally, to my knowledge, nobody professes to doubt that, so far forth as we possess a power of bettering things, it is our paramount duty to use it and to train all our intellect and energy to this supreme service of our kind.'[3]

The most important contribution of evolutionary theory to the discussion of political and social problems was probably the renewed emphasis on the possibility of change and readjustment both in conditions and individuals and consequently in their relations and the outcome thereof. In a volume of essays of very

[1] *Man's Place in Nature and other Anthropological Essays* (London 1895), p. 151
[2] *Evolution and Ethics*, p. 36
[3] *Evolution and Ethics*, p. 31

great significance for twentieth-century social thought and political practice, Sidney Webb wrote: 'Owing mainly to the efforts of Comte, Darwin and Herbert Spencer, we can no longer think of the ideal society as an unchanging State. The social ideal from being static has become dynamic. The necessity of the constant growth and development of the social organism has become axiomatic. No philosopher now looks for anything but the gradual evolution of the new order from the old, without breach of continuity or abrupt change of the entire social tissue at any point during the process.'[1]

.   .   .   .   .

It is not, indeed, wholly true that evolutionary social thought has superseded more violent and revolutionary plans for social development. But this latter tradition derives from a distinct pattern of thinking which must be left to our final chapter. Meanwhile, it may be said that political thought in the democratic nation-states of the west, as they customarily think of themselves, has, with different emphases, conformed increasingly closely to Webb's estimate of modern trends.

Changes in practice have contributed as much as theoretical developments to this general substitution of what Webb calls a dynamic ideal for the older philosophies. But these practical changes are themselves the outcome of earlier advances in modes of thinking. If the economic revolutions of the last century and our own owe their inception to the application and effects of scientific thought, this phenomenon itself began to be apparent from the very outset of the modern era. The traditional social and economic pattern has had to be modified to meet a succession of new developments: increased economic productivity, a rapidly rising population, the extension of education to all citizens, and a revolution in transport and other means of communication. The opportunities for realigning the relations of social groups with one another and for redistributing a no longer static fund of wealth had reached the point where some at least of the dreams of the past might be transmuted into the experience of the future.

But, together with this modern vision of a malleable and

[1] *Fabian Essays in Socialism*, edited G. Bernard Shaw (London 1889), p. 31

developing social structure, we have inherited also from the nineteenth century a theoretical dilemma inseparable from a progressive doctrine of society. It may be stated briefly as the contrary convictions that progressive values are finally evident only in the lives of individual citizens and that at the same time they are to be created only by the citizens acting in concert as an organized social body. Two nineteenth-century British thinkers addressed themselves particularly to this problem: John Stuart Mill, whom we have already had occasion to mention, and the Oxford philosopher, T. H. Green. Mill was more impressed by the importance to the community of the moral development of individuals; Green placed his emphasis on the value to all the members of a state of their possession and exercise of the rights and duties of citizenship.

Mill thought historically, a debt which he owed and acknowledged to his acquaintance with the Saint-Simonian school of French thinkers. This fact alone marked him off from the abstract reasoning of earlier utilitarian thought. He saw himself living in an age of transition, as indeed it was pre-eminently, an age, as he says, 'of loud disputes but generally weak convictions', from which he looked forward to an era which should combine the best of each type of Saint-Simonian historical periods: critical and organic. From the first Mill expected 'unchecked liberty of thought, unbounded freedom of individual action in all modes not hurtful to others'; and from the second firm moral convictions, grounded in reason and unanimity of sentiment.[1] It was much to expect.

Mill's second and equally significant divergence from the utilitarian school in which he was trained was the result of his early discovery that 'Those only are happy . . . who have their minds fixed on some object other than their own happiness; on the happiness of others, on the improvement of mankind, even on some art or pursuit, followed not as a means, but as itself an ideal end.'[2] Self-concern was no longer to be only self-interest, but the first and necessary step in the improvement of others. The development of individual character for the sake of its social effects and because it was good in itself became Mill's substitute for Benthamite felicity. This was the chief ingredient, he tells us,

[1] *Autobiography* (5th edition, London 1875), p. 166
[2] *Autobiography*, p. 142

of individual and social progress and also one of the principal ingredients of happiness. This cult of the individual, 'the highest and most harmonious development of his powers to a complete and consistent whole', as Mill quotes from Wilhelm von Humboldt,[1] was the theme of Mill's famous essay *On Liberty*, published in 1859, which was prefaced by another citation from Humboldt in praise of 'the absolute and essential importance of human development in its richest diversity'.

These restatements by Mill amount to a sort of credal affirmation of a humanistic faith. There is nothing to show that they are necessarily true. But if there were difficulties and impediments, of which Mill himself was acutely conscious, the times were hopeful and many of the traditionally accepted evils of human living might be seen as no longer inevitable accompaniments of the human lot. Poverty, disease and ignorance could be conquered. No one can doubt, says Mill in his essay on *Utilitarianism*, 'that most of the great positive evils of the world are in themselves removable' and that 'All the grand sources, in short, of human suffering are in a great degree, many of them almost entirely, conquerable by human care and effort.'[2]

This immense possibility of radically altering the human environment, opened out by the advances in applied scientific knowledge, brought with it, however, a sharpening of the age-old political problem of the division of duties between the political authority and other centres of initiative, which in the circumstances of the nineteenth century was correlated with the distinction between the state and the individual. Mill valued spontaneity in the individual and the largest possible area of free decision in which to express himself. But he feared that decisions made centrally might diminish the use of all faculties except 'the apelike one of imitation'. The conflict which Mill's analysis brings to light is, in his own words, that 'The spirit of improvement is not always a spirit of liberty.' These attitudes were at one in being in opposition to the dead hand of custom and unthinking traditional behaviour, but Mill was not in favour of improvements forced on

[1] *On Liberty*, edited J. W. Gough (Oxford, Basil Blackwell, 1946), p. 50
[2] John Plamenatz: *The English Utilitarians* (Oxford, Basil Blackwell, 1949), p. 177. This essay prefaces a re-edition of the text of J. S. Mill's *Utilitarianism*.

an unwilling people; and although he believed that the despotism of custom was a hindrance, the despotism of a central authority, interfering at the wrong time and in the wrong way, was decidedly worse.

Mill's antipathy to political control was the obverse of his deep-set belief in diversity of character and the importance 'of giving full freedom to human nature to expand itself in innumerable and conflicting directions'.[1] More specifically, Mill lists three domains of free choice which he treats as sacrosanct: liberty of conscience, thought and feeling; liberty of framing the plan of our life to suit our own character; and liberty to unite for purposes not involving harm to others. 'Mankind are greater gainers by suffering each other to live as seems good to themselves, than by compelling each to live as seems good to the rest.'[2] Human nature, he says, is no machine, but like a tree, living and spreading and developing. But Mill buttresses his positive dogma with a rational philosophical scepticism. Individuals should be allowed to practise their opinions at their own cost because, in the last resort, no one else knows, for sure, any better. Every truth is no more than an imperfect assertion; and divergence in judgment, like its political counterpart an organized opposition, is a necessary corollary of advancing knowledge and developing standards of behaviour.

In fact, Mill supposed that diversity and argument would tend inevitably towards general harmony and a feeling of social unity; and he agreed with Comte that an ennobled sense of serving humanity could become an effective secular religion. At the same time he castigated Comte for his despotic control of the individual by social organs: 'a monumental warning to thinkers on society and politics, of what happens when once men lose sight in their speculations, of the value of Liberty and of Individuality.'[3]

But this eventual harmony was ideal and, meanwhile, Mill recognized that some duties fell to the central authority, far more indeed than would have been tolerated by Spencer. Mill's problem, then, was where to draw the line beyond which political control stifled the exquisite moral flower of self-development. The limit

---

[1] *Autobiography*, p. 253
[2] *On Liberty*, p. 11
[3] *Autobiography*, p. 213; and see also *On Liberty*, p. 12

required to be applied equally to encroachment by collective public opinion as by political despotism, but not so rigorously for actions as opinions. It is thought, above all, which must be free. It cannot be said that Mill deals at all satisfactorily with this very difficult issue. He makes a distinction between what chiefly interests the individual and what chiefly interests society, which is neither clear nor altogether intelligible. If society has jurisdiction, as he says, over conduct which prejudicially affects the interests of others, it is not easy to find cases where this would not be so in some sense either immediate or remote. Mill uses Locke's example and says that no person ought to be punished simply for being drunk, but if a soldier or a policeman be drunk on duty, then he is properly brought within the law. But it is not so easy to decide the limits of a citizen's duties to his neighbours, by distinguishing between official and unofficial occasions. Mill does not limit state interference along any of the traditional moral or religious lines, except for freedom of conscience. Positively he upholds the greatest possible degree of free decision; negatively, he holds that every conclusion is open to argument.

'The worth of a State, in the long run,' Mill writes at the conclusion of his essay *On Liberty*, 'is the worth of the individuals composing it'; and 'with small men no great thing can really be accomplished'.[1] These statements, valid and important as they are, nevertheless leave open for discussion the difficult question of how exactly the composition of the political body is to be envisaged. For upon the character of the composition of the state might well depend the quality of the men composing it.

In the thought of T. H. Green this question whether the political relationship is somehow adventitious or on the contrary central to the moral life of men comes to the fore. It is a question as old as political speculation; but, as we have seen, other issues of religious faith, administrative convenience, economic necessity or the claims of self-interest have repeatedly through the centuries thrust it aside. This is not to say that Green went the whole way with those German philosophers who saw moral fulfilment nowhere but in the political life of the state. His words are very close to those used by Mill. 'The life of the nation has no real existence except as the life of the individuals composing the

[1] *On Liberty*, p. 104

nation.' Progress, improvement and development have meaning only in relation to the worth of persons. But the spirit in which Green penned these phrases was different from Mill's. He saw the civic life of the community, the extent to which the citizens pursued purposes in common, as the prime component of their moral discipline, an aid rather than a threat to moral integrity and freedom.

Green spent his working life in the eighteen-sixties and seventies as an Oxford tutor and for a few years before his early death as Professor of Moral Philosophy in the university. His mind, as with many academic thinkers, was a meeting-place for diverse traditions. Something of his conviction that the life of citizenship was the path to virtue is of Greek origin, though he expressed it democratically; still more derives from that English Christianity which is still permeated with mediaeval thought and the Thomist contention that the temporal power should positively support the life of grace by arranging the conditions for its proper exercise. Surrounding and greater than the political system of legal rights and obligations lay a realm of moral values, not perhaps fully embodied, but like mediaeval natural law, mediating the divine will to the measure of human conditions. The outside world of public relations was no alien and hostile country for Green, but a means whereby God, working unseen, transformed men's capabilities into realities, through truth and love. Moreover, 'The progressive apprehension of the divine idea must ever be closely connected with the hope of its fuller manifestation, and to one who is full of sympathy with his fellow-men, the most welcome manifestation would be in the political life of mankind.'[1]

Aristotle's account of the life of virtuous citizenship was neither progressive nor democratic. The Christian pursuit of salvation, though progressive and egalitarian, customarily concentrated on a citizenship within the world but not of it. It is the fusion of these two traditions which marks out Green's thought as at once of special interest and also representative of the most persistent political theme in European history. Imperfection, for Green, was to be found in the failure of the human will to seek its own highest satisfaction in a perfect purpose presented to it by

---

[1] *Works of Thomas Hill Green*, edited R. L. Nettleship (London 1888), vol. iii, p. 17. *The Influence of Civilisation on Genius*

reason. There is a disunity between possibility and realization, not present in the divine life but to be observed in man whose 'will at best only *tends* to reconciliation with itself in the form which it takes as reason'.[1] This interpretation of human life as a process of perfecting the will has an Augustinian ring; but Green goes on to see the political life in this world partly in the Christian tradition as a remedy for imperfection, but partly in the classical tradition as a school of moral discipline. It is the institutions of civil life which enable the capacities of will and reason 'to be really exercised'. At the same time one of their principal exercises is to organize society in such a way that the obstructions which impede the moral life, arising from past ignorance and sin, shall be progressively removed.

It is in this context that Green faced the contemporary problem of how far political authority should intervene in controlling or modifying individual decisions; but it did not present itself to him as it had done to Mill, for all actions had moral relevance both to the agents and to the society in which they lived. 'All virtues are really social'; as he puts it, 'or, more properly the distinction between social and self-regarding virtues is a false one'.[2] Green's distinction is both more intelligible and more satisfactory than Mill's. Political control must be limited to that sphere in which alone it can operate effectively, the direction of external behaviour, the realm of acts as distinct from motives. It is not for the state itself to make those moral decisions which are properly the business of individuals. But where individuals fail to maintain the conditions necessary to the moral development of their neighbours, the political authority, acting for the common good, may enforce through the law the maintenance of all those legal rights which safeguard the lives and set free the virtuous energies of all the citizens. Beyond these legal rights lie moral rights, dependent for their embodiment on the perfected motives of individual wills; and these lie beyond public control. It is the conditions for their encouragement, the removal of the obstacles to their full realization, which concern the state.

Progress, for Green, was the moral advance wherein that which must now be legally enforced might come increasingly to

[1] *Lectures on the Principles of Political Obligation* (London 1931), p. 21
[2] *Political Obligation*, p. 244

be done willingly, in which the realm of morality gradually
diminished the sphere of law by transmuting enforced decisions
into free choices. What the law now guaranteed was that development should be in a morally desirable direction. The sinful or
irrational life, for Green, was somehow less than real. He was
imbued with the Greek teleological sense of a completed purpose
being the governing motive of every action. It was not the present
which was real and the future a hypothetical field of possibilities,
but the other way round. 'To anyone who understands a process
of development, the result being developed is the reality, and it is
in its ability to become this that the subject undergoing development has its true nature.'[1]

It was not, however, the state itself which was being developed.
Reality pertained to the moral life of its members who pursued
common purposes in and through political institutions. The
political body, as for Aristotle, was the necessary precondition
of the life and the good life of the citizens. Political power, says
Green, is derived from the development of institutions for the
regulation of a common life without which men would enjoy no
rights at all. But Green goes further in interpreting this doctrine
democratically. The citizens at one and the same time foster their
own moral growth and create the conditions for a similar exercise
for all their neighbours. There is an important difference between
what Green calls loyal subjects, such as might be found in Bodin's
state or even Locke's, and intelligent patriots, ready to take an
active interest in the service of the state. But this state is no Hegelian
absolute for Green; he thinks of its attracting devotion rather as
does a family. The man with a higher feeling of political duty must
take part in the work of the state. 'He must have a share, direct or
indirect, by himself acting as a member or by voting for the
members of supreme or provincial assemblies, in making and
maintaining the laws which he obeys.'[2]

It will be seen that Green does not think of the state as an
aggregation of individuals, still less as a system of government and
no more, but as an organized community, presupposing lesser
communal groups with their special relationships and specific
rights. Nor is there the same emphasis, as in Mill, on individual

---

[1] *Works*, vol. iii, pp. 224–25. Fragment of an address
[2] *Political Obligation*, p. 130

diversity for its own sake ; for Green's insistence on the importance
of free moral decisions assumed that these decisions would
converge on a common good and that this common good, in so
far as it had been attained, was embodied in the established order.
The law demanded respect and obedience as the approximate
expression of the divine purpose in much the same spirit for Green
as had been the case for Burke. This essentially moral relationship
was projected in political terms as a guarantee on the part of the
state of all those rights of persons and groups enshrined in the
law in return for the performance of social duties. Even punishment had as its object a purpose beyond the maintenance of rights,
for their restoration was required for the general well-being of the
individual, and such well-being, for Green, was essentially moral.

Moral well-being was summed up by Green in a single term :
freedom. He meant by this not exemption from control and the
ability to do as one likes, but an assertion of the self in accordance
with its true nature, freedom from sin in devotion to self-imposed
duties. 'It would seem indeed that there is a real community of
meaning between "freedom" as expressing the condition of a
citizen of a civilized state, and "freedom" as expressing the condition of a man who is inwardly "master of himself".'[1] Freedom was
thus both a social and a positive concept. The political life was
concerned properly with building the preconditions of the good
life for all men and in exercising the desired virtues in the process.
'When we speak of freedom as something to be so highly prized,
we mean a positive power or capacity of doing or enjoying something worth doing or enjoying, and that, too, something that we
do or enjoy in common with others. . . . When we measure the
progress of a society by its growth in freedom, we measure it by
the increasing development and exercise on the whole of those
powers of contributing to social good with which we believe the
members of the society to be endowed ; in short, by the greater
power on the part of the citizens as a body to make the most and
best of themselves.'[2]

---

[1] *Political Obligation*, p. 16
[2] *Works*, vol. iii, p. 371. Lecture on 'Liberal Legislation and Freedom of
Contract'

CHAPTER VI

FREEDOM

'IN PLACE of the old bourgeois society, with its classes and class antagonisms, we shall have an association, in which the free development of each is the condition for the free development of all.' These words from the *Manifesto of the Communist Party* may serve to remind us that the idea of progress in terms of freedom belongs equally to that tradition of thought which has come to rely for social development on revolution rather than evolution. In this context, freedom is a condition which, far from being guaranteed by existing social institutions, is thought to be impeded by them.

This concept of freedom as a release from the hindrances and imperfections of experienced living, for the enjoyment of a richer moral life, more just, less inequitable, more rational and enlightened than the political achievements of the past, is one aspect of a dream or ideal vision at least as old as Plato. There is a sense in which all political speculation has been concerned with improving social conditions physically and morally; with recommending that much or little or nothing could be done about them, or that it would be best to concentrate on learning how to live in a more abiding city. While the vision remained discarnate, it was an open question whether, historically, experience reflected the penalties of ignorance or the wages of sin, the laws of an indifferent cosmos or a stage in a developing process. Most human societies have changed so slowly as to seem like glaciers unmoving and immovable. Only comparatively recently have advancing knowledge of the natural order, increasing wealth and health, and the spread of literacy, perhaps the profoundest revolution of all, opened up such possibilities of reform that social thinkers could, to use Marx's terms, give up trying to interpret the world in order to concentrate on changing it.

This shift of emphasis may be remarked long before Marx gave it a revolutionary impetus and T. H. Green incorporated some of its more urbane implications in his arguments in favour of extended democratic citizenship. Among the earlier progressive thinkers, and particularly in Condorcet, we find the advance of natural knowledge being seen as freedom from servitude to ignorance, and increasing moral awareness implying a freedom from temptation which would make the virtuous life easy and natural. Both Condorcet and Saint-Simon had seen how the ignorance of previous eras had set hard in institutional forms which, whether in their procedure or in the officials who operated them, constituted a vested interest in conservative practice and developed a resistance to new, and presumably better, patterns of life. Earlier imperfections were preserved, whether from habit or, as some thought, as part of a deliberate plot, by the religious, legal and political systems surviving from the past.

Continental thought tended, on the whole, to be more revolutionary than in England, as indeed it still is. There is a notable division of conviction between those for whom the established order is the repository of the wisdom and practical experience of the past, not lightly to be criticized or altered, and those for whom it enshrines all the follies and wickedness of ignorant and perverse generations, whose handiwork should not be permitted to survive them.

For this latter group, the question was not in what way social and political institutions could best be developed and used in new settings, but by what forces they could be overthrown, superseded, and reorganized in keeping with the dynamic changes of a transformed social order. The least revolutionary suggestion was that increasing knowledge of the natural order and of man as an integral part of it would bring with it in the course of historical evolution a transformation of the social order and of the political institutions which belonged to the past. But there is the further suggestion that if social evils are the effect of conditions, fatally distorting the good life, and certain of these conditions are themselves the petrified effects of the sins and ignorance of the past, then it should be possible by an enlightened act of will to overthrow this regime and set free all those imprisoned under it.

Freedom in this sense was to be the moral fruition of a social and political revolution whereby, either inevitably or by taking thought, the members of existing historical societies would transform their institutions so that all traces of the imperfections which they could be held to embody would be purged away. Statements which enshrine this belief are, not surprisingly, often phrased as battle cries or passionate assertions of faith. 'L'homme est né libre, et partout il est dans les fers,' reads Rousseau's famous declaration; and he seems to have meant that whereas man was born, or destined, for freedom, we find him in practice always enchained. Rousseau does not pretend to explain why this has happened, although he makes one not very successful attempt to do so, but he is particularly concerned to ensure that if there must be chains they should be legitimate, that is that they should support the free life and not impede it. In an equally famous announcement, Marx and Engels cry: 'Let the ruling classes tremble at a Communist revolution. The proletarians have nothing to lose but their chains. They have a world to win. Working men of all countries, unite!' This echo of Rousseau's words a century later also represents a development of the theory, for Marx would have the chains removed as constituting an absolute impediment. If the last words of the *Manifesto* echo Rousseau a century back, its first words might have been written for our own day, a century ahead. 'A spectre is haunting Europe—the spectre of Communism.' Indeed it is because the doctrine of social and political freedom in its peculiar sense of release from the chains of ignorance, poverty, oppression, injustice and man's own evil will is so closely bound up with questions of present-day topical concern that it behoves us to examine its implications with special care.

The tradition is an old one. That a few people, the philosophers, could attain freedom in the sense of becoming their own lawgivers, was already hinted by Plato, but the theory had no wider implications for other citizens. In Christian social thought, the belief that political institutions were themselves the outcome of man's sinful aberration is insistently repeated, particularly with regard to property and government. But the condition of the new life of perfect freedom found in the service of God was submission to the thraldom of sin in this world in the hope of final redemption in the next. To transform these suggestions into a serious political theory with revolutionary implications, it was essential that it should be believed that the offer of freedom was open to all men not only in the heavenly kingdom or vicariously in this world in the church, but within the framework of their normal political relationship. This belief took the form that the normal framework could itself be transformed, not by the remote influence of philosophers, but by a revolutionary act of self-redemption on the part of the whole people or at least of that section of it not fatally involved in maintaining the existing, but doomed, political regime. In one sense, this suggestion was an alternative resolution of the mediaeval tension between the spiritual and temporal powers. Like Calvin's fusion of church and state in principle, the secular counterpart to this policy gave the spiritual power in fact to the secular authority and with it something of the despotic and absolute concentration of sovereignty which tends to result from any failure to keep a fair balance, whatever the disguise, between the two realms of human government.

Of the different post-mediaeval attempts to provide workable substitutes for the uneasy dyarchy of pope and emperor, the protagonists of secular freedom come nearest to choosing a simply heretical version of Christian belief in their repudiation of the crucially important doctrine of original sin. It is significant, though not widely enough known, for his writings were put on the index in 1775, that it is in the unpolished composition of a renegade catholic priest of the early eighteenth century that is to be found one of the clearest sources of later communist and Marxian theory. Jean Meslier, who never had the courage to confess his apostasy in his lifetime, came to the conclusion that his sacramental ministrations were vain. For it seemed to him that the first need of his parishioners, mostly the poor peasants in a French country district, was to be given real bread to eat. They could not live by grace alone. Upon this simple reversal of the mystery of transubstantiation, Meslier proceeded to construct a new heaven on earth in the course of which church and state were superseded and the whole galaxy of their administrators consigned to the gallows. Meslier's *Testament* is an extravaganza which was known only in a severely truncated form in the eighteenth century, from editions prepared by Voltaire and Holbach. But his comment on the story of the Garden of Eden is deeply significant. Could not God be satisfied, he asked, with all the evils, miseries and afflictions of this life, by way of vengeance for what Meslier called 'le prétendu crime d'avoir indiscrètement mangé quelque pomme ou quelque prune dans un jardin ?'[1]

This simplified, crude, but persuasive re-edition of the Genesis myth was later elaborated in what was perhaps Rousseau's most characteristic essay, the *Discourse on the Origin of Inequality*, a document of hardly less importance in modern political thought than the *Communist Manifesto* itself. In the course of his often intemperate denunciations, Meslier accused Christian society of sanctioning the maintenance not only of inequality, but of private property, tyrannical government, and a class of useless and idle men. He took no account of the traditional attitude of the church to these imperfections. He was convinced that they were due not to an ineradicable flaw in human character, but to a deliberate manipulation of social conditions. It was, in particular, economic conditions that were exploited by the lucky, clever or unscrupulous few to the detriment of the majority of their fellows, who thereby became enslaved. It was this unnatural division of society into the rich and the poor which necessarily provoked moral evils : pride and ambition and luxury on one side, hatred, envy and a desire for vengeance on the other. The situation was unnatural because Meslier saw his ideal society in the language, Christian in origin but contemporary in phrasing, of what God and nature must obviously have intended, but of which they had been baulked. But the frustration arose not from the evil will in all men but from the distorting effects of the deliberate wickedness of a particular class.

It followed that if this class and the institutions in church and state which it had fashioned to maintain its hegemony were finally disrupted and dismantled, the prime causes of poverty, oppression and inequality could be removed for ever; and the surviving majority secure in their goodness of heart need concern themselves only with avoiding a recrudescence of the social institutions and structure which had formerly enslaved them. Christians, said Meslier, had substituted an unreal communion of spiritual goods for the genuine communal sharing of material

[1] *Le Testament de Jean Meslier*, edited Rudolph Charles (Amsterdam 1864), vol. ii, p. 142. It is not known exactly when Meslier died; both 1729 and 1733 have been suggested. But it is reasonable to suppose the *Testament* was composed in the seventeen-twenties.

goods enjoined by nature. Once all men had sufficient for their needs, social evils would inevitably decline from lack of motives to commit them.

These sentiments were couched in the form of an appeal to revolution and Meslier correctly estimated the likely reaction of the governing powers when he took care to conceal his views until after his death. His diagnosis of the political relationship was simple. All public institutions were manned by Augustinian brigands, unmitigated in either church or state by any pretence of justice. For Meslier also, the innocence and natural peace of the heavenly garden had been destroyed by the devil, but he located his garden in the contemporary world and he identified those who came to be called in later communist theory the ruling classes as the devil.

In the belief that moral freedom consisted in a return, or among some thinkers an advance, to a condition of innocence and social harmony following a radical revolution in political relationships and institutions, we may detect two distinct themes. First there is the identification of the causes of disharmony and enslavement and recommendations for their removal or transcendence; secondly there are the arrangements to prevent any relapse, to preserve the new-won freedom in supposed perpetuity. This second contribution is a reiterated and important contention; for it is the belief that imperfection is somehow a mistake and could in different circumstances be avoided which sustains the enthusiasm necessary to overturn the established order before creating the new world. Less extravagant radical thinkers than Meslier laid particular stress during the eighteenth century on the importance of avoiding those conditions which might expose the sufferer to irresistible temptation, as one might recommend a man to beware of risking infection.

Another French reformer, the Abbé de Mably, cited with evident approval a classical story in which Agesilaus is made to say 'To be a good man without effort . . . I avoid exposing myself to temptation'.[1] It was this condition, in which the natural goodness of men should be submitted to no further disturbing tests, which lay beyond the revolution and which justified the ending of the property system and the full democratization or even

---

[1] *Œuvres* (Paris 1794–5), vol. ix, p. 35. *De la législation*

abolition of government. Morelly, a contemporary of Mably's, wrote in his *Code de la nature*, published in 1755, that '*where no property existed none of its pernicious consequences could occur*'.[1] Some of these prophetical writings were frankly utopian, envisaging an ideal society devoid of all governmental direction; but in others, and here Mably is an example, political authority was to become the prime means for ensuring the maintenance of a social life free from vice and the conditions which provoked it. Both views are to be found in the better-known expositors of secular redemption. The possibility of transforming government into something specifically non-political finds a place in some passages of Marxian literature; and the resolution of the moral disharmony in human society through the medium of a revolutionary recreation of political authority in which all should be sovereign and all at the same time subject was Rousseau's contribution to political speculation. If Rousseau was the major political prophet of the movement and doctrines which we are considering in this chapter, Marx and Engels may be said to be their economic interpreters. This distinction reflects once more the divergent emphasis between the measures necessary to prevent the repetition of social disorder and the root causes of its occurrence. Rousseau, however, tells us very little about how the new order is to be planned or administered, except in his constitutional sketches for Poland and Corsica which were *ad hoc* compositions rather than general treatises. In our own century, however, the principal architect of one of the great social revolutions which have been modelled on this tradition of thought has left us his views on the achievement and preservation of freedom. From Lenin we may learn something of the role of a new ruling class purged of all taint of desire to oppress and opportunity to exploit.

Mr. Weldon has suggested in a recent essay that this use of the term free, to mean a condition which can be forced upon those who do not or will not enjoy it, is odd, paradoxical, confusing and dangerous.[2] He may well be correct in this estimate. But, perhaps regrettably, it is a usage which is also persuasive, influential, revolutionary and even intelligible. To call it also heretical, which is well-merited, is to do no more than underline the very important

[1] Op. cit., p. 30
[2] T. D. Weldon: *The Vocabulary of Politics* (Penguin 1953), p. 74

difference between this mode of thinking about society and politics and the Augustinian original from which it has derived its more meaningful assertions.

．　　．　　．　　．　　．

It was a citizen of Calvin's Geneva, significantly enough, who provided the blue-print for a new church-state, in which spiritual and political authority met together in a single sovereignty, in which every member participated and to which all were to be rigorously subject. This vision, for it was not a description of any existing society, has provoked more discussion and argument and had profounder and more far-reaching effects than any other politicial treatise in European letters. Yet, it cannot even now be said, almost two centuries after the publication of Rousseau's *Social Contract*, that there is precise agreement as to what Rousseau meant by the terms he used or how his proposals should be interpreted or understood. It follows that any brief account of his thought must be lamentably partial and imperfect and can do little more than hint at the subtlety, complexity and profundity of the issues which he raised and sought to resolve.

Attention is often withdrawn from the importance of what Rousseau was trying to say by the very evident, or some might say, morbid, fascination of his character. More than for other social thinkers, Rousseau's life is closely linked with his thought, for he came to reflect upon politics accidentally almost, in the course of resolving the moral enigma of his own personality. The effect of this interest was that the self is his most frequent analogy for the discussion of society; and his recommendations for recreating a city in which the good life can be assured are phrased according to the same principles that he would recommend for the recovery of a balanced and morally harmonious person, with the proviso that, finally, the achievement of the latter depended on membership of the former.

The second distortion which is to be met in studies of Rousseau arises from the very difficulty of understanding what he meant by holding that a political group could be possessed of a general will and that the precondition of a harmonious society was that this will should exercise the sovereign authority. Does such a will exist, and, if so, how can it be known, what is its object, how can it be reconciled with divergent minorities, and is it always to be identified with the majority? These questions are weighty and interesting and deserve to be considered. But their discussion too often diminishes concentration on Rousseau's own principal concern and interest which was the characterization of the moral condition which he calls freedom, the analysis of the causes of its loss and the description of the conditions within which it might be regained. The operation of the general will plays an important role among the measures suggested for creating a free society, but it is not the only factor involved and it is almost unintelligible except in the wider context of Rousseau's search for freedom.

Other French-speaking social reformers in the eighteenth century were also in search of freedom, by which they meant usually the end of arbitrary government and the substitution of a rational regime in which the laws would accord with empirically ascertained social trends, naturally tending towards harmony once political interference had been checked. The rational individuals who made up such a society would similarly be naturally in accord and co-operative, by reason of that benevolent sociability, as Diderot called it, which was only awaiting free play for its enlightened influence. Rousseau, when he first came to Paris in the seventeen-forties, was attracted to this viewpoint as he was to Diderot; but he lived to repudiate them both. In his rejection of the principles of the enlightenment, Rousseau stands almost alone in the eighteenth century and he began a movement of reaction from French individualist rationalism which has not yet expended itself.

Society as he experienced it could not, Rousseau thought, be improved and perfected by altering the pattern of government and trusting to harmonious rational co-operation. On the contrary, it required to be radically transformed; and as there seemed very little hope of this reorganization being undertaken, Rousseau's first reaction was to recommend escape and a withdrawal to a primitive existence with a minimum of social contacts. This rejection of contemporary theories may be seen as partly the distaste of a man of strong feelings for the dry, rational self-interest of the encyclopaedists, partly the provincial's spurning of Paris, mostly perhaps the uprooted neurotic's longing for the perfect peace which is not of this world. At all events, Rousseau set out alone, or virtually alone, to frame a new social theory in which freedom should mean the harmony of a self whose will, reason and emotions all co-operated in balanced perfection, and who was able to live happily in company with others, for together they mirrored in their common concerns the same harmonious self-control.

In his first well-known published work, the *Discourse on the Moral Effects of the Arts and Sciences*, which came out in 1751, Rousseau was aware that he would not readily be forgiven for adopting a position which he describes as 'setting myself up against all that is nowadays most admired'. This rhetorical denunciation of the alleged advantages of intellectual progress suggested that the great advance in civilization so vaunted by contemporary thinkers was better understood as a failure. In Rousseau's view, the original and native goodness of man was sacrificed in this process and he found no place in the conditions of the time for the carefree, happy and unfrustrated life of his dreams, the life which, he argued, all men ought to be enjoying. Already, we find a special insistence on the characteristic of social independence as a mark of the free and natural life, on not being in a position where a man's decisions were directly or indirectly dependent on someone else.

Having stated and underlined the contrast between the enslaved life of civilized society and the free life of nature, Rousseau in a second Discourse set out to trace the origin of inequality, the condition of subservience and dependence which distorted and frustrated the lives of the great majority of men in historical societies. He pursues this investigation by using the metaphor of a state of nature much as Hobbes and Locke had done. Like Hobbes's state of nature, the condition is an abstraction from the normal political setting, but like Locke's it is designed to illustrate the abiding moral characteristics of human character. Unlike Hobbes, Rousseau does not suggest by implication that the conditions he is describing are impossible; and unlike Locke, he does not use the language of contract to support a system of individual rights which take precedence of political relationships. Indeed for Rousseau the anarchy of Hobbes's natural man from which he is rescued by a sovereign government corresponds to the historical societies in which he lived. But there is a vital difference in Rousseau's method of escape. He never recommends that the sovereignty be vested in the executive power, but that it should be jealously retained by the whole people.

At the outset, Rousseau is not suggesting a political answer to his question, but trying to describe the character of the free man and, though not very convincingly, the factors which have robbed him of his natural independence. Here again, there is a close resemblance, psychologically, between Rousseau's vision of freedom and Hobbes's description of felicity. For both, the most significant characteristic of human beings is their pursuit of purposes in the satisfaction of desire. To be in a position to do this successfully and continuously is, for Hobbes, the condition of felicity. The morality of the purpose is not an issue for the individual, except legally in subjection to political authority. But, for Rousseau, the morality of the purpose is all important. A man is free when he makes a good choice, makes it for himself and controls the means to fulfil it. For both of them, power, the control of circumstances, is paramount; but in Hobbes the analysis of power is factual, in Rousseau it is also moral. He who makes an evil choice is as much enslaved as one whose good intentions are thwarted by lack of means to fulfil them. 'All wickedness comes from weakness.'

Rousseau's plea for a return to nature has consistently been misinterpreted by some of his critics ever since it was first denounced by Voltaire. It is a philosophical plea for the reinstatement of moral control in the self and society rather than an appeal for an impossible return to historical conditions, which may never, as Rousseau himself says, have in fact existed. In the unreformed society in which Rousseau was compelled to live, a withdrawal to the simple life of the countryside, an avoidance of the false, seductive, artificial manners of metropolitan life was doubtless the best course for a wise man. But Rousseau's final message is not one of escape; withdraw only if there is no chance of reform; but reform, he saw, must be undertaken by all together if each was to remain as free as he would have been, ideally or naturally, in conditions in which a proper balance could be maintained between desire and achievement.

Rousseau here agrees with Aristotle. There are two ways in which a lack of balance can be set right, by increasing the means of satisfaction or by reducing or altering the pressure or character of the desires. This suggestion was not open to Hobbes for whom all desires, naturally, had equal weight and could therefore be limited and controlled only by an external power, itself the source of moral distinctions and rules. For Rousseau, this moral distinction could be made, and in theory was always being made, by individuals, whose conscience, reason or good will would always make right choices unless prevented by circumstances from doing so. This good will was never, in Rousseau's view, permanently distorted or rendered inoperative. At worst it was eclipsed, frustrated and impeded by conditions. Wrong choices were concomitant with unfavourable situations in which needs outran strength; they were not constitutive defects of the naturally good individuals who found themselves thus misplaced. There was, indeed, a kind of fall, though not in accordance with orthodox doctrine, in Rousseau's Garden of Eden. Man had been led astray from his primitive innocence. But, unlike God in the Genesis story, Rousseau was prepared to accept the excuses proffered by Adam and Eve. The good life was not possible with women and serpents in the garden; and in making this excuse for himself, Rousseau accepted it for all men.

We may say that Rousseau's psychological view of human nature differs from that of Hobbes in two vital respects. Man's will is both free and good, which leads him to try to create conditions in which he can live in a morally satisfactory way; and secondly, a man has a fellow-feeling for his neighbours, what Rousseau calls *pitié*, which helps him to pursue purposes in common with them whenever circumstances allow. In historical societies these faculties are eclipsed and distorted; and, thus, in his picture of the natural life, Rousseau is not painting an isolated individual abstracted from a political setting, but man imaginatively rescued from a fallen world, man without sin, without disharmony and division in his own person, no longer subject to inequality and social dependence.

Man is born innocent, but not perfect; and it is in his capacity for self-improvement that Rousseau detects the possible source of all human miseries. To seek change is to risk deterioration. For change might involve wants in excess of those immediately satisfied by nature; and improvements mortgaged the present in return for uncertain future satisfactions. Man remained good and free through ignorance of vice, calmness of passion, absence of temptation. The natural man possesses nothing and is beholden to no one.

This free, natural man became fatally involved in a distorting social relationship at the point at which someone 'having enclosed a piece of ground, bethought himself of saying "This is mine", and found people simple enough to believe him'.[1] This first intrusion of the idea of property is identified by Rousseau as the beginnings of civil society. But although he agrees with other early communist thinkers in seeing an uncontrolled property system as one of the causes of inequality and moral slavery, he does not simply suppose, as they did, that to abolish all holding of property where men are living in social contact would be to eradicate the main source of evil. The property relationship represents a wider kind of disharmony, in that it weights personal preferences in favour of a narrow self-interest, exclusive of other people, which Rousseau calls *amour-propre*, and diminishes that desire to make the best of oneself in the service of one's neighbours, to use Green's words, which Rousseau calls *amour-de-soi*. This distinction is very important, for Rousseau never simply blames circumstances for bad social impulses. There is nothing contradictory in his later acceptance of a property system under the law, when any misuse of its privileges by individuals could be controlled by the political authority, which is to say the general will. Indeed, no one could properly be said to own anything except as part of a recognized social order.

Men might be naturally good, but nevertheless they were liable to be perverted. In its broadest definition, the good will became perverted whenever it succumbed to the temptation to allow the means at its disposal to dictate the ends being pursued. But, specifically, Rousseau detected in the self a division of interests which corresponded to the higher and lower nature of

[1] *The Social Contract and Discourses*, edited G. D. H. Cole (Everyman), p. 192. *Discourse on Inequality*

classical psychology. We can understand the concept of the general will in its political setting only if we first see that its character and intentions are identical with the good will in the individual and that this good will, though sometimes disregarded in favour of a particular selfish will, motivated by *amour-propre*, not only characterizes the natural state of innocence and freedom, but remains a permanent, underlying human disposition at all times. The will can only become general in the body politic, if it is first general in the individual, by which Rousseau meant that all men must be supposed to have a common moral interest distinct from their personal concerns, which can be pursued freely only when they are rescued from dependence on conditions. Rousseau did not in practice think the first primitive conditions could be restored, except for isolated and exceptionally strong-minded persons. His so-called return to nature is really an advance, a redemptive transformation of a fallen world by means of joint action, possible only because the good will, eclipsed but unspoilt, was available in everybody to undertake the task.

Man had lost his innocence, but he could attain morality, the deliberate recreation of the free life, not in another world but in this, not in a separate spiritual society but in a single undifferentiated community with all his fellows, and not in subjection to any authority whatsoever except his own free good will. Morals and politics are never separate subjects for Rousseau, just as he does not seriously recognize a distinction between church and state, or the sort of distinction between individual and society about which his fashionable contemporaries were wont to argue. The unity of both the theory and the structure of Rousseau's reformed state is formally almost identical with that of Hobbes. But the sovereign authority is within and not external, moral not pragmatic; it enables the society to live, not just to function: *vivre* not *agir*. As he writes in *Emile*: 'Society must be studied in men, and men in society: those who would like to treat politics and ethics separately will never understand anything about either of them.'

Rousseau recognized the chains; he was concerned in his *Social Contract*, which would be better called by its sub-title *Principles of Political Right*, with reorganizing their disposition and control, so that political society became a means to live the free moral life for all its members, and not the cause of its frustration. Chains imposed by alien despots in a divided society necessarily enslaved; chains self-imposed by common decision might have all the advantages of the shared rope for a party of mountaineers. On what terms, Rousseau was asking, should men submit to obeying the laws; and he answered this question as others had done by saying that it depended who made them. But in his attempt to describe how in his view the laws should be made, Rousseau set forth a revolutionary democratic creed which has left no state of the modern world unaffected and has radically altered the structure of many of them. Hitherto, it had been argued that laws should be obeyed if they were seen to be just, or if they were issued by a power with recognized divinely sanctioned authority, or if they did not overstep certain defined areas of ecclesiastical or individual concern, the realm of rights. Hobbes, admittedly, had suggested that even when the law-making authority held its position by force, in some sense all the subjects were authorizing this rule. But it was a negative concept; for the Hobbesian sovereign rescued his subjects from chaos, but made no attempt to lead them forward to freedom. Any positive pursuit of felicity fell to them as individuals.

Rousseau, on the contrary, argued that all the members of a political body should equally share in common responsibility for making the law, for they had a common interest in living together, a common positive interest which was not only to escape from the slavery of historical conditions, but to ensure the future pursuit of the good life. Their positive interest was freedom. Rousseau begins the *Social Contract* by telling us that his enquiry will consider men as they are and laws as they might be, and he concludes that laws of a morally satisfactory kind are the primary means of transforming men from what they are into what they, also, might be.

It was a platitude that a human society represented a system of division of labour such that each member was richer for his neighbour's efforts. The excess wealth produced by the co-operation of all left each in an infinitely better position than he could have reached alone. Similarly, Rousseau saw the moral co-operation of the state as the way to restore the disturbed balance in the individual whose good will had become submerged by frustrating and inimical conditions. Thus the law in a reformed state, the new wholly democratic city of Rousseau's dreams, would act redemptively, guiding and preserving all the citizens so that they acted only from socially harmonious motives.

Rousseau was quite clear that this desirable result could be attained only in one way, by making the sovereign authority in the state the general will. Only if the laws expressed the aims of the good will, and aims which were common to all the members of the society, were those who obeyed them exercising their freedom and limited only by their own decisions. It was possible for him to argue in this way theoretically because of his belief that natural goodness was never forfeited but only lost to sight. Rousseau allows that conflicts will still occur between the general and particular wills of citizens, but in this case the general will, enshrined in the law, will have the last word. The erring citizen, 'forced to be free', is governed only by his own good will writ large, made to do morally what he ought to do, but for which he lacks either the physical or moral strength or full understanding. There is no conflict here between state and individual, only a moral conflict between communal ends in which all share and individual ends of the selfish, anti-social sort, better in any case abandoned.

There are many difficulties in this conception, mostly arising from its being an ideal pattern of a reformed society and not in all its details able to be reproduced experimentally. Rousseau himself explains that he does not mean the final authority to be a mere consensus of opinions, the will of all, for this might be erroneous or even evil. Nor does it follow that the majority is always right. The will for Rousseau was, when directed to a good general end, a rational will; but it might be less than rational in practice either by reason of ignorance or sin. In civil society, the law would control the deviations of the sinful, but it was a problem primarily of education to correct the ignorant. Education, for Rousseau, represented the negative path of redemption, the training in avoidance of wrong choices and selfish temptation, as it was also seen by Mably and which both of them had learned from Plato. This possibility of initial lack of accord between will and reason is always taken seriously by Rousseau; and he even suggests that at the outset a reformed society might need a Platonic philosopher-

king, whom he calls a legislator, to guide the new city in the way
it should go. For the time being this leader might represent the
general will; for whatever else Rousseau means by this term, he
always suggests that there is a right answer somewhere, even if
only one man knows it. His decisions, embodying the common
good, ought to be imposed on the same principle that the sober
man of a party has a duty to rescue his drunken comrades
from burning themselves in carefree ignorance of their true
interests.

Rousseau never satisfactorily answers the question where we
are to be sure of finding the general will, but he asserts intelligibly
that there must be a common interest in a political group; and
even if the only common aim of the general will in all men is to
declare and maintain themselves free, this might conceivably be
realized if Rousseau is correct in holding that the good will in
man is never finally defaced. But he does explain very clearly
where the general will is not to be found, although it often mas-
querades in this quarter improperly. It is not to be found in the
executive government.

The idea that the executive government should properly be
subordinate is the one aspect of Rousseau's theory which has
exercised almost independent influence since his day, by reason
of its being able to be detached from the rest of his theory of the
state. No modern government, however authoritarian in practice,
can afford not to pretend that its authority is delegated to it,
even by a prearranged ninety-nine per cent. vote in its favour.
But in fact Rousseau's argument is an integral part of his general
theory. Sovereignty residing in the general will is embodied in the
legislature, which ideally should be a direct democracy of the
whole people. But by definition the laws must apply equally to
all the citizens, so that all particular administration falls to a
smaller body of executive officials, to whom authority is delegated
but never transferred. The government in this executive sense is
the principal means whereby the citizens as sovereign apply their
common decisions to themselves as subjects. It must, according to
Rousseau's idea of freedom, remain strictly subordinate, always
a means, never distorting the end by substituting its own will or
decision for the general will whence its authority derives.

Rousseau recognized that in practice governments are prone

8

to usurp the role of sovereign authority. They develop, he remarked, a general will of their own. But in relation to the state, this remains a particular will and ought not to be permitted any of the freedom inalienably attached to the sovereign people. The tyranny of governments was the political hub of Rousseau's moral reflections. His answer is to redefine, in a way never now likely to be forgotten, the concept of citizenship. A citizen is properly neither a ruler nor a subject, neither above the law nor merely subservient to it, but both at once. While obeying a government in particulars, he is its sovereign lord by participation in the general will. While subject to the law, he also creates it. As in the self, so in society, obedience becomes reconciled with freedom, at once its precondition and its expression.

'We always will our own good, but we do not always see what that is. The people is never corrupted, but often deceived.'[1] Men may fail to achieve their moral or physical well-being, either from being misled, or while they are children, or because they live in a corrupt society. But by joining with their neighbours in an act of common self-redemption, they can acquire again the strength and conditions to be free. This seemed possible for Rousseau because he believed not only in the freedom of the human will, but also in its abiding natural goodness, indestructible, pure and unchanged, however defiled by wrong choices, corrupted by society, paralysed by weakness or constricted by ignorance. All these defects could be remedied by man himself, if only he would boldly advance, in agreement with his fellows, to establish conventionally a political order in which they might be communally insured against the temptation of their own *amour-propre*.

This redemptive transformation, which has never taken place, but the vision of which has moved every generation since Rousseau's day to attempt to incorporate its message, is described in *The Social Contract* in the following words : 'This passage from the state of nature to the civil state produces a very remarkable change in man, by substituting justice for instinct in his conduct, and giving his actions the morality they formerly lacked. It is only when the voice of duty replaces physical impulse and right supplants appetite that man, who up till then had considered only

[1] *Social Contract*, II, iii

himself, finds that he is forced to act on different principles, and to consult his reason before listening to his inclinations.'[1]

.   .   .   .   .

Rousseau's arguments for constructing a society in which there shall be complete scope for the citizen genuinely to make his own laws, not in the sense of doing what he likes, but in the sense of willing or learning to will the morally good ends he holds in common with all other citizens, have influenced all modern states affected by the French revolution. But the great revolution was not the progenitor of the new society Rousseau had described; and, indeed, he hardly believed it was possible except in a small city-state territory; moreover he was convinced that however else the general will was to be expressed, it never lends itself to representation. An extension of the franchise has, however, in western states particularly, been one of the principal means whereby democratic citizenship has been encouraged. But the attempt to follow out Rousseau's theoretical interest in freedom and its realization was prosecuted more vigorously by German thinkers. Two German professors, Kant and Hegel in succession, bear witness to Rousseau's influence, though Hegel, not altogether fairly, criticized Rousseau's doctrine of freedom as inadequate, and on similar grounds also criticized Kant's political views.

The spread of Rousseau's views to the very different political setting of eighteenth- and early nineteenth-century Germany explains to some extent the different emphasis which we find in the German writings. Both Kant and Hegel reject the validity of Rousseau's exaltation of innocent, uncivilized nature as a moral model. Hegel thinks the spiritual is submerged in simple nature and Kant that all man's higher capacities would slumber eternally if he were not disturbed from this state. They look rather to the perfection of rational institutions, to the freedom which lies in a moral society which, in Kant's view, has much to achieve beyond the present level of cultivation and civilization. We find, too, a more traditional concern with the need for strong and decisive rule. Kant, at least, is more insistent than Rousseau on the contrariness of man and his need of a master, as he puts it, 'to

[1] *Social Contract*, I, viii

break his self-will and compel him to obey a Will that is universally valid, and in relation to which everyone may be free'.[1]

Rousseau's criticism of contemporary political institutions had been concentrated on the highly organized and developed nation-state, as represented by France, which lacked what he called patriotism and was characterized above all by a strong central government. The Germany of the time was in rather the opposite condition, its constitution still largely feudal and mediaeval in form, with no adequate central authority, but a lively sense of cultural unity. When German thinkers read Rousseau, they applied his ideas to the resolution of a very different problem, to the sort of political difficulties which had faced western Europe in the sixteenth century and been considered, for instance, by Bodin.

Kant, who was a contemporary of Rousseau, acknowledged his debt to him in framing his moral philosophy and, in principle, at any rate, expressed an almost identical point of view in putting forward the fundamental conditions of the institution of the state. It should be founded, he said, on three rational principles: the liberty of every member of society as a man; the equality of every member as a subject; and the self-dependency of every member as a citizen.[2] These were not laws to be enacted by the state but the principles which should inform it. They are the political expression of Kant's moral maxims: that every man should have respect paid to his personality and be treated as an end, never as a means; that the will should make decisions according to a universal principle which could equally apply to all other men; and that the universal maxims reached in this way should constitute a body of general legislation. The free will was thus characterized by autonomy and universality. All were to be equal under the law as subjects and though not all might precisely enact the law, it must proceed from a public will, which alone, says Kant, can do no wrong to anyone. This is the same principle as Rousseau's even if does not issue in practice in a demand for direct democracy. The legislator, says Kant, should enact such laws as might have arisen from the will of a whole people; and

---

[1] *Kant's Principles of Politics*, edited and translated W. Hastie (Edinburgh 1891), p. 14. *The Natural Principle of Political Order*
[2] See *Principles of Politics*, p. 35. *Principles of Political Right*

the subject shall regard the law as if he had consented to it of his own will.

Kant is thus making a plea for a common good as the ground and end of the state, which he denies to be happiness, for this is the private concern of separate individuals to pursue as they think fit. But they must do so within a legal constitution guaranteeing liberty to each through the laws applicable to all. The maintenance of this constitution is the first duty of the state and constitutes the common end of the citizens. Only such a rational end would exclude all individual conflict; and when Kant calls the state a moral person, he means the same as Rousseau when he calls it a 'moi commun'.

It was one of Hegel's less obscure purposes to improve upon this doctrine shared by Rousseau and Kant. He argued that its basis was the capricious will of the individual, not an absolute and rational will consonant with the true spirit. Kant's theory of right thus achieved no more than a limitation of each man's freedom so that it harmonized with that of others according to a universal law. This was a negative idea of rationality, external and formal, but not inherent. In short, Hegel found it philosophically inadequate. But it is to be doubted if he had fully grasped the significance of Rousseau's contentions. Nevertheless, he set about the task once more of asking how man could be free in the conditions of an organized society. How could the state rationally guarantee the objective expression of that capacity for subjective freedom which pre-eminently distinguished man as a spiritual being?

It is idle to pretend that Hegel is not a very difficult thinker to understand or interpret. J. S. Mill tells us he 'found by actual experience of Hegel that conversancy with him tends to deprave one's intellect'.[1] In our own day, Mr. Weldon has accused Hegel of systematic confusion, irretrievable muddles, and the use of a 'cumbersome and high-sounding terminology which has a mystifying effect'.[2] It is easy to feel antipathetic to Hegel, but difficult to ignore him. Few important philosophers lend themselves less easily to citation; no great work on politics is so unsuitable for summary exposition as Hegel's *Philosophie des Rechts.*

[1] *The Letters of John Stuart Mill,* edited H. S. R. Elliot (London 1910), vol. ii, p. 93. Letter to Alexander Bain of 4th November 1867
[2] *The Vocabulary of Politics,* p. 107

We must, therefore, limit our consideration here to one or two of
Hegel's more important arguments and in particular his attempt
to show the necessity of the state to the life of freedom.

Hegel's interest in political questions, as was true also of Plato,
St. Augustine and St. Thomas, was subordinate to a religious or
metaphysical interpretation of the universal order. He differed
from them in that the revelation of the divine purpose and the
precise character of its operation in history seems very largely to
have been private to himself, though it had some affinity with
earlier German philosophic thought, notably with that of Leibniz.
Thus reason was the essential character of what Hegel called the
world-spirit or the absolute, very much in the Greek sense of an
idea or form, the universal character of which may be recognized
in its material manifestations. But he also saw the rational spirit
developing through time to ever greater perfection in terms of
self-consciousness and the free co-operation of self-conscious
individuals in this divine process, as they became aware of its
reality and direction. Hegel thus opposed knowledge of this
divine, spiritual, rational development, which alone is real, to the
disordered, fragmentary empirical knowledge of events in time.
This experienced life of succession, accident and personal wishes
was therefore unreal on Hegel's definition and, he was inclined to
argue, also unimportant. Only the rational was real; and the
individual partook of this reality as he came to understand it and
participate consciously in the divine purpose.

This participation, whether willed by the individual or imposed
on him by those who knew its necessity more clearly, was freedom;
and freedom, Hegel assures us, is one of the principal rational
purposes of the absolute. We are all like children, creatures of
momentary caprice, prime promulgators of disorder, as has been
said of the devil, because we do not grasp the principles and
purposes which govern behaviour in the adult world of the gods.
But Hegel is not dismayed by human imperfection, firstly because
he divined that the principle of this development was what he
called dialectical, by which he seems to have meant that there must
be opposition and discord as a prelude to moral advance, on the
doubtful analogy of the advantages of argument and contradiction to the elucidation of truth; and secondly because whatever
situation is reached in fact at any point in history is the best

attainable, not in the sense that whatever is, is right, but that whatever has developed could not have developed otherwise. Philosophical insight leads us to see, says Hegel, that the real world is as it ought to be, that the universal divine reason is capable of realizing itself in time so that it may be said that the carrying out of the divine plan is the pattern of history. But in this contention, Hegel has predicated reality not of the rational interpretation or understanding of events, but of the events themselves. It is a confusion which constantly distorts all his arguments.

It was in this metaphysical setting that Hegel considered the character of political relationships. But, historically, it was in a Germany largely mediaeval in structure and in strong reaction against the success of French ideas and French arms that Hegel lived his professional life. Finally, Hegel brought to his task a mind even more strongly influenced by Plato than Rousseau's had been, so that when he is most strongly criticizing his master, he remains imprisoned in the idealism and functionalism of the Platonic tradition.

Society, for Hegel, was an exemplification of the process of the realization of freedom. This process had a succession of phases which included the earlier developments, though transformed, in the achievement of the later. It was not simply biological, from acorn to oak or caterpillar to moth, but rational in the sense that its significance could be understood only in retrospect and philosophically. The earlier phases were inadequate and incomplete without the later. For Leibniz, the present was always pregnant with the future; for Hegel, it was heavy with the past.

Hegel thought in triads, which fitted in with his dialectical pattern; and he distinguishes three conditions of society, the family, and what he calls civil society, and the state. Thus, at the outset he sees the state not as the totality of the community but as a special principle of organization or control informing the other activities which are both other than political and less than political. Each of these three forms of social relationship provides scope for the individual's freedom. In the family he can satisfy his natural instincts; in the external economic world he has the opportunity to express what Rousseau called his particular will and what Hegel calls caprice; only in the state, or so Hegel insists, is there manifest a public, universal will which actualizes, objectifies and fully expresses the freedom of the human spirit.

Hegel's criticism of Rousseau and Kant was that they tried to construct their whole community on the basis of the selfish wills of individuals operating in the economic sphere, which conformed to a universal law perhaps, but unconsciously and not because they made decisions in accordance with their knowledge of it. This is certainly not what Rousseau meant by the general will, though doubtless Hegel's refusal to accept the arguments in Rousseau's *Discourse on Inequality* precluded his understanding the later argument in *The Social Contract*. Hegel himself allowed a special social arena for the economic realm of private property, free contract, and individual choice. This was the field of operation of the self-concerned, particular will, in accord with the universal will of the state but not directly and in detail ordered by it. This in fact was little different from the situation in Rousseau's state in which particular decisions were free to be made within the wider legal control of the general will. In Hegel's words: 'The particular interest shall in truth be neither set aside nor suppressed, but be placed in open concord with the universal. In this concord both particular and universal are inclosed.'[1]

It is in an assertion of this kind, for example, that we can see how Hegel is preoccupied with an earlier historical problem: the maintenance of a free market for capital and enterprise, in which money payments replace service in labour and kind and contract displaces status as the determinant of economic activity. Within this world of primarily individual choice there was room for associations, trade guilds, the corporations of the mediaeval world, to conduct their business as groups; and all this activity allowed for the second kind of freedom, the freedom of satisfying the caprice of individual desire while at the same time serving a general social end, the satisfaction of wants.

Had Hegel confined this realm to economic activity or, formally, to individual conflict of desire, it would have corresponded in a sense to the state of nature as envisaged by Locke or Hobbes. But, at this point, he introduces a serious confusion, partly evident in his use of the term civil to describe this phase of social life. It is not yet the state, but it is a society subject to civil

[1] *Philosophy of Right*, translated S. W. Dyde (London 1896), 261, note

order, an order which does not suppress the free play of individuals but holds the ring as it were, keeping a watching brief for the general interest. This, in different terms, was what Locke's government and, indeed, Hobbes's sovereign were required to do. Property must be protected by the administration of justice in order, says Hegel, to actualize the general freedom required for the satisfaction of wants. The civil society must also include general public administration, for which Hegel uses the eighteenth-century term police, which covers much of what we should now call welfare services. The problem thus arises of why Hegel needed a state to complete his structure other than to satisfy his preference for triadic synthesis.

In the developing expression of freedom, Hegel posited a higher form which at once negated the lower and expressed it more completely. The particular will, the freedom to satisfy desire, must be transcended and taken up in a freedom to will according to a rational knowledge of the emerging divine principle. Thus the economic individuals of the civil society are already in a sense members of a city because their actions are circumscribed according to a universal law. They do not make this law, but they are capable of recognizing it rationally and in this recognition are free. Hegel, in submission to the linguistic needs of his idealism, constantly uses the indicative 'is' where most other theorists would use ought. This universal law is not a moral desideratum to be aimed at by the citizens nor a set of standards against which their actual performance may be judged, but is in some sense already there, able to be known and in being known to be obeyed, for Hegel's use of will in this context is closer to a conformity to reason than to a moral imperative.[1]

Hegel calls both these kinds of freedom able to be enjoyed in civil society subjective, although they are subjective in different ways ; and he therefore envisages the state as a further dialectical stage in which freedom shall finally become objective. There is administration of justice and the maintenance of order in civil society, both customarily treated as political activities, but there

[1] The difficulties into which Hegel's rationalism leads him in his attempt to define objective freedom in the state are too numerous and complex to be considered in detail here. For an illuminating unravelling of this confusion, see M. B. Foster's *The Political Philosophies of Plato and Hegel* (Oxford, Clarendon Press, 1935), particularly chapters IV and V.

is no legislation or final sovereign authority. It is these activities, and in particular the latter, which characterize the higher development of a social body. The state is thus at once transcendent and beyond the criticism or control of most of the citizens, and also immanent in their lives as the rational presupposition of even private and family activities. It is in this sense like the world-spirit of which it is an emanation. The whole is greater than the parts and the parts are not, as Rousseau would have said, members of the sovereign but members of subordinate classes or organs. 'The concrete state is the whole, articulated into its particular circles, and the member of the state is the member of a circle or class. Only his objective character can be recognized in the state.'[1]

Hegel had already included in his civil society a universal class, whose business was not economic but to represent the state's legal interests by administering justice or keeping order. Correspondingly, the groups, not the individuals, of this society are represented in the state's own sphere in a legislature. It is conceived closely on the lines of a mediaeval parliament of estates, in which it is interests not persons which are represented. This body does not exercise the sovereignty of Rousseau's legislature, which is reserved by Hegel solely for the executive government, headed by and symbolized in a constitutional monarch. They enjoy only the freedom, not unlike that demanded by Bentham, of having decisions of policy explained to them, not as one might expect from Hegel on rational grounds but in relation to the historical expediency of passing events. The executive government which is the centre of this political system, and the only group in the community completely free in Rousseau's sense, is also in touch with the citizens through public opinion. But Hegel is careful to add that public opinion must not affect their decisions in any way. Freedom of speech and a free press are little more than devices for releasing emotion, safety valves for private feelings, a sop to the irrationality of the multitude.

But even Hegel's government is not free quite in the sense of Rousseau's citizenry. It is not free either against God, as is a Christian, nor willingly in concord with goodness as for Rousseau, but necessarily by the divine propulsion of the rational world-spirit. Hegel sees states as modes of expression of this rational

[1] *Philosophy of Right*, 308, note

principle, which the blindness of men may perhaps delay but never altogether frustrate. This march of God on earth, as he calls it, proceeds on its mysterious dialectical way and freedom can never be more for those subjected to its demands than rational insight into its necessity.

Necessity, for Hegel, included acts of individual self-assertion on the part of the state by which it became more self-conscious and organically united. The most revivifying of these acts was war, which Hegel happily calls 'a necessary commotion'. But because for him the state was the final form of the divine wisdom in human affairs, he does not see this further pattern of dialectical conflict as the prelude to a wider and superior unity. This use of the dialectical method was bequeathed to Hegel's communist successors, Marx and Lenin, for whom the state was rather a negative phase in man's attempt to achieve social freedom. For Hegel the state was transcendent and he could not accept that it might be transcended.

.   .   .   .   .

Hegel's idealism, despite its difficulties and its comparative lack of influence in English thought, was destined to have a profound and far-reaching effect on the continent and particularly in Germany and Russia. For many decades it provided a philosophical orthodoxy which recalls the dominance of mediaeval scholasticism; and the measure of Hegel's importance is to be seen no less in the debt owed to him by those who rejected his particular arguments than in those who were whole-hearted in accepting them. Marx's collaborator Engels, though he is as lavish as Hegel's English critics with impolite epithets, does not stint his praise of Hegel's merits. He can write that 'there is much that is botched, artificial, laboured. . . . The Hegelian system, in itself, was a colossal miscarriage.' But he recognizes that, though Hegel may not have solved the problem he set himself satisfactorily, at least he propounded the vital question. What was the inner law governing the universal process of change and transformation, which unified the natural, historical and intellectual world? Had Hegel achieved nothing else but to provide a metaphysical framework for Marxian thought, this alone would serve to rank him among the most influential of European social theorists.

But it was not only the fundamental problem which Marx learned from Hegel. He accepted also some part of the Hegelian methodology in order to suggest his own solution. In the first place, Marx retained his allegiance to the dialectical interpretation of history. Historical forces in conflict with one another gave birth to new social forms. Secondly, he continued to hold that the understanding of this process was rational and that its inevitable development could be predicted. Lastly, he always thought of society in terms of groups interrelated with one another, the membership of which served to define the individuals who made them up; and treated the state not as a political relationship which constituted the citizens as a community, but as an addition or superstructure, to use his own word, attached to an economic society whose disharmony had demanded its creation.

All these formal aspects of Hegelian thought are provided by Marx with a content and interpretation very different from their German original and often with a close affinity to French thinkers of the immediately preceding generations. Marx himself is indeed a meeting-place for theoretical influences from widely divergent sources. His originality consists in much more than eclecticism, but his manifold sources provided an unusually firm substructure for the massive theory which he erected upon it. Marx, for one thing, was always looking forward in revolutionary expectation of the next stage in social evolution. In this he is like Saint-Simon rather than Hegel. The significant changes in the industrial world were providing conditions in which corresponding social changes could take place, particularly for Saint-Simon's lowest class of the poorest and most numerous. This expectation of change derived too from an awareness that social institutions were no longer in harmony with the new modes of production and exchange, which led to the unhegelian conclusion, in Engels's words, 'that existing social institutions are unreasonable and unjust, that reason has become unreason, and right wrong'.

Marx had French roots deeper than Saint-Simon, for together with an acceptance that the established superior classes are linked with an outdated economy and way of life, he saw them also, in the spirit of the early eighteenth-century communist writers, as perverting society morally by standing in the way of economic and social progress. Much of the moral fervour of Marxism is linked with the belief that the political and economic domination of a particular class, however inevitable historically, is also morally wrong. The Marxian term exploitation combines an economic theory of misappropriated wealth with an ethical theory of unjustified enslavement. The classless society is to be defined as one in which the sources of economic power and production are communally owned, so that the phenomenon of class division can no longer distort the conditions of living, subjecting, as Mably had believed, both groups in society to irresistible temptation.

Thus it came about that the Hegelian dialectic, transposed from its ideal realm, provided a pattern of argument leading to a conclusion wholly different in content from the original, though concerned finally with discovering the conditions of human freedom in history. Marx signalized this transformation by calling his theory historical materialism, for which he owed some of the inspiration to the influence of Feuerbach's theories. This was not the aristocratic materialism of the eighteenth century condemned by Robespierre, which held that there was no reality but matter in motion, but it was similarly a substitute religion, a form of devotion to man defined as a thinking animal and to the successful conditions of his survival. Marx substituted this humanistic faith for Hegelianism, as earlier materialism had filled the theological gap left vacant by former Christians. It was not man's being, said Engels, which was to be explained by his knowing, but his knowing by his being. In place of the Hegelian world-spirit exerting its hidden rational power on the lives of men, Marx put a similarly occult power, the forces of economic production which satisfied human wants, and which developed dialectically in social life, altering its forms and structure through successive historical periods. Historical materialism is defined by Engels in the Introduction he wrote to the three chapters of his *Anti-Dühring*, as it is known, separately published in English in 1892, as 'that view of the course of history, which seeks the ultimate cause and the great moving power of all important historic events in the economic development of society, in the changes in the modes of production and exchange, in the consequent division of society into distinct classes, and in the struggles of these classes against one another'.[1]

[1] *Socialism, Utopian and Scientific*, edited E. Aveling (London 1892), p. xix. The pamphlet was first published in French under this title in 1880.

It was this belief Engels held in his 1888 Preface to the *Manifesto* which was destined to do for history what Darwin's theory had done for biology.

This primary assertion of Marxian social theory, being couched in the form of a metaphysical proposition, cannot be satisfactorily proved or disproved in its status as a social law. But it acquires added importance from the fact that as a working hypothesis, and Marx at times claimed no more for it, the theory has helped to explain many of the economic and social changes of western Europe since the emergence of this area from mediaeval society. As a hidden influence, the forces of economic production can scarcely claim a universal status; as a basis for prediction, they are of doubtful value unsupported by current empirical evidence; but as a primary factor of historical interpretation these assumptions were used by Marx with considerable insight and profit.

The social vehicle of the productive economic forces was the class. The group-terms in which different theorists define social relations are always significant; and the Marxian use of the concept of economic class is of the first importance in understanding the theory. It is through their membership of an economic class, whether owning and exploiting or disinherited and enslaved, that individuals achieve or forfeit the freedom they desire. As individuals they can do nothing significant. In the Hegelian sense, they are unreal. But as organized groups the economic classes can, through conflict and dialectical development, finally overcome their inherent disharmony and emerge into a world in which the hidden powers are rationally controlled by a no longer divided society. This unity of the citizens is something which lies beyond the revolution. It comes after an act of social self-redemption not unlike that which inaugurated Rousseau's ideal city. In the interim historical period, society is characterized by a simple division between those who own and control the primary means of production and those who do not, and because they do not, are necessarily enslaved by the first group in order to acquire their daily bread. This division of society, for which Marx had some empirical evidence particularly in mid-nineteenth century England, was assumed by him to be becoming ever sharper and more exact. All those minor groups of uncertain definition, who lay between the exploiting few and the proletarian masses, were being compelled, he thought, to declare their allegiance to the ruling class or be forced by economic pressure into the proletariat. This prognostication fitted in better with the demands of dialectical theory than with the later development of industrial society.

For Marx, as for Hegel, this inharmonious society has a form of political control which he also calls the state. The control is exercised in terms of order and justice by a special class of economically unproductive persons, and for the time being, that is between revolutions, successfully prevents the implicit conflict in society from becoming violently disruptive. The difference is that the state is not the servant of the rational idea but an expression of the will of the ruling class to continue to reap the rewards of its superior position by maintaining the existing property relations sacrosanct. The state arises out of the clash of class interests, for it is a necessary curb to the violence which economic inequality would otherwise engender. Control is exercised by force, and continental thinkers thought of force in terms of a standing army, with the direct intention of preserving the privileges of the few at the expense of the many. The law and justice practised in any community is no more than the sanctified self-interest of the ruling group; and religion itself part of the hypocritical system for encouraging passive obedience. Engels calls the state the official representative of capitalist society and, in the *Manifesto*, the executive government is described as 'a committee for managing the common affairs of the whole bourgeoisie'.

A certain confusion arises in interpreting communist political thought because the concept of the state has this special characteristic of being at once external to the economic process and yet constitutive of a given period of exploitation. In this sense, it is an interim political theory. The state controls the whole society but does not represent the common interest of all its members. It is destined to be superseded; but this is not to say that communist theory recognizes no political relationship in post-revolutionary society, only that it will not take the form of a repressive force allegedly used solely in the interests of the superior class. Marx was convinced empirically that the tensions generated in capitalist society would reach a revolutionary pitch and involve the creation of a proletarian community. He also believed *a priori* that this was what always happened and ought to happen. He was not against central, social control, but determined that it must not be exercised violently and contrary to the interests of most of the citizens. The revolution, then, was bound to come, though Marx came slowly to see that the best conditions for its occurrence might be found in less highly developed countries such as Russia. The inevitability of the final resolution of class conflict in a new social synthesis did not preclude the need for all those who understood the pattern of events to help to further the good cause. It is the communists, as a revolutionary party, who have the advantage over the great mass of the proletariat 'of clearly understanding the line of march, the conditions, and the ultimate general results of the proletarian movement'.[1] This special position of the party later received renewed emphasis from Lenin.

It is worth remembering that Marx was opposed by other champions of working-class freedom concerning the advantages of centralized control, even when purged of bourgeois bias. Proudhon, for instance, became involved in direct and acrimonious argument with Marx in the eighteen-forties over this very question. Proudhon also accepted that governments distorted social relations, that the economic activities of different groups were likely to provoke a measure of discord and opposition, and that the working classes did not require to be regimented. But he was not concerned to achieve a Hegelian synthesis and he welcomed the diversity of activities and interests in a society in which he believed that the family rather than a whole economic class was the significant unit. Proudhon, however, was still attached to the rational freedom of the great revolution and held that liberty was not the daughter but the mother of order. His followers tended towards a theory of anarchy, one of his own terms, and repudiated the monolithic community of later Marxian theory. Marx condemned Proudhon as a petit-bourgeois, which, of course, on Marx's own theory is just what he was; but it was this class, condemned by Marx to absorption, which has in fact played an increasingly important role in western European politics.

For Marx and his followers on the contrary, the state, defined as a system of organization with force at its command, was

[1] *Communist Manifesto*, II

destined itself to play an important part in the revolutionary process. Because he thought of political power as economic power exercising repressive force, the first action of the victorious proletariat would be to employ what Marx precisely calls its political supremacy 'to wrest, by degrees, all capital from the bourgeoisie, to centralize all instruments of production in the hands of the state, i.e., of the proletariat organized as the ruling class'.[1] Not until the completion of the revolutionary process, when class distinctions have disappeared and the community as a whole controls all productive power, will 'the public power . . . lose its political character', which is to say have no more need to use force to repress dissension. As society takes over productive forces, Engels tells us, the producers will have a perfect understanding of the social character of the process, and what was once a source of disturbance will become a spur to productivity.

This intervening period is known as the dictatorship of the proletariat. It is thought of as a prelude to the final consummation of the revolution in which all repressive measures will have ceased and everyone will be free. Marx never allowed himself to prophesy how long this period would last, but Lenin, in the pamphlet he wrote on the eve of the 1917 Russian revolution, speaks of 'the entire *historical period* between capitalism and "classless society" communism'.[2] The transition, he says, 'must obviously be a rather lengthy process'.[3] While it was correct, then, to speak of the inevitable withering away of the state, there was no evidence to say how long it would take, and he was prepared to leave 'the question of length of time, or the concrete terms of the withering away, quite open'.[4]

Lenin constantly uses the term machine when writing of the state. He thought of it as a kind of tool for getting something done, as characteristically repressive in its functions, and as incompatible with any condition of freedom. It was improper, he thought, to speak of a free state or a people's state. The two terms, as Engels had said, could not be combined. 'While the state exists

[1] *Communist Manifesto,* II
[2] *State and Revolution* (Little Lenin Library, London 1933), p. 29. Lenin wrote this in August and September 1917, and it was first published as a pamphlet in 1918.
[3] *State and Revolution,* p. 64
[4] *State and Revolution,* p. 73

there is no freedom. When freedom exists, there will be no state.'[1] But this rejection was partly linguistic, for he also argues that as bourgeois democracy becomes proletarian democracy, the state is transformed 'into something which is no longer really a state'. Lenin had no words for the new political form which he himself helped to create. But we cannot doubt that both during the period of proletarian dictatorship and after the achievement of the new order, some kind of political relationship is envisaged. The dictatorship might better perhaps be called leadership, for Lenin is insistent that one of the needs for central organization is so that the party may lead the great mass of the population in the work of organizing socialist economy. It is just this role which the party has played in Russian politics since the revolution.

The final condition of a free, classless society is sketched in rather lightly; and for all the tendency of Marxist apologists to repudiate utopian theories, the picture has something of the utopian quality of eighteenth-century communist visionaries. Engels envisaged a gradual decline in the need for state interference in social relations until the time when this interference would die out or wither away and, in the oft-quoted phrase, 'the government of persons is replaced by the administration of things and the conduct of processes of production'.[2] Engels attributes a similar view to Saint-Simon, as though administration by scientists and economists was in some sense non-political, which is true only in the restricted sense that it is assumed that they will not use repressive measures. Lenin was inclined to simplify the whole process of administration. It could be reduced to 'registration, filing and checking', he said, 'easily performed by every literate person', a job which should not command more than a workman's wage. But his more serious suggestion was that the sphere of government would contract because the need for 'the *subjection* of one man to another, and of one section of the population to another, will vanish, since people will *become accustomed* to observing the elementary conditions of social life *without force* and *without subordination*'.[3] He expected individuals here and there to behave anti-socially, but with the removal of the

---

[1] *State and Revolution*, p. 73
[2] *Socialism, Utopian and Scientific*, pp. 76–77
[3] *State and Revolution*, p. 63

social causes of their misbehaviour, the exploitation, want and poverty of the masses, even this amount of social disharmony would cease.

The higher phase of communist society for Lenin would come only when the necessity of observing the simple fundamental rules of human intercourse became a habit. This might be put, in Rousseau's words, as the time when no one had to be forced to be free. But the rational understanding of social and economic forces is no less an integral factor in the final communist utopia. Active social forces work, said Engels, destructively like natural forces, until we understand them and in so doing subject them to our will. Only then does the struggle for individual existence disappear. Man emerges from mere animality into truly human conditions. 'Man's own social organization, hitherto confronting him as a necessity imposed by Nature and history, now becomes the result of his own free action. The extraneous objective forces which have hitherto governed history, pass under the control of man himself. Only from that time will man himself, more and more consciously, make his own history—only from that time will the social causes set in movement by him have, in the main and in a constantly growing measure, the results intended by him. It is the ascent of man from the kingdom of necessity to the kingdom of freedom.'[1]

*   *   *   *   *

The uncertain terminology in which both Engels and Lenin describe the social organization of the period of proletarian democracy and of the final free community is itself significant of a serious attempt to escape from the categories of political thought appropriate to a period of history which we can now see is drawing to a close. Possibly Lenin will be proved to have been right when he saw its end in 1914. The significance is not diminished because the communist ideal may be just as utopian as any of the other ideals we have considered in this book, nor because the social and economic conditions which govern the creation of political forms to suit the modern industrial era may be very different in fact from what Marx told us they were. It remains true that whatever

[1] *Socialism, Utopian and Scientific,* p. 82

we call modern Russia, it is not a nation-state in the traditional sense of the term current since Bodin. If we are honest, we should perhaps have to admit that the United States of America was not one either. What the British Commonwealth is politically in the mid-twentieth century defies definition, though not perhaps description. From Marx we can learn at least that in a dynamic, changing world, all the social and economic factors involved are interacting and interdependent and that political forms are not exempt from these effects.

The impact of the continuing scientific and industrial revolution, for it has never ceased, but rather grown swifter and more complex, not only in established industrial centres but over the whole world, has made any simple diagnosis of social change outdated. We may detect in modern political studies a marked reversion to what can only be called an Aristotelian outlook, a withdrawal of interest from ideal purposes or the taking of these ends for granted, in favour of concentration on the possible, on what can be achieved in given conditions. The comparatively new disciplines of social science and psychology and of economics, divorced from the political framework which gave it its earlier designation of political economy, devote themselves to the collection of factual data and the assessment of possible trends in human behaviour and reaction. Thus the pattern of the interrelations between social institutions and the conditions in which they must function may be laid bare and, if possible, understood.

This necessary adjustment of interest in twentieth-century society does not mean that the age-old concern with human purposes and ideals can be neglected. It may be doubted whether any of the patterns of thought which we have reviewed is wholly dead and lacking in influence. But the complexity of modern conditions does compel us to recognize three distinct tasks in the realm of political speculation. Firstly, we must clarify our awareness and understanding of those systems of value and purpose which, in the last resort, quite apart from their truth and whether it can be certainly known or not, alone empower common human action and evoke social allegiance and service. Secondly, we must increase our knowledge of the facts. Finally, recalling Hume's lesson that we must never confuse the indicative and the imperative, we have to maintain these two objects of social study in balance with each other, neither over-stressing their division nor under-estimating their interaction. Every purpose must be correlated with its conditions if it is to be more than a mere dream; but no account of conditions which leaves out the human ends which irradiate them is other than an uninspiring catalogue.

'The true progress of political thought,' wrote L. T. Hobhouse towards the end of the first world war, 'lies in the cultivation of imaginative power.' It is this quality, above all, which has characterized the great thinkers whose works we have briefly scanned in this essay. It is also a gift no less in demand in our own day. We are faced with an unprecedented problem of matching our political institutions to our moral and economic purposes. It is perhaps not altogether new in principle, though immensely wider in scope than earlier cases of a similar nature. The end of the period of the nation-state has, formally, much in common with its beginning. At the close of the middle ages the serious theoretical difficulty was to try to understand a political world of embryonic nation-states within the conceptual framework of an empire sharing authority with a universal church. To-day we are beset with the troublesome task of comprehending a nascent international society with the help of political concepts almost wholly limited to the needs of national sovereignty.

It may seem anachronistic, but it is singularly to the point, to close this essay with a comment of an eighteenth-century philosopher, very pertinent to the theoretical problems of our own day. The words come from Kant's *Principle of Progress*: 'Human Nature appears nowhere less amiable than in the relations of whole nations to each other. No State is for a moment secure against another in its independence or its possessions. The will to subdue each other or to reduce their power, is always rampant; and the equipment for defence, which often makes peace even more oppressive and more destructive of internal prosperity than war, can never be relaxed. Against such evils there is no possible remedy but *a system of International Right* founded upon public laws conjoined with power, to which every State must submit— according to the analogy of the civil or political Right of individuals in any one State. For, a lasting universal Peace on the basis of the so-called *Balance of Power in Europe*, is a mere chimera. It is like the house described by Swift, which was built by an architect so perfectly in accordance with all the laws of equilibrium, that when a sparrow lighted upon it, it immediately fell.'

SUGGESTIONS FOR FURTHER READING

It is not really necessary, and would be impossible in the available space, to record all the books on the themes treated in the text which students might profitably read. Most of the works listed below have themselves often extensive bibliographies. Among general studies of political thought, the only short essay comparable in length and treatment with this volume is C. Delisle Burns: *Political Ideals*, first published in 1915. The standard full-length study in English is G. H. Sabine: *A History of Political Theory*, of which there has now been a second edition. An earlier study in three volumes, also by an American professor, covers the period from Plato to Spencer: W. A. Dunning: *A History of Political Theories* (1910–1920); it was completed by a fourth volume in 1924, covering recent times and contributed by Professor Dunning's students, edited C. E. Merriam and H. E. Barnes. An even earlier general study, to which I have been much indebted and which remains valuable, is Paul Janet: *Histoire de la science politique dans ses rapports avec la morale* (2 volumes, 1887). Among the general essays on social and political thought, attention should be drawn to Sir Ernest Barker: *The Principles of Social and Political Theory*; C. E. McIlwain: *The Growth of Political Thought in the West*; Ernst Troeltsch: *The Social Teaching of the Christian Churches* (2 volumes, translated Olive Wyon); and John Bowle's two volumes, valuable for their historical background: *Western Political Thought* and *Politics and Opinion in the Nineteenth Century*.

Two series of volumes devoted to political thinkers are valuable for more detailed treatment of particular authors: the Home University Library's *Political Thought in England* series; and the series edited by F. J. C. Hearnshaw from 1923 onwards beginning with *The Social and Political Ideas of some great Mediaeval Thinkers*. This latter series, originally published by Harrap, has recently been re-issued by Barnes and Noble of New York. It includes in addition: *Great Thinkers of the Renaissance and Reformation*; *Great Thinkers of the Sixteenth and Seventeenth Centuries*; *English Thinkers of the Augustine Age*; *Great French Thinkers of the Age of Reason*; *Representative Thinkers of the Age of Reaction and Reconstruction*; *Representative Thinkers of the Revolutionary Era*; and *Representative Thinkers of the Victorian Age*. The Home University Library includes: Christopher Morris: *Political Thought from Tyndale to Hooker*; G. P. Gooch: *Political Thought from Bacon to Halifax*; H. J. Laski: *Political Thought from Locke to Bentham*; H. N. Brailsford: *Shelley, Godwin and their Circle*; and Sir Ernest Barker: *Political Thought from Herbert Spencer to the Present Day*, which is to say up to 1914.

Several general studies cover only part of the historical field, but nevertheless treat wider concerns than are subsumed under the separate chapters of this volume. The classic study of mediaeval social thought is by R. W. and A. J. Carlyle: *A History of Mediaeval Political Theory in the West* (six volumes, 1930–36), but it is to be recommended to specialists rather than beginners. C. E. Vaughan: *Studies in the History of Political Philosophy before and after Rousseau* (2 volumes), treats thinkers from Hobbes to Mazzini. R. H. Crossman: *Government and the Governed* begins with Machiavelli.

J. W. Allen: *A History of Political Thought in the Sixteenth Century* is a standard textbook. Crane Brinton: *English Political Thought in the Nineteenth Century* and Roger Soltau: *French Political Thought in the Nineteenth Century* are companion volumes. Another valuable study of this period is J. P. Mayer: *Political Thought in France from the Revolution to the Fourth Republic.*

Students new to the subject will also find some of the published lectures valuable as introductions, notably: G. D. H. Cole: *Scope and Method in Social and Political Theory*; D. W. Brogan: *The Study of Politics*; M. Oakeshott: *Political Education*; and Bertrand Russell: *Philosophy and Politics.*

.   .   .   .   .

For the classical period the two volumes in the *Legacy* series are valuable : *The Legacy of Greece* and *The Legacy of Rome.* F. M. Cornford's translation of Plato's *Republic* is particularly suitable for beginners; and Sir Ernest Barker's edition of Aristotle's *Politics* has been specially prepared for those who have not had a classical education. The same author's *The Political Thought of Plato and Aristotle* covers the wider field. G. Lowes Dickinson: *The Greek View of Life* is helpful for beginners. G. Glotz: *The Greek City* and W. W. Tarn: *Hellenistic Civilisation* fill in the historical background. Cicero's *De Republica* and *De Legibus* may be read in the Loeb edition, as also may Seneca's *Epistulae Morales.* M. B. Foster's *From Plato to Machiavelli*, which is Volume I of *The Masters of Political Thought* series, covers most of the authors considered in the first two chapters of my essay and has a valuable introduction. The same author's *The Political Philosophies of Plato and Hegel* is intended for more advanced students.

.   .   .   .   .

The Elizabethan translation of Augustine's *De Civitate Dei* by John Healey, originally edited and abridged by Bussell and published in Dent's Temple Classics series in three volumes, is now produced in one volume with a new introduction by Sir Ernest Barker. J. N. Figgis: *The Political Aspects of S. Augustine's 'City of God'* is an invaluable commentary; and advanced students may also consult E. Gilson: *Introduction à l'étude de Saint Augustin.* The social thought of St. Thomas Aquinas has been collected in the volume of Blackwell's Political Texts, edited by A. P. d'Entrèves: *Aquinas: Selected Political Writings.* Professor d'Entrèves's *Mediaeval Contribution to Political Thought* should also be consulted for this period and for Marsilius and Hooker. Dante's *De Monarchia* is translated in the Temple Classics edition (Dent) of the *Latin Works of Dante.* For the mediaeval theory of natural law, see A. P. d'Entrèves: *Natural Law* in this present series; and for the intervening centuries between Augustine and Aquinas, J. M. Wallace-Hadrill: *The Barbarian West*, also in this series. Other valuable essays on mediaeval thought are F. W. Maitland's translation of Otto Gierke's *Political Theories of the Middle Age* together with Maitland's introduction; B. Jarrett: *Social Theories of the Middle Ages*; R. L. Poole: *Illustrations of the History of Mediaeval Thought*; J. N. Figgis: *From Gerson to Grotius* for the fifteenth and sixteenth centuries; and *The Legacy of the Middle Ages* in the *Legacy* series.

.   .   .   .   .

Bodin, Locke and *The Federalist* are all edited in Blackwell's Political Texts. Montesquieu's *De l'Esprit des lois* is translated by Nugent, revised by Prichard, but is better read, by those who can, in French. Joseph Dedieu: *Montesquieu, l'homme et l'œuvre* is a valuable exposition. Hooker's *Laws of Ecclesiastical Polity* is included in his *Works*, edited by Keble, as revised by Church and Paget. Other original works, not mentioned in the text, which are worth consulting, are Milton's *Areopagitica* and *The Tenure of Kings and Magistrates*; Grotius: *De Jure Belli et Pacis*; and Alexis de Tocqueville: *De la démocratie en Amérique.* Two general essays cover the subject-matter of Chapter III: Otto Gierke: *Natural Law and the Theory of Society,* 2 volumes, translated with an introduction by Sir Ernest Barker; and D. G. Ritchie: *Natural Rights.* Other essays to which attention should be drawn are J. W. Gough: *The Social Contract*; A. S. P. Woodhouse: *Puritanism and Liberty*; G. P. Gooch: *English Democratic Ideas in the Seventeenth Century*; T. H. Green: *Four Lectures on the English Revolution,* reprinted from his *Works*; R. H. Murray: *The Political Consequences of the Reformation*; Crane Brinton: *The Political Ideas of the English Romanticists*; C. E. Merriam: *American Political Theory*; and J. N. Figgis: *The Divine Right of Kings.*

. . . . .

Hobbes, Bentham and John Stuart Mill are all edited in Blackwell's Political Texts. There is also an earlier edition of Bentham's *A Fragment on Government* with a valuable introduction by F. C. Montague (1891). Machiavelli's *The Prince* is translated in the World's Classics series and his *Discourses on the First Ten Books of Titus Livius* is in the four volumes of his *Works* translated by C. E. Detmold (1884). Hume's *Treatise* is edited by L. A. Selby-Bigge and the relevant sections may be found also in *Hume's Theory of Politics,* edited Frederick Watkins, which includes the political essays. Burke is edited in six volumes of the World's Classics series, in which the *Reflections on the Revolution in France* appears in vol. IV. J. MacCunn: *The Political Philosophy of Burke* is a useful commentary. There is an edition of James Mill: *An Essay on Government* (Cambridge University Press 1937) with an introduction by Sir Ernest Barker. John Stuart Mill: *Utilitarianism* is reprinted in J. P. Plamenatz: *The English Utilitarians* in Blackwell's Political Texts together with a long critical essay on this movement of thought by Mr. Plamenatz. Other studies include E. Halévy: *The Growth of Philosophical Radicalism,* translated Mary Morris; F. K. Martin: *French Liberal Thought in the Eighteenth Century*; and C. Becker: *The Heavenly City of the Eighteenth-Century Philosophers.*

. . . . .

The theme of Chapter V is covered in J. B. Bury: *The Idea of Progress.* Condorcet's *Esquisse* has been edited by O. H. Prior (1933); and selections from Saint-Simon are published in Blackwell's Political Texts, as is J. S. Mill: *On Liberty.* There is a recent study of Mill's life and thought by M. St. J. Packe: *The Life of John Stuart Mill* (1954). Of Spencer's voluminous writings, the most important politically are *Social Statics* and *The Man versus the State.* Bagehot's *Physics and Politics* and Sir Henry Maine's *Ancient Law* express different points of view from mid-nineteenth-century thinkers which should also be considered. T. H. Green's *The Principles of Political Obligation* is also

226   THE DEVELOPMENT OF POLITICAL THEORY

published separately from his *Works*. A recently published study, R. V. Sampson: *Progress in the Age of Reason* has appeared too late for me to consult.

.   .   .   .   .

The Everyman edition of Rousseau's political writings, translated with an introduction by G. D. H. Cole, contains the *Social Contract*, the *Discourses* and the *Political Economy*. The French text of *Du contrat social*, together with a valuable appendix of extracts from other writings, has been edited with an introduction in English by C. E. Vaughan. Vaughan's two-volume edition of *The Political Writings of Jean-Jacques Rousseau* covers a much wider field. A more recent edition of the text of *Du contrat social* (Geneva 1947) is prefaced by an extremely valuable essay by Bertrand de Jouvenel, to which I am much indebted. Critical and expository volumes on Rousseau's thought are very numerous indeed. The following may be recommended as valuable in themselves and as expressing points of view differing both from each other and to some extent from those of the editors already mentioned. E. Faguet: *La politique comparée de Montesquieu, Rousseau et Voltaire*; E. H. Wright: *The Meaning of Rousseau*; Alfred Cobban: *Rousseau and the Modern State*; C. W. Hendel: *Jean-Jacques Rousseau: Moralist*; René Hubert: *Rousseau et l'encyclopédie*. Hegel's *Philosophie des Rechts* is translated into English by Dyde and also by Knox. His *Philosophy of History* should also be consulted. The reflection of Hegelian thought in England is to be found in B. Bosanquet: *The Philosophical Theory of the State*, and a criticism of this viewpoint in L. T. Hobhouse: *The Metaphysical Theory of the State*. A more recent reconsideration of Hegel is to be found in Herbert Marcuse: *Reason and Revolution*. Two volumes of the Home University Library are especially valuable in the study of Marxism. H. J. Laski: *Communism* and I. Berlin: *Karl Marx*. The latter has a full and helpful bibliography. The development of socialist thought has been covered in the present series by Norman Mackenzie, who gives an extensive reading list. There are also now available the seven volumes of G. D. H. Cole's *History of Socialist Thought*.

.   .   .   .   .

Of other works written in the present century with some bearing on the themes discussed in this book, it is impossible to do more than pick out a few of those which I have myself found most useful. Sir Ernest Barker: *Essays on Government* and *Traditions of Civility*; E. F. Carritt: *Morals and Politics* and *Ethical and Political Thinking*; G. D. H. Cole: *Some Relations between Political and Economic Theory* and *Essays in Social Theory*; B. Croce: *Politics and Morals*; J. N. Figgis: *Churches in the Modern State*; L. T. Hobhouse: *Morals in Evolution*; B. de Jouvenel: *Du Pouvoir*, translated as *Power*; H. J. Laski: *A Grammar of Politics*; A. D. Lindsay: *The Modern Democratic State*; J. D. Mabbott: *The State and the Citizen*; M. Oakeshott: *The Social and Political Doctrines of Contemporary Europe* (1938); R. H. Tawney: *Equality* and *The Acquisitive Society*; D. Thomson *Equality* (Current Problems series); Graham Wallas: *Human Nature in Politics* and *The Great Society*; and T. D. Weldon: *States and Morals* and *The Vocabulary of Politics*.

INDEX

ALEMBERT, Jean-le-Rond d', 141, 154
Alexander the Great, 22, 33
American revolution, 96, 111, 114, 137
Anarchy, 216
Arbitrary power, 97, 104–6, 111, 142, 159, 163, 167, 193
Aristocracy, 20, 23, 162, 163, 165
Aristotle, 10, 13, 19, 21–31, 32, 33, 34, 35, 36, 37, 40, 41, 49, 57, 58, 63, 64, 65, 66, 67, 91, 97, 99, 107, 181, 183, 196
Aristotelian tradition, 65, 66, 67, 73, 82, 89, 90, 94, 118, 119, 120, 220
Augustine, St., 11, 50, 53–63, 65, 71, 99, 122, 153, 175, 206
Augustinian tradition, 73, 74, 75, 89, 91, 94, 118, 119, 127, 135, 182, 190, 192

BARBARIANS, 34, 63, 72, 75, 79
Barker, Sir Ernest, 34
Beccaria, Bonesano Cesare, Marchese di, 142, 144, 147
Bentham, Jeremy, 139, 142, 144–9, 210
Blackstone, William, 144
Bodin, Jean, 85, 89–92, 93, 107, 155, 183, 204, 220
Bolingbroke, Henry St. John, sometime Viscount, 104
Boniface VIII, Pope, 70
Bracton, 72
Burke, Edmund, 130, 135–9, 141, 144, 152, 184
Bury, J. B., 151

CALVIN, 87, 188, 192
Carlyle, R. W. and A. J., 71
Cartesianism, 121
Charlemagne, 67, 81
Cicero, 55, 97

Citizenship, 26, 28, 34, 38, 51, 177, 181, 183, 186, 202, 203
Classless society, 213, 217, 218
Common law, 75, 76
Communist theory, 160, 187, 188, 190, 197, 215
Comte, Auguste, 152, 165–9, 171, 173, 176, 179
Condorcet, M-J-A-N. Caritat, Marquis de, 33, 154, 157, 158–61, 167, 174, 186
Consent, 76, 86, 92, 95, 101, 134, 205
Cosmopolis, 31, 35, 38, 39, 40, 43, 46, 51, 55, 72
Covenant, 98, 128, 129, 130
Custom, 74, 75, 76, 78, 86, 130, 135, 138, 152, 178, 179
Cynics, 35, 38

DANTE, 70, 71, 77, 81
Darwin, Charles, 170, 171, 176
Darwinianism, 172, 174, 214
Declaration of Independence, American, 113
Declaration of the Rights of Man (1789), 114, 115
Democracy, 23, 29, 30, 101, 115, 149, 161, 167, 176, 181, 186, 191, 199, 200, 201, 203, 204, 218
Despotism, 32, 53, 109, 110, 121, 149, 150, 167, 179, 180
Dialectical development, 206, 207, 211, 212, 213, 214
Dictatorship of the proletariat, 217, 218
Diderot, Denis, 140, 141, 154, 155, 157, 193
Diocletian, Emperor, 53
Diogenes, 35
Divine law (See Revealed law)
Divine right of kings, 86, 89, 96, 98, 123, 167
Donatism, 54

227

For Product Safety Concerns and Information please contact our EU
representative GPSR@taylorandfrancis.com
Taylor & Francis Verlag GmbH, Kaufingerstraße 24, 80331 München, Germany